The Wisdom of Women

CANDIDA BAKER

The Wisdom of Women

Intimate stories of love, loss and laughter

inspired LIVING

ALLEN&UNWIN

First published in 2012

Copyright © Candida Baker 2012

All rights reserved. No part of this book may be reproduced or transmitted in any form or by any means, electronic or mechanical, including photocopying, recording or by any information storage and retrieval system, without prior permission in writing from the publisher. The Australian *Copyright Act 1968* (the Act) allows a maximum of one chapter or 10 per cent of this book, whichever is the greater, to be photocopied by any educational institution for its educational purposes provided that the educational institution (or body that administers it) has given a remuneration notice to Copyright Agency Limited (CAL) under the Act.

Inspired Living, an imprint of
Allen & Unwin
Sydney, Melbourne, Auckland, London

83 Alexander Street
Crows Nest NSW 2065
Australia
Phone: (61 2) 8425 0100
Fax: (61 2) 9906 2218
Email: info@allenandunwin.com
Web: www.allenandunwin.com

Cataloguing-in-Publication details are available
from the National Library of Australia
www.trove.nla.gov.au

ISBN 978 1 74175 953 2

All internal photographs are by the author, except:
pp. 31, 126, 180, 264 © Jacklyn Wagner

Internal design by Christabella Designs
Set in 12/20 pt Centaur MT by Midland Typesetters, Australia
Printed and bound in Australia by Griffin Press

10 9 8 7 6 5 4 3 2 1

The paper in this book is FSC® certified. FSC® promotes environmentally responsible, socially beneficial and economically viable management of the world's forests.

For my sisters and women friends who encircle my life with love, support, encouragement and kindness.

Contents

	Introduction	1
1	A mother's love	3
2	It takes all sorts	9
3	Standing out from the crowd	26
4	The importance of fitting in	32
5	The friends we find and the friends who find us	41
6	Grandmothers	46
7	A Mother's Day present	57
8	Mothers-in-law or the absence of them	62
9	The kindness of strangers	71
10	Who are we?	79
11	Sometimes we just don't feel quite right	84
12	The dark word	90
13	Things are not always what they seem	99
14	Which comes first?	105
15	Learning that love is enough	112
16	Women who inspire us	119
17	A mother's instinct	127
18	A road less travelled	137
19	Home cooking	153
20	The creative touch	164
21	Becoming a mum at forty-five	169

22	Magic mothering	176
23	The call of mysticism	181
24	Soulfulness	187
25	The many faces of motherhood	197
26	Sisterly love	206
27	Old friends and changing times	215
28	A woman's welcome and a nice cup of tea	220
29	Losing the women we love	225
30	The healing touch	246
31	Hormones rule	249
32	Aunts and great aunts	256
33	Forever young	265
34	Growing old gracefully—almost	271
35	Time flies	282
36	Taking time out	287
37	Leaving children	303
38	As mothers move on	308
39	The importance of rituals, writing and nurturing	318
	Biographical details	323
	Acknowledgements	342
	Notes	344

Introduction

I don't think it ever occurred to me when I was young to think about the importance of being a woman, how we differed from men, what our needs were or how we met those needs. I was simply busy getting on with the business of existing. It took me a long time to reach beyond a superficial understanding of 'womanhood' and come to terms with what my sense of being female means to me. As I grow older, however, it has become more and more important.

So perhaps it was inevitable, being one of five sisters, that I should turn my attention to the idea of the journeys women face throughout their lives, and begin to collect those stories—the women's stories we tell each other—that chart the triumphs and tragedies, the innermost longings, the broken dreams and the realised goals.

I am extraordinarily grateful to all the women who have shared their stories for this book. They have reached deep into their memories, their hearts, even into wounds never quite healed, to give me their pearls of wisdom, and I appreciate their generosity more than I can say. They have given me their stories with a breathtaking honesty, humour and warmth.

During the course of writing and compiling *The Wisdom of Women*, much has happened in my life. Three other books, just for starters, plus a year spent as director of my local writers' festival.

Then of course there's life at home, with children, animals and a series of creative projects always demanding attention. And somewhere within all this are my friendships with the women in my life, and my continuing connection with my four sisters. The presence of all of them in my life means that someone is never far away if I need a chat, a cup of tea, a cuddle or just someone to moan to on the phone for a while!

Within my family I have been a daughter, a sister, a stepmother, an auntie, a cousin, a niece and a mother to a daughter. All of these relationships, rich in emotion and meaning, have made my life the full-bodied, complex vintage it is today, and for that I am ever grateful.

The importance of strong, powerful women in a woman's life cannot be overestimated. When women encircle another woman with their kindness and support, it leaves a space in which grace and love can grow.

Candida Baker

I
A mother's love

The first and most important woman in my life was my mother. As it should be, in an ideal world.

When I was born, my world must have seemed, to those who observed it, pretty close to ideal. My father was a well-known actor; my mother, Julia Squire, a costume designer whose career was taking off. For myself and my younger sister, born two and a half years later, life was a beautiful flat in Belgravia, a stone's throw from Buckingham Palace, nannies and au pairs, walks to St James's Park to feed the ducks and smocked dresses made by the Queen's own dressmakers.

Even now, so many years after my mother died, when I think of those early days I can still smell her perfume on the air as she bent to kiss me goodnight, dressed in some beautiful off-the-shoulder gown she had designed, her pearl-covered bag in her hand, her hair swept up and her nails immaculately painted. Dad would be in the background, tall, handsome, his dinner suit gleaming black, already by then a somewhat scary presence in my life—not like my mother, warm and soft and comforting.

To be honest, I think she was a bit soft as a mother. I remember once when I was small, five or six I think, I had been behaving badly—badly enough for me to know it as well. Mum, who absolutely never punished me, got cross with me and hit me on the hand with a wooden spoon. I remember looking at my hand in astonishment, but at the same time feeling that it was fair enough, when my mother burst into tears, knelt on the floor beside me, covered me with kisses and apologised to *me*! Hmmm, this is interesting! I thought, putting the knowledge somewhere into a 'mustn't forget' file.

Although we lived in the city, both my parents had grown up in the country and from the time I was a baby we went away almost every weekend, first of all to my godmother's cottage in the Cotswolds, and later to our own cottage. When I was little my parents were in their element at the weekends. They both loved to garden, and Mum's gradual creation of our beautiful garden was a testimony to her love of design and colour. She was also a brilliant dressmaker, designer and cook, but her passion was painting, which she did at every spare moment. I know that in some ways I was a disappointment to her—she never could quite reconcile the fact that her eldest daughter appeared to have brown thumbs, could not sew to save her life and had no particular skill in art. This was partly because her taste in art was beautifully crafted drawing and classic painting, and mine, as I grew older, was large messy abstracts, but she tried to forgive me my 'modern' inclinations.

Where we met each other fully was with a love of books and writing. Her father, my grandfather, was a poet, essayist and editor, and her mother had been a reader of children's books for a publishing company. Our house was full of books, and from my earliest years one of my strongest memories is of my mother and me reading together and discussing books of all kinds. There was one taste of mine she couldn't abide, however: Georgette Heyer. She thought that Heyer was a poor man's Jane Austen and was disparaging about my habit of disappearing into yet another Regency romance. But apart from that, and her mystification at how I could read books about horses over and over and over again, we had a rich and full communication running through our lives on the subject of books.

In some ways I had two mothers during the very early years—the smart city Mum, beautifully dressed in clothes of her own design and making, her hands carefully French-polished. The Mum who would pick me up from my first very expensive private school in London and take me to Peter Jones to the cafe where we would have afternoon tea before walking home through the city streets, and my weekend country Mum, who wore old shirts and jeans and gumboots, and liked nothing better than to be working in her garden or renovating the house.

By the time I was eight, life in our family was beginning to fray at the edges. My father's career had temporarily dive-bombed, and with four children under eight it was impossible for my mother to keep working. The decision was made for us to move to the country, and for my father to keep working in the city during the week.

This was a time of strange upheaval, but my mother was determined to make it work. I, of course, was delighted to be living in the country—anything that meant I could be nearer horses was OK by me, and for some time it seemed as if she would keep alive her dream of a happy family and her country life with freelance work and painting on the side.

She put a lot of effort into our lives, working incredibly hard at creating the picture of a happy country life.

I remember a particular few years, probably when I was around ten or eleven, when everything—to my child eyes—seemed to be as it should be (apart from my father's black moods, that is). We had an enormous vegetable patch that fed us; we had a small orchard of fruit trees and bushes—blackberries, redcurrants and cherries included. Our garden twinkled and shone with rockeries, flowerbeds and a pergola covered in roses. Mum made chutneys and jams and preserves of all kinds. With the help of a gardener, a cleaner and live-in help, life ran relatively smoothly—frozen pipes, cracked slate roofs, pet disasters, snow, slush and mud notwithstanding. The silver got cleaned, the lawns mowed, the red tiled floors polished and the firewood chopped. Dusting happened on a regular basis and the ironing, with my mother's insistence on ironing absolutely everything, including face flannels, sheets and underpants, was downright scary—particularly to me, since it was often on my list of Saturday morning chores. Hospital corners were paramount, as was calling things by their right names—napkins not serviettes, sofas not settees, supper not tea.

I loved my mother so. I loved her gentleness and kindness, and her constant availability for cuddles. When I was about ten I was struck with the notion suddenly that she might die, and I spent a long time one night when she was putting me to bed trying to subtly ascertain the state of her health. She didn't know whether to laugh or be offended. 'Candy,' she said, 'I'm only thirty-eight!' Well, that seemed a great age to me, I can tell you, and didn't allay my fears in the slightest. Thirty-eight!

I had a wicked habit of slipping downstairs to be with her after we children had gone to bed. I would tell my unfortunate younger sister that she was not under any circumstances to follow me because the witch who lived on the landing would eat her, then I would persuade Mum that Tessa was sound asleep and she should let me sit on the sofa with her. If she gave in we would drink hot chocolate, eat biscuits and watch television together. She was very interested in what was going on in the world, and she also loved to watch sport on TV—in fact it didn't really matter if it was Kenneth Clark's *Civilization* or Wimbledon, it was all information to her and she shared it with me, or at least until Tessa would overcome her fear of the witch and appear crying at the door, at which point I would be summarily sent straight back to bed.

So that was my mother for the first decade of my life. She was the first of many women to fill my life with love. The love of a mother for a daughter and a daughter for a mother is a wonderful thing, and I was lucky to know the very best of her when I was small.

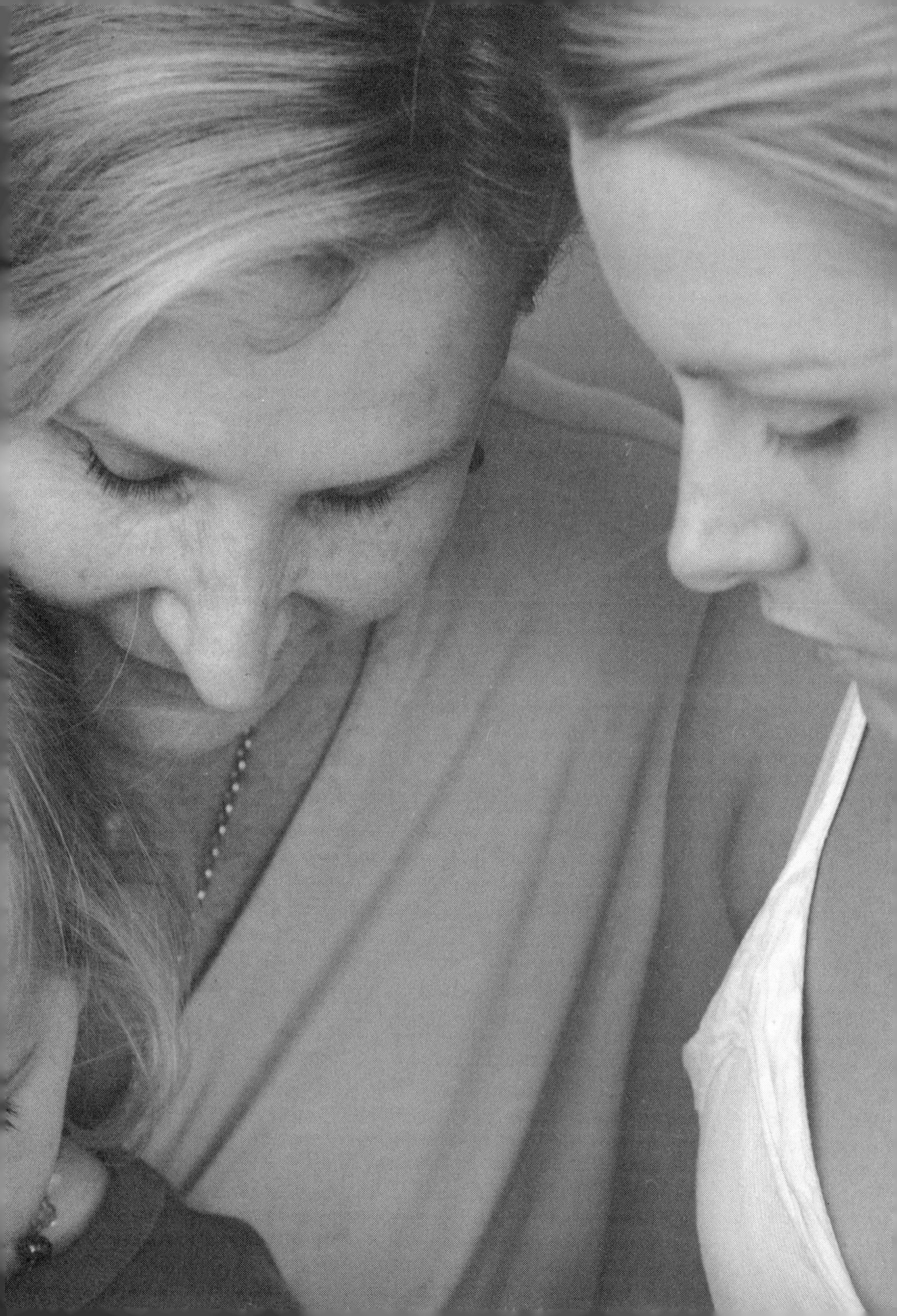

2

It takes all sorts

What does the ideal mother look like? I have absolutely no idea! I hope that despite the flow of constantly cheerful beautiful women in TV ads making sandwiches, cleaning houses, sending children off to school and driving in spotless cars we have come far enough to know that mothers are far more than any stereotypical media version of what or how we should be.

Certainly that was the case for composer Yantra de Vilder, whose mother, Faith Reid, was a trailblazer for women in the media.

I always wanted a normal mother—you know, the kind that makes cross-over curtains and bakes cakes—but this was not to be. I grew up in the fifties, a time when women had not even begun to burn their bras or question the domestic status quo.

My mother, Faith Reid, was different. She had a high-powered career in the early days of television and radio, working as a presenter and journalist. From a young age she had been instilled with the virtue of service. Indeed, her school motto, *Ut Prosim*—'To Serve'—has run a strong course through her life, and now, in her twilight years, her sense of herself and her place in the world is as inspiring as ever. These days she finds joy in the simple things.

But this was not always so. Faith was endowed with a searching soul and an intelligent mind. After winning a scholarship to Sydney University, she was chosen for a Cadetship at ABC Radio, where she later joined the nightly broadcasting team for the National Children's Hour. Married women were not eligible for employment in the public service in those days, but on her wedding morning Faith received a telegram from Sir Charles Moses, then the head of the ABC, welcoming her back as a freelance artist. She became a regular acting and writing member of the team that produced the Argonauts Club—a cult radio phenomenon in those days.

Domestic bliss was never high on my mother's list of priorities. I constantly struggled with this, as I had quite old-fashioned views of what a mother should be. All I really wanted was for her to be at home, cooking and cleaning like a 'normal' mother. I was highly embarrassed that she was on television at all, and if any of my friends recognised her on TV I would deny that it was her. How times change—now I am so proud of the work she was doing then and I wouldn't have it any other way.

I find it interesting now that all the things Mum was doing revolved around children—the bigger picture of children's needs. Mum even had the foresight to send me to a Rudolf Steiner school, as I was clearly more interested in creativity than academia at the time. And of course I was never neglected; I had a loving family home on the leafy north shore of Sydney.

Looking back, I can see that without Mum's influence I wouldn't be where I am today. It is through her example that I have been able to carve out my own niche in the music world, and constantly reinvent myself in my career and lifestyle. I also realise just how important my mother's influence on me has been in terms of my sense of service to the world. More and more I have chosen work that I feel makes a difference. To me it has been a wonderful experience of continuity and the power of lineage.

Recently, I have been fortunate to be deeply immersed in projects that have meant a great deal to me, such as working for the BBC as a composer on a wide range of TV and radio series. I have worked with Burmese refugees, Afghani musicians and Bangladeshi people. Many times I have heard my mother's voice in my head guiding and encouraging me: 'We may never know the consequence of our care for each other, or the far paths which our kindness may travel. Behind every working volunteer in an underdeveloped country lies the inspiration received from another being.'

Naturally, there are times when my career has been particularly challenging, and yet I feel that the path that my mother has walked has somehow smoothed the road for me. I have found (like my mother) that more often than not doors tend to open for me by virtue of being in the right place at the right time with the right attitude. Once again I see a parallel between Mum's life and my own, where she was battling with the 1950s status quo that said that most women stay home, and I on the other hand chose the life of a composer—a predominantly male-dominated arena.

My mother's words have been heard and seen in many different forms: radio, television, books and public speaking. In a speech she gave in 1951 she said 'It is your capacity to live life to the full in the best sense of the word that counts.' It is her engagement with this inner world that is deeply embedded in my mother's influence on me—the importance of quiet time, the need to walk the middle path, to 'listen to a beautiful piece of music, to read a fine piece of poetry and to do something for someone else every day'.

And now, when my mother's life is becoming quieter and infused with a deep stillness, I am blessed with the moments of time we have together. Both of us understand the world of deadlines and pressure, but are also impelled to sit by the lake and feed the ducks, watching the play of light among the reeds and reflections.

We are also making the most of our shared talents. For many years Mum has been collecting words of wisdom, and her old and tattered book of sayings has been a constant companion to her throughout the years. Now we have joined forces, me with my watercolour painting, and her with her quotations, to create a book together. Called *Wisdom Writings*, this special project is truly a meeting in the finest sense of the word, and has been a process that we both cherish.

After a life of incredible highs and challenging lows, I watch with a mixture of sadness and inspiration as my mother becomes more restricted in her mobility and lifestyle, and am humbled when she says: 'One appreciates Shakespeare far better when one has withstood, or experienced, the "slings and arrows of outrageous fortune".' And yet this difficult time of ageing also seems to provide her with an inner depth and strength that it is a privilege to witness.

Writer and journalist Liz Porter also had a working mother, Rose Porter, who was a biochemist, and, according to Liz, as precise with her work as she was experimental with her cooking. Rose was obviously a 'supermum' long before the phrase was fashionable, and her cool ability to deal with children was something Liz admired in her as both a parent and a grandparent.

'If I tell you what happened,' my thirteen-year-old daughter asks me. 'Do you promise not to go mad at me?'

I agree, of course. Thinking of my mother, who never lost her temper with me when I was a teenager, I also make a silent vow to keep my word. Lying on my daughter's bed, I listen to the story— mouth clamped shut. It is five days before Christmas 2004. It's been a ghastly day. And this evening is not improving it. I have spent most of the afternoon in a hospital foyer, getting Mum admitted. She has cancer, and has suddenly become much weaker.

It is also my birthday—a detail that is only relevant because Mum has forgotten it, and that means she is seriously ill. Panic rises in my throat. But I contemplate her stoicism in the face of illness and I remain calm.

'Calm' is always the word that comes to mind when I think of Mum. A working mother years before the words 'double shift', 'stress' or 'supermum' entered everyday parlance, she worked as a biochemist in the pathology department of Melbourne's Royal Women's Hospital.

Every night at six she'd walk through the front door, straight-backed, her bag full of shopping she'd done on the way home, ready to cook dinner. She was 'part time', meaning she finished at 4 p.m. instead of 5 p.m., allowing time for the tram ride from Carlton into the city, a stop at a shop or two, then the bus ride to south-east suburban Caulfield.

Now, more than five years after her death, I close my eyes and remember her sitting at the grey laminex table in the kitchen, buttering sandwiches for my school lunch. It's night time and our cat perches on a chair, gleaming eyes watching every move of the butter knife, ready in case Mum might set it down for her to lick clean (as if!). Aged sixteen, I am also sitting at the table, doing homework.

I have always made a point of making my daughter's school lunch. Unlike Mum, I do it in the morning—but it's one of the many things I do just because she did them. It's one of the ways I keep her alive.

I talk of 'channelling Mum' every time I urge my daughter to—please, darling—wear a coat, as she heads out bare-armed on an icy Melbourne winter's night. But when I talk seriously of emulating my mother's behaviour I mean that I wish to follow the example she set by the way she lived her life.

My mother lost everyone except her immediate nuclear family in the Holocaust. Yet she expressed none of the intolerance towards modern Germans that I have heard in many who lost less at the hands of the Nazis.

She was also always, of all her siblings, the one with the most open-minded view on the (for most Jews) vexed question of the Arab–Israeli conflict. She was 'the sensible one', as all my cousins called her, approvingly.

Mum's tolerance was shaped by the fact that she was one of that large group of Australians who, arriving here before World War II, had their lives saved—literally—by immigration.

Fortunately for her and her five siblings, her father, Abraham Wysokier, was prescient enough to leave Poland more than a decade before the Holocaust destroyed his and his wife's entire extended families. With Mum's older brother Raphael he travelled to Belgium and then Paris, seeking a place where Jews might live in peace. Finally, father and son left for Australia, sending for the rest of the family after they found work.

Mum's journey as a migrant began with the excitement of a train trip from Warsaw to Marseilles, during which she met the first of a group of Polish Jewish girls with whom she would remain friends for her whole life. With her mother and siblings (and her new friend Esther) she then boarded the French liner, SS *Commissaire Ramel* for the voyage to Australia.

The Wysokier family arrived in Melbourne on 30 January 1930 and were welcomed into the close-knit migrant Jewish community of Carlton—the social landscape remembered by writer and Wysokier family friend Judah Waten in his book *Alien Son*, and again, more recently, by writer Arnold Zable.

'Everyone helped one another,' Mum always used to say.

I can only imagine how traumatic it must have been to be dumped, aged thirteen years and eleven months, and speaking no English, into the eighth grade at the local state school. 'Miss, she don't know,' was the first English phrase Mum learned. Her deskmate said it whenever a teacher looked in her direction. In Poland, I remember Mum telling me, she had been quite the extrovert—the sort of kid who'd go in the school play.

But immigration changed all that, robbing Mum of her native language and, therefore, her confidence. Acutely shy, Mum battled to improve her English by ploughing through the English translations of Tolstoy, Turgenev and Proust that her older sisters brought home from the library. Two years later, after repeating the eighth grade at Princes Hill Central, she was able to pass the entrance exam for the selective Melbourne Girls' High, soon to be reborn in new premises as MacRobertson Girls' High School. One teacher told her she would 'never make it' at university.

But within five years of her arrival, Mum was one of a minority of women doing a Bachelor of Science degree at the University of Melbourne, following that up with a career as a biochemist, first at the Alfred Hospital's Baker Institute and then at the Royal Women's Hospital.

Mum had always wanted to work in a hospital pathology department but such jobs were scarce. Initially she worked in an industrial job and then as a science teacher. But, determined to get the experience she needed, she worked for nothing in the Royal Women's pathology department. Impressed, a senior scientist recommended her when the war broke out and the Baker Institute needed a replacement for a male scientist who had enlisted.

Mum was a quiet achiever. And a quiet rebel. She loved and respected her Orthodox Jewish parents, but followed her own path. Seeking alternatives to her mother's kosher cooking, she led her elder sister Hela on Saturday afternoon expeditions to the restaurant of the Victoria Hotel in Little Collins Street for decidedly non-kosher sausages and mash.

Her ultimate act of rebellion was her marriage to my father, Norman Porter, whom she met in 1938 at the home of Judah Waten. She always referred to the occasion as 'one of Judah's drunken parties'. Waten was a central figure in a colourful Melbourne group of left-wing bohemians. It included the journalists Brian Fitzpatrick, Theo Moody and Alywn Lee, the artist Noel Counihan, and my father—a wharfie's son who, at fifteen, had been apprenticed to the artist Max Meldrum. After doing a brilliant philosophy MA at the University of Melbourne, my father had been a philosophy lecturer at Sydney University under the legendary libertarian philosopher John Anderson. But his contract had not been renewed under controversial circumstances largely brought on by the over-exuberant behaviour of a young man enjoying his first good salary and the opportunity to spend it wining and dining a crew of very hard drinkers. By 1938 he was back in Melbourne, unemployed, divorced from his artist first wife, studying Chinese in Chinatown, and generally worrying his hardworking Catholic mother to death.

His first meeting with Mum was the 'coup de foudre'—love at first sight. In sweet and gentle 22-year-old Rose Wysokier he found an intellectual peer and a woman with the capacity to calm his restless spirit. Mum found him interesting intellectually. But she thought he was, at thirty-four, too old, and, as a gentile, entirely unacceptable to her parents.

Mum was always unconventional enough to question the decisions made by peers of hers who heeded their parents' disapproval of relationships with gentiles, but it still took her a while to work up the courage to defy her own parents and put them in a situation where, if they were to follow custom, they would end up saying the 'prayer for the dead' for her. (They never did, but she wasn't to know that then.)

My father persisted, writing long, passionate letters to her at the university. By late 1939 they were an item. And finally, with the war breaking out, my father had a job. With his knowledge of twenty European and Asian languages, he was welcomed into the war effort as a translator in intelligence.

On her wedding day in 1942, Mum left the family home without telling her parents of her plans. She eventually reconciled with her father three years later, but not before she missed out on her own mother's funeral. And true to her quietly unconventional nature she defied the custom that a woman should stop working after her marriage. She stopped only when my older sister was born, and returned when I was six, so I was always one of only a few in the class with a mother who worked.

Mum kept on with her education through her sixties, seventies and eighties, doing CAE and University of the Third Age courses in history, Latin and Italian, and making significant new friendships along the way. But despite all these interests, she always had unlimited time for her daughters and her grandchildren. Whenever my daughter was ill and I had to go to work, I would always ring Mum and ask if I could bring her over. But the question was only a courtesy. I knew the answer would always be 'of course'. And she didn't just 'mind' grandchildren; she helped them. At eighty-seven, and diagnosed with cancer, she was coaching my daughter in Year 7 maths.

My mother's patience made her the perfect person to handle a tantrum-throwing toddler, using skills that, it seems, have already been passed on to a third generation. When my daughter was a toddler her response to getting overtired and hungry was to refuse to eat, sending her blood sugar even lower and making her crankier and more irrational than ever.

Other adults would make things worse by trying to persuade her to eat. But Mum would just prepare some food, put it on the table and wander out of the room, apparently oblivious to the small child huffing and puffing a few feet away. Alone, and with no position to defend, my daughter would, of course, attack the food with gusto—and her good mood would return.

Now seventeen, my daughter recently found herself babysitting a younger relative, who was throwing a tantrum and refusing to eat her dinner.

'Remember what Rose used to do when I wouldn't eat?' my daughter said, when she got home. 'I did the same. I made her some food—and then left the room. She ate it all up.'

I am always intrigued by the many stories I hear these days about grandmothers resenting being 'used as babysitters'. I was never in a hurry to have children, but I always knew I wanted to have at least one child, and that my main reason had less to do with notions of 'creating a family' than with replicating the closeness I had enjoyed with my mother.

Because of Mum, I now look forward to my own daughter being a mother, and to looking after her children the way Mum looked after my Alice and my sister's children. I will do well if I manage the task with half the grace she brought to it.

Liz Porter's story has a lovely feeling of continuation about it, that the lessons Rose taught have been learned and passed on. Liz and her daughter still enjoy the sense that Rose would approve of what they are doing.

Talking of 'looking after', I love the following piece by Kerry Littrich, a mum to two soccer-crazed boys who also teaches Buddhism and meditation—it seems to me to sum up exactly what we all want from our mothers. Perhaps if we are lucky we have experienced this feeling from time to time. If not, then perhaps we can give this feeling to our daughters or to girls we know.

> As I open the door, rock'n'roll music plays through the crackly speakers of our old stereo. My mum walks barefoot into the lounge room. She wears a loose summer house-dress and the sun streams in through the window behind her. I drop my school bag and she takes my hands in hers, gently bouncing them up and down.
> 'Feel it,' she says.
> She looks down at our feet, listening, concentrating, then up into my eyes with a slight smile on her lips. She swings me a little from side to side, pushing one hand back and pulling the other forward. The smell of dinner cooking wafts through from the kitchen. The movements get bigger and faster. Now we are both smiling. She pushes me to turn, letting go of one hand, and I duck under her arm and spin around on my toes. She smells of cooking and woman. It is delicious.

This little piece too, by writer Jessie Cole, is a testament to the smell and feeling of our mothers—that indefinable essence that is perhaps our first taste of sensuousness in the world; the comfort of smell, and touch, and the feeling of motherly safety.

On a quest for socks I happen into my mother's room, lit up in the half-light. The rack of her clothes hangs up against the wall, muted earthy colours. I think of the comfort of her long, flowing skirts, and how I had once climbed beneath them, shielded and shrouded. When I was small, my mother's gaze was a constant presence, an endless beaming light. I had talked and played and laughed within this soft sun-gaze, but sometimes, overwhelmed by brightness, I searched around for shade. Curling myself against my mother's soft frame, I hid my face beneath her clothes, nuzzling in the shadowed darkness against her warm, dry skin.

And now, reaching out a hand, I trace the edge of the silk scarf that hangs down beside the door, remembering.

I read Jessie's and Kerry's stories with a touch of sadness because by the time I was twelve my beautiful mother had begun to disappear, fading at the edges slowly at first, then quicker and quicker as the years went by until she was nothing like the mother of my early childhood.

How quickly adult life went wrong for my mother. By the time I was eight she had four children under eight, my father's acting career had dive-bombed, and the time she had spent away from her career was looking irreversible. Unbeknown to her, my father had started a long affair with the woman who would later become his second wife (my stepmother Sally, who was the love of my father's life and mother to my wonderful half-sister Sarah), and it suited him for my mother and the four of us to move to our rented weekend country cottage.

So, having worked with people like John Ford and Ava Gardner, whose bust Mum used as a model for her own clothes because they were exactly the same figure, there she was in an isolated hamlet, two miles from the nearest village shop, initially without even a driving licence, with two children and two tiny babies, her husband in London during the week.

I wonder now how she coped at all, because although she loved the beauty of nature, she was very much a woman of the city—how she must have missed her work, which she loved, and the shops and restaurants and the theatre, and how she must have missed her friends.

Of course, I didn't see any of this then. I was busy starting a lifelong love of country living and horses, and was entirely swept up in my childhood concerns—except that even then it was obvious that my father's occasional presence was disturbing. If he was happy, and friends came for Sunday lunch, the house seemed alive with joy and laughter—actors and actresses, directors and producers and playwrights, family and extended family came to our cottage and all received a warm welcome. But how quickly it could change. A few too many drinks and my father's mood would plunge, and off we would whirl on the merry-go-round of his anger, recriminations and tantrums.

I remember once, many years later, asking my mother how on earth her drinking became a problem in the first place. It was a gradual progression, she said, from the odd drink with lunch and dinner to too many to cope with the weekend, to the prop that it became in order for her to cope with the lonely weeks, with her lonely life. She drank to drown her sorrows, but for those of us around her, the sorrow was the drink.

We would manage to laugh, sometimes, at the stories. Mum drunk out of her brain, waving the car key across the lock, fortunately incapable of inserting it. How long it would take her to butter a piece of toast, or us finding yet again that the vodka bottle had water in it, and the whisky bottle had cold tea, or that she had bought alcohol in place of the food she had gone out to buy.

There was also her absolute refusal to countenance AA. 'Not in the country,' she told us once. 'Now if it was Belgravia ...' As if *where* you were an alcoholic counted! Her brother, my uncle, was a generous and wonderful soul, and he took over much of her care financially, and relieved us of a burden we were unable to handle. In the long run my sisters and I all recognised that being supported in such a way is not the best thing for someone with an addiction, but at the time, with my younger sisters still at home and suffering from their mother's lack of care, I did not know what else to do, or where to turn.

In reality, these stories were not funny, and my heart bleeds for every child whose mother becomes emotionally absent due to an addiction of any kind.

When she died, falling down the stairs of our cottage when she was drunk, the second cause of death was cirrhosis. She was lucky it was not the first—the angels took pity on her, I believe.

By the time my sister and I got back to England from Australia, she had been dead a few days and was lying at the funeral home.

I decided that I wanted to see her body, which was in an open casket.

It was the strangest experience, looking at her body and realising that she simply wasn't there. She'd left her body behind, it seemed to me, and that feeling led on to the absolute belief that she was still around, but in a different form.

It is a feeling that has never left me.

Don't compromise yourself. You are all you've got.

JANIS JOPLIN

3

Standing out from the crowd

*I*t's hard to stand out when you're a child, isn't it? After all, what you want more than anything else in the world is to be accepted. Even if you're not lucky enough to be a 'cool' kid, at least perhaps the middle group will take you in, you hope. The last thing you want is to be left on the sidelines, to be noticed for being different in any way, shape or form. And yet, for many of us, to a greater or lesser degree that does occur.

I know that I often felt like an outsider as a child. My family's fluctuating financial fortunes didn't help. I spent half the time at private schools being bullied because my father couldn't pay the school fees, and then at government schools being bullied because I spoke in a posh accent. I often felt that there was nowhere I belonged. For me, nature was my sanctuary, and the place I received no judgement was with my country friends and my animals, and I guess that feeling has stayed with me all my life.

Of course, I know that I'm lucky—the sense of being an outsider was an emotional sense, not something brought about because of an extreme physical difference. Yet even these differences, handled and supported properly, can encourage people to live the fullest lives imaginable, as Elaine, a broadcaster and writer, describes.

> You wouldn't think loneliness possible when growing up as the second child in a family of five, would you? The early childhood equivalent of being lonely in a crowd, perhaps? Well, in the early years it wasn't much of a problem, but being the only child of the family to attend boarding school did have its drawbacks.
>
> The school wasn't my parents' choice but just the way things were done then. The first primary school was close enough for me to go home every weekend. Mum would collect me on a Friday afternoon, then the whole family would pile into the car to take me back on Sunday evening. Friday lunch was almost invariably fish, followed by lemon meringue pie; I am allergic to the one and at that stage hated the other, so was inevitably starving by the time classes finished. Mum generally arrived with a treat for us to share during the long bus trip home and it felt like manna from heaven. The family also attended the annual Christmas plays, carol services and sports days, as well as many concerts. Some of it must have

been deadly dull for my brothers and sisters but I heard not one word of complaint—Mum would never have allowed it.

The high school was the only one of its kind catering to blind students such as me, and much further from home than the primary school. It had exacting academic standards and provided invaluable, if stringent, social training, not always appreciated at the time. The anguish of those first nights back there at the start of each term haunts me still. Holidays were longed for, looked forward to—and boring. Reading, writing letters, listening to radio serials and playing solitaire scrabble can fill only so many hours, and it was during this time that Mum and I became firm friends. She followed the radio serials with me, shared an afternoon treat, and took me with her on shopping trips that were fun simply because we did them together. The friendship survived the usual domestic battles between mother and teenage daughter, and it occurred to me only recently that her hostility towards my husband during the early years of our marriage probably stemmed from the fear of losing that precious bond. Mercifully they were more than reconciled before leukaemia claimed her.

It was when I returned to live at home after years away at school that I saw my first example of multi-tasking, long before the expression was invented. Mum was a miracle worker, I was sure of it. How else could she get everyone out of bed, fed and through the door on time for their respective jobs or schools, and still be ready by nine o'clock to open the shop she owned at the time? Living on the premises was practical and convenient.

I learned countless things from Mum over the years—though knitting remains beyond me and I still need recipes where she never did—but it was during the troublesome teens that she offered the wisest counsel. Group interaction with strangers can be challenging enough during puberty, but add blindness to the mix and there are even more unseen traps and hurdles, if you'll pardon the pun. I had much to learn about eye contact and body language, and it was Mum who taught me that just because someone did not address me directly by name it did not mean they were excluding me from the group.

'They include you with their eyes, Darling.'

I can still hear her say it and feel the untold, palpable relief offered by that simple revelation—something I was unable to know for myself. She also taught me the vital lesson of always looking at the person to whom I am speaking, something else I had not managed to work out for myself. Obvious lessons, you might think, but without her assistance I may never have learned them. I have since worked in the communications industry for more years than I dare to count: radio, television, print, extensive public speaking and some teaching, as well as serving on various boards and engaging in theatrical performing; without Mum's timely intervention, all this would have been a great deal more difficult. Striving to be accepted on merit and on equal terms is a constant battle, and the advice given to a troubled teenager added valuable weapons to the armoury.

Mum also possessed that rare gift of loving all five of us siblings equally while still managing to make each one of us feel unique and cherished—a lesson in itself.

Money was tight when we were growing up but this did not prevent Mum learning braille and acquiring the necessary equipment in order to write to me when I was at school. She and Dad also had the phone installed before I went to high school; it wasn't the norm in most rental housing in England in the late 1960s. Before that, Mum had trudged to the nearest public phone to maintain contact if ever I needed to stay at school over the weekend.

I was twelve years old when my younger brother was born. As he grew older we worked our way through many books, from the *Mr. Men* books to the Narnia series and on to *Watership Down*. Mum would creep in to listen as I read aloud, enjoying the stories as much as we did, particularly when I put on different voices for the various characters. Audio books were not as popular as they are now, but even then she believed I deserved a wider audience.

Mum died in March 1993, leaving a void that can never be filled. I think of her often, talk to her and ask her opinion. I think I am still mentally seeking her approval even after all this time.

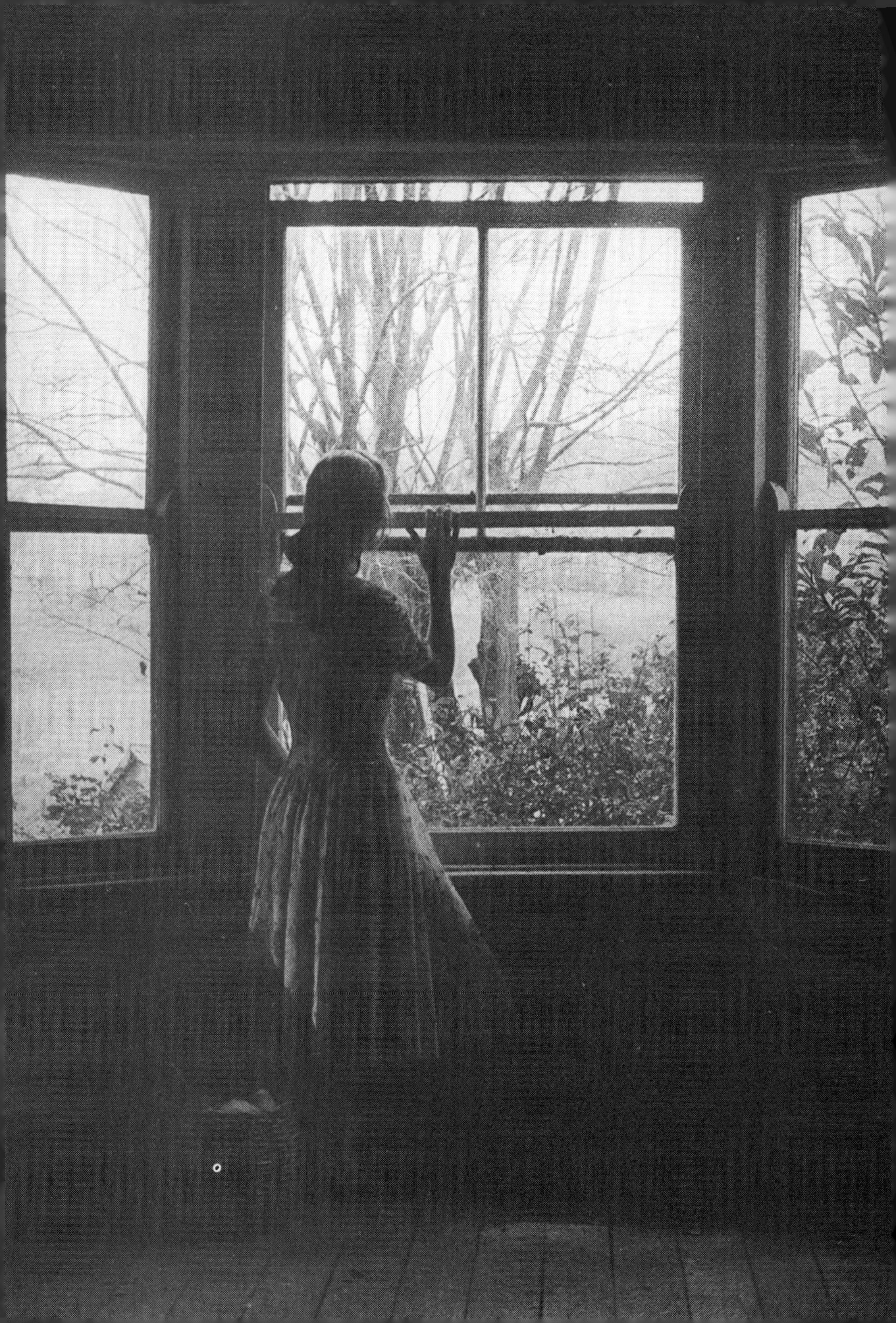

4
The importance of fitting in

As a teenager the importance of parties looms large on the horizon, doesn't it? In fact the importance of parties probably begins much earlier. I know for me the childhood parties—who to invite, would they come, should I ask boys ('no way' and 'yuk' being the answers to that question)—were as important as the teenage parties, although of course by then boys had become obligatory, desirable and essential!

I don't think there would be a single one of us who would not have had a great or even dreadful party moment. You know, those parties where everything is perfect—music, dancing, food and company—and those parties were everything goes wrong, including your love life.

The importance of fitting in

And of all those parties, New Year's Eve carries the most freight—who wants to be left alone on New Year's Eve? The stigma attached to nothing to do and nobody to be with is too horrible to contemplate. As for the first New Year's Eve with the first kiss with the first boy, well, as Susan Wyndham recalls, that is something to remember.

I could tell you about the office Christmas party where I first kissed my husband, or the New Year's Eve party where I kissed someone else's husband. Both were the beginning of grand love stories.

But those parties are a blur: Michael Jackson's new *Thriller* album, raspberries dripping with cream, daggy fancy dress ... nothing else remains.

The same with the party where I met my ex-husband's boyfriend. My manic friendliness and post-party sobs drown out the rest.

There have been plenty of baggage-free parties where I danced a lot and drank a lot. But one long-ago night hovers above the rest with a magical aura. It rushes back whenever I smell jasmine.

New Year's Eve 1972 was looking grim. My mother had a party to go to but no invitations had come for me—social death for a fifteen-year-old. And then, sweet relief, I discovered my friend Virginia was also going to be alone. With the house to myself, I asked her to come and stay the night. Two outcasts are less pathetic than one. We could eat, drink, sneak a cigarette and giggle our way into 1973.

Once she arrived we had a better idea: why not invite some boys around? I can't recall who rang whom or if we got any rejections.

All that matters is we found three desperate sixteen-year-olds with nowhere better to go.

One of them had taken me to a school dance that year and thrust his tongue in my mouth (I wouldn't call it kissing). He had gone out with Virginia too, but neither of us liked him in 'that' way. One was a country boy from aristocratic stock who hung around our group. And one was a cutie we both vaguely fancied. We anticipated their arrival as if Mr Darcy was about to ride through the front door.

My mother, looking beautiful, left for her party. We waited. The boys were late. I don't know how we filled the time. Eventually they arrived with a bottle or two of Cold Duck. We sat facing each other, on two sofas and the floor, in the tiny living room with a sandstock brick fireplace. My mother had bought the house a few months earlier after years of rented flats. This was my first 'party'.

The night's music was my small pile of LPs: Rod Stewart, Joe Cocker, Bette Midler, Elton John, America, Santana. We drank cheap wine and smoked a few cigarettes. Our uneven numbers meant there was no pressure to pair off and pash. Flirtation breezed through the room just lightly enough to remind us we were teenagers. Mostly we talked and talked and laughed at anything.

Some time before midnight we moved onto the little wooden deck at the back of the house. One of the boys shook a bottle of Cold Duck so the cork burst out and the syrupy wine fizzed round the courtyard. I'm not sure if we could hear anyone else as we noisily toasted the New Year. It was long before Sydney's fireworks and mass celebrations. We all kissed and laughed a whole lot more.

The wine ran out and the boys went home at some point. Then the best part of the night began. Far from being social rejects, Virginia and I were buoyed by our triumph. We might have lain on our beds in my attic, but we didn't sleep. There was a whole event to relive, with commentary.

By dawn we were light-headed. We decided we should be the first people to leave our footprints on the year. Virginia pulled on her rolled-up grey velvet Sportsgirl pants. I wore something with cork-soled white clogs. As we walked out the front door, my mother opened the gate and crept in carrying her shoes. We were all giddy teenagers caught in the act.

The streets of Woollahra and Paddington were silent. Even the most hardened partygoers had given up. We walked without a plan, up empty lanes and around unknown corners, past terrace houses spilling jasmine over their fences. We picked sprigs and carried the sweetness with us.

The sun seemed to rise with epochal slowness, softly warming the air. No day could have been more beautiful, no sky more blue, no year more full of possibility. 'This is the morning of the Earth!' we shouted. Like most teenagers, we had seen a new Australian surf movie that was about more than waves. Alby Falzon's *Morning of the Earth*, with its rock soundtrack, showed surfers at one with nature and youth as a kind of Eden. We were there.

Singing and twirling through the streets, smiling at strangers, we were as joyful as we ever would be. At fifteen, life was still to come. We were probably awkward, pimply and uncertain. But we were also gorgeous, powerful and wise enough to savour perfection.

Some time in the bright morning we drifted home and went to sleep. The year sped up. We fell in love, got part-time jobs, smoked our first joint, did the School Certificate exams. I spent the next New Year's Eve with my boyfriend, though I can't remember where.

I don't know, either, what happened to the boys who shared that night with us. To them it might have been a disappointment. No-one got drunk. No-one scored. It wasn't even a real party. But I'm still grateful for their good-natured company and low expectations. They were the chorus to our celebration.

All these years I thought I'd clung to the myth on my own. Then I asked Virginia how much she recalled and out poured the details: phone calls, boys' names, velvet pants, jasmine, Morning of the Earth, elation. That's why we're friends. She said: 'It would be wonderful to walk again that morning...'

We both know you can't go back. And you can't plan spontaneity. The best parties, like the best kisses, happen when you least expect them. You just have to be ready to seize the night.

For most of us, life—particularly during the working week—is a well-trodden routine. We go about our daily tasks of getting ourselves to work and/or our children to school in such an automatic fashion that we can become quite oblivious to our surroundings. There's a certain shut-down face, isn't there, of the people on the buses and the trains as they listen to their music or read their papers and just, well, get on with what they have to do.

The importance of fitting in

But just sometimes something will pierce the mundane routine, take us out of ourselves—remind us that the world is beautiful, and not always the same. Here is a story about the opposite of fitting in, or how everybody on a bus was arrested in their normal routine by the arrival of someone 'different'. Linda Walker describes a simple moment while travelling into work and how it was transformed into something special by the arrival of a girl who was transfixed by the fun and, to her, the beauty of the bus and the journey.

Sometimes your path crosses with someone and they may not even know of the impact they have upon the way you will view the world after just a fleeting moment in their presence. This story is a treasured one that I sometimes take out of the memory box in my mind, and I never fail to recall without a smile.

Some years ago I was living and working in the centre of Sydney. I took a bus to work daily and would spend most mornings sitting in silence cursing the public transport system. This particular morning was worse than usual. It was a Monday for a start, and it was cold and raining heavily. The seats were wet and workers were unhappily filing onto the bus after a weekend off, grimly ignoring each other, sitting with glazed expressions on their faces. I'm afraid I was one of them. I don't think one person wanted to be on that bus, facing the start of another dreary wet week. As the bus began to get crowded, rude messages were muttered under breaths and rude looks given as wet bags brushed past people. You could feel it in the air, a trapped feeling of being somewhere you didn't want to be. We all in turn stared blankly out the windows as the rain came down, not willing to even pass the time by talking with each other. Then we stopped for a new passenger.

I craned my neck up to see who the hold-up was, why the big delay in getting us moving again. A girl with Down syndrome had got onto our bus, and her mum was nervously trying to explain to the bus driver where she was to get off, and that someone would be waiting for her at the other end of her ride.

This girl's face was so different to ours. She was so excited to be on this bus ride by herself. Her face was optimistic and hopeful, joyful even—so different to the expressions we all wore. There were no seats left by then, so she stood alone near the front luggage area, smiling around. Most people ignored her, but I watched her, fascinated. Waving her arm around indicating the streets outside, and with a huge smile, she announced to the bus in general that everything was pretty now, it was wet, see how it shines? Like fans uniting with a Mexican wave, smiles and warmth seemed to flow around our bus.

We looked again, but this time with her eyes. Where we had seen greyness, she was seeing glitter. She kept pointing it out to us. The shiny trees, the shiny cars, the shiny road. Pretty soon our bus was full of shiny, happy people as we got caught up in her delight at something so simple. You could almost feel the mood lift as we all became a little less cynical about things for just a while.

I think sometimes life just sends you little moments like that to surprise you. A little warm fuzzy moment for you to tuck away and take out again when it's needed. The memory of the girl and the happiness she brought to that bus is as vivid in my mind as the day it happened. That simple enjoyment and the reaction it caused in us all, lifting and lightening our mood.

I don't know where she is now, that smiling happy girl, but I hope she is out there, continuing to be the sunshine of someone's life, and still seeing the glitter through the grey.

Seeing the glitter through the grey—what a lovely expression! All too often if we are in a place of sadness or depression, or of simply getting on with life, we forget to lift our heads a minute and see the glitter through the grey, but if we do take the time, we *will* see it.

Find out who you are and do it on purpose.

DOLLY PARTON

5

The friends we find and the friends who find us

I made my very first best friend when I fell into a blackberry bush in her garden at the age of five. My howling was only stopped at the sight of a girl, slightly older than me, with white-blonde hair and the bluest eyes I've ever seen. In next to no time Lyn and I were firm friends, and it was a friendship that extended to all my younger sisters. My next best friend, Sally, also lived in the village and she had a pony! I was desperate to learn to ride, and desperate to be friends with someone who had a pony, and quite soon Sally and I became inseparable. Over the years we spent hours together riding and staying over at each other's places or just hanging out. We would make up stories in which it was discovered that we were actually sisters, or in which something awful would happen to one of our families so the other family would adopt the lonely orphaned child.

In fact, our collective imaginations were pretty gruesome—my mother had a wonderful dress-up box full of cast-off costumes and clothes from her mother that went back to Edwardian-style fashion. We invented a never-ending game called Aunt Emily. Aunt Emily was a cruel harridan and we took turns to play her. Our gang of four or five, made up of sisters, a visiting friend and the two other village girls, would be the orphans left behind when our parents died (a strangely recurring theme now I think about it!). Aunt Emily would be unimaginably awful to us, locking us up in attics and punishing us for the slightest misdemeanour, and we would spend hours plotting how to escape her, which of course in reality simply meant walking away from the game.

We invented and performed endlessly boring plays and made our parents and other innocent bystanders pay money to watch performances that had no beginning, middle or end. But what we mostly did—and how lucky were we—was to roam the several thousand acres our little rented cottages were on, pinching apples from neighbours' gardens, swimming in the river, playing chicken on the train tracks and daring ourselves to crawl across the slippery pipe suspended across the river. In the winter we would toboggan down the hills in the snow and wait for the pond to be frozen enough to slide on, or inevitably try it before it was frozen. And if we were bored with everything else there was always Sally's grandad's farm just up the road, with its herd of Friesian cows and its one very friendly Jersey cow, Beatrice. It also housed the hay shed, the feed shed and the stables.

At one point we decided to make a club, and we met in the feed shed at the weekends. We called ourselves the Rousham Girls Friendship Club, which my father unkindly but somewhat truthfully renamed the Rousham Girls Frenzied Club, due to our unfortunate habit of falling out with each other almost as often as we were friends.

Even though these friendships were formed fifty years ago, and I have lived in Australia for thirty-four years, I still see Lyn and Sally on the odd occasion I visit England, and the memory of those early friendships will burn brightly through my whole life.

Jean Linderman started the program Women Writing Women in 2003 from her home town of Medina, Ohio, as a way to promote understanding between American women and Muslim women in the Middle East. They send letters of friendship two to three times a year from women all over the United States. They also welcome letter-writers from other nations. Very few women have received replies, but the purpose of the group is simply to plant the seeds of friendship, as this letter from Sarah, a member of the group, shows.

> Dear Friend,
> I am sending you this letter as a participant in a program called Women Writing Women. We are American women who want to extend friendship to Muslim women in the Middle East. We hope that by exchanging letters over the years we will better understand each other.

I am writing to you from the coldest part of our winter here in Vermont. We live only about 35 miles from the border with Canada, and snow is a big part of our life in the winter. It's beautiful, it's fun to ski on, but it also gets a bit monotonous! We look forward to spring in April, when the trees start to get leaves and the grass grows again.

I have two daughters. My younger daughter will turn 20 on Saturday, and she is in her second year of college. She lives at her college and comes home for vacations. My older daughter is 22 and studying psychology at the University of Toronto, which she loves. She will graduate in June and we are very proud of her. We talk often on the phone, but she likes to live independently from us and practice being a grown-up.

My own job is at the university in my town. I work as a medical editor for a group of surgeons doing research on cancer. We hope that our work will improve treatment for women with breast cancer. When I am not at work, I cook, visit neighbors and family members, think about starting my garden in the spring, and read as many newspapers as I can so that I can understand what is happening in this wide world.

I hope you are well, that your family is safe, and that peace will come. I would love to correspond with you. If you would like to write to me, I will write back to you.

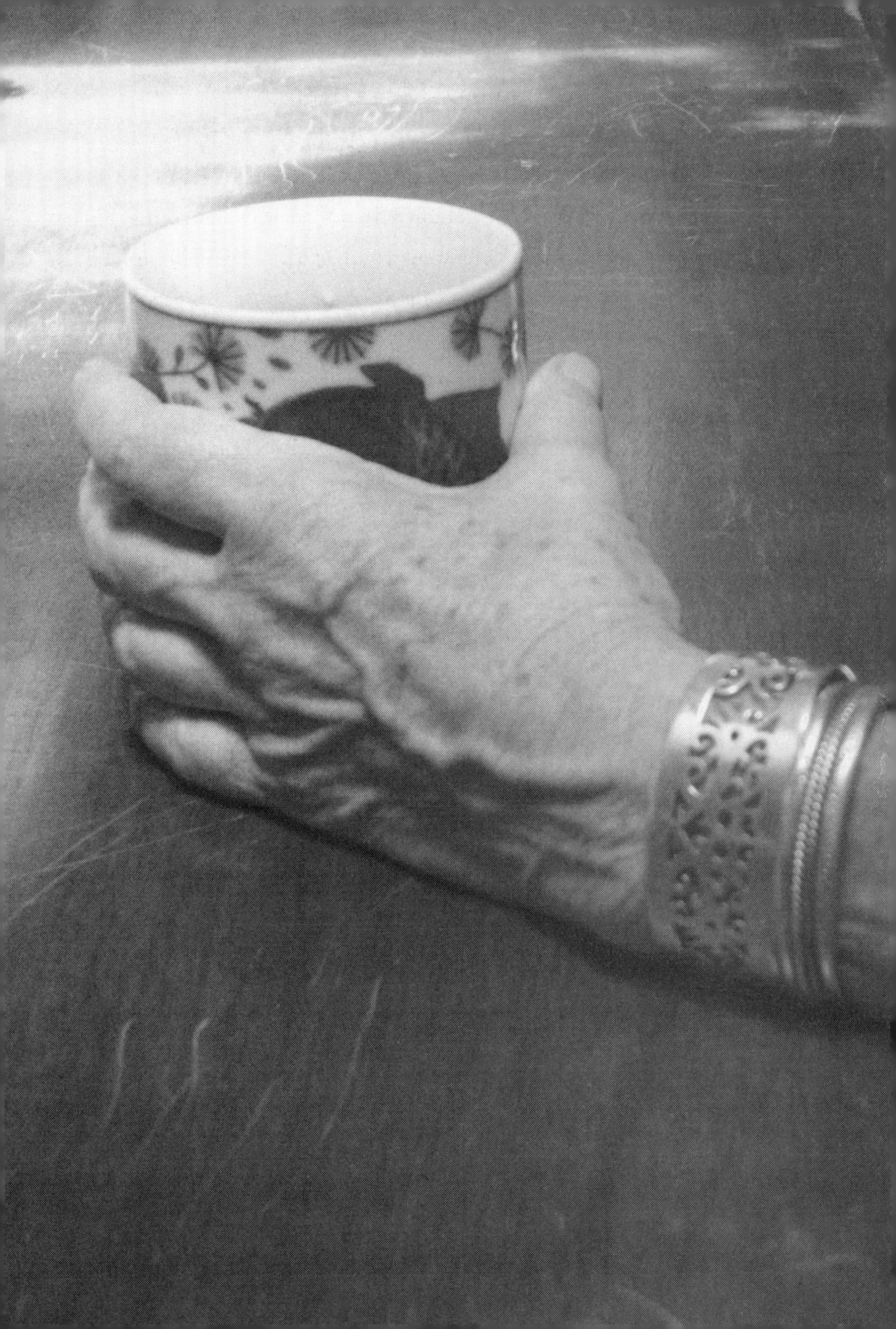

6

Grandmothers

My grandmother. She is babysitting me. I am five or six. My little sister is tucked up in bed and asleep, which is quite the right place for her.

My grandmother has TV dinners. My parents hate them, don't even like buying them for her. But we—she and I—love them. I love the tiny compartments. She lets me pinch from each pile of sloppy colour mashed potatoes, carrots, beans and something that may once have been meat. We curl up together on the sofa and watch TV—black and white, of course. While we watch, I suck my thumb with one hand and clink her lovely chunky necklace with the other. She wears beads, and they make this noise that I know, and I can hear it even as she arrives in the house. I call her my Granny Kindley after the beads, because that is the sort of clicking 'kindley' noise they make and you have to click in your mouth to mimic it.

My other grandmother, my mother's mother, is jealous of the fact that Granny Kindley has a nickname. She wants one too. She is much more everybody's idea of a Granny. She is stoutish and a bit scary, with a certain authoritarian way about her; she somehow doesn't lend herself to a nickname. I tell her that I think she should be my Ordinary Granny; my mother turns away to hide a smile. Ordinary Granny, as she is now forever more, puts a brave face on it. My mother, whose relationship with her mother is vexed, changes it behind her mother's back to Ornery Granny.

My Granny Kindley is Irish and she is my father's mother. My father has a temper. He fights with everybody, including me, and quite often with his mother, who storms out of the house and disappears from our lives for a while, but she always come back. When the family fortunes suffer disaster after disaster and we move to our tiny weekend cottage, Granny Kindley arrives, her six-foot tall body bent into her tiny Mini. I fly into her arms and hug her.

When she was young, this lass from Dublin, she was a beauty, tall and striking with long curly black hair and green eyes, and freckles and a ready laugh. She went to London to train as a nurse, and then in a search for adventure she joined the Red Cross, who sent her to Bulgaria.

'When they interviewed me they said to me, "Now, don't you be forgetting your gumboots",' she would tell me, her Irish phrasing still there after all the years.

THE WISDOM OF WOMEN

'I said to the head of the Red Cross, "Excuse me ma'am, but I believe Sophia is very elegant and has an opera house and hothouse flowers and a railway station",' and at this point she would throw her head back and laugh and say, 'Those silly English people, they just said, oh no that can't be right. Bulgaria is not at all civilised. You must take your gumboots for riding on the mules.'

She never did think much of the English, and in all of her children and grandchildren there was, and is, some maverick blood that caused us to never quite belong to a stereotypical notion of what it is to be English, I think.

Her father disappeared when she was young. A walk-down-to the-shops job and the next you thing know he's gone forever. The family heard he had gone to Canada, but for some reason Granny always thought he had actually gone to Australia.

Granny fell in love with a diplomat, Francis Baker, when she was in Bulgaria—and didn't once need her gumboots. They married and had five children, and built a house overlooking the sea at Varna, surrounded then by vineyards and countryside. My father was born during a fire in the house. Granny would describe how she was busily having a baby while firemen were traipsing through the bedroom trying not to look. She reckoned it was a dramatic entrance into the world, and should have alerted her to the fact that he would grow up to be an actor.

When my father was ten, war broke out and the family was sent back to England for safety, leaving their beautiful house and rose garden for the small grey island with its distinct lack of Mediterranean climate and food, and from then on they lived in a succession of rented accommodation.

When Frank was killed, it broke my grandmother's heart. Now I wonder about it—her father and her husband—the sudden break with both of those men in her life, never more to be seen. She became, according to her children, quite mad during this period. My father always said she had suffered a severe nervous breakdown. My grandmother insisted that she spent the rest of the war working as a spy breaking secret codes on the wireless.

I believe it was this time that created in her a certain detachment from life. She would fling herself into causes with great relish, but I think human relationships were hard for her. My father kept the letters that his father had written to Eva before his death, and they are the most beautiful love letters—in one he talks about the fact that they will build once more a rose garden together and she is not to despair. But I think she did despair, even though her wonderful sense of humour and her increasingly eccentric ways saw her through the many decades to come.

She never ceased to surprise—and annoy—her offspring. I remember a huge row when she suddenly decided to move to Inverness, in Scotland, because that is where she could afford to buy a house, she said. One of her letters to my mother started:

Dear Julia, I am writing this to you surrounded by my washing which is draped about me on the floor. This is one of the many advantages of having underfloor heating…

She came back to London some years later and found a flat in the middle of busy Victoria. There she fought a campaign to have traffic lights installed at the intersection below her, where carnage was wreaked on a regular basis. When letters to the editor did no good, she took her sleeping bag and pillow, called the newspapers and slept out there for the night. That did the trick.

Her cooking was as eccentric as the rest of her. Visiting her one day I found her making mackerel pate. As she was chatting and waving her arms about in her wonderfully expressive fashion, she casually threw a couple of teabags into the blender.

'Granny!' I remonstrated.

'Now darling,' she said, conjuring up one of her favourite phrases: 'The thing is, it adds a bit of flavour!'

I lived with Granny Kindley for a year when I was nineteen. I was working in nightclubs and jazz clubs at the time—not the healthiest of lifestyles, and I was often not home until 3 or 4 a.m. But often when I got back she would be up, working on her 'book', a constant occupation for her. Unfortunately it was a huge tome, and due to her habit of getting sidetracked into almost any subject she could think of, not ever publishable. But it did allow us to have endless cups of tea early in the morning and discuss world affairs, King Boris of Bulgaria, her childhood in Dublin, and her rose garden in Varna, and how she spied for UFOs while she was living in Inverness, among many other subjects.

When I moved to Australia at the age of twenty-two, I missed her terribly. I remember the word got out one time about a phone box in Sydney that was letting everyone make free calls to anywhere in the world, and it was Granny I called for several days before the telephone company worked out what was happening.

We wrote, often, in the beginning, but life intervened and contact became less regular. I lost touch with her in the last years of her life, although she was living with my uncle by then and I always knew from my father how she was. When my mother died very suddenly and I had to go back for the funeral, my grandmother had been very sick, but was better and had been allowed to go home. I made a decision not to see her before my mother's funeral, but to go and get all of the family business out of the way. Only two days after my mother's funeral, Granny Kindley suddenly died. She was sitting at the kitchen table, and my uncle had just given her a glass of wine.

She looked up at him and smiled, and he must have sensed something because he asked her if she was OK, and she nodded, slipped forward and died.

I found it very hard that I had not been able to say goodbye to her.

Sometimes circles are completed in the strangest of ways. My father, who is now eighty and in a nursing home after numerous strokes, has reverted to quite frequently speaking in Bulgarian. When I visited him one of his favourite words was 'metchka', which he would say quite often—'metchka, metchka, metchka …'

Around the same time, I was contacted through Facebook by a young Bulgarian woman, Valeria, who said to me she thought she was living in what had been my grandparents' house. She and her family had been renting it for some years and now the state was planning to sell it. She thought that the family should reclaim it somehow, which was sadly not a practical idea. She sent me photos of the house, and they matched up totally with the pictures that my father had of the place he had grown up in. Then she sent me pictures of the rose garden, and herself and her daughter in it, and there it was, just as my grandparents had planted it and loved it all those years ago.

I told Valeria that I had been to England to see my father, and she wrote me back a message saying that she had always felt there was still a strong presence from the family in the house. 'In Bulgarian,' she wrote, 'we have a word for care of the family, it is "metchka" …'

Of course we know that grandparents are hugely important for children—my daughter is quite cross that due to the advanced age of her parents she has been carelessly brought into the world with a distinct absence of grandparents.

Children feel the lack of them, as Melissa Sanghera, a lawyer and writer, describes in her story about growing up without her grandmother.

> I only met my grandmother twice in my life. Once when I was born. Once just before she died.
>
> As a child, I used to dream about meeting her. My dreams were filled with feelings that she was strong, calm and kind, like a big warm hug.
>
> We never really spoke much, either in my imagination or in reality. We always had a language barrier overshadowed by an age barrier. As a baby, I couldn't speak, and as an adult, she couldn't hear. I wrote her a letter in Punjabi once, but didn't receive any reply.
>
> Still, we shared something special.
>
> Bibi lived with our family on our lychee farm in the hinterlands of Byron Bay about twenty-five years ago. I've seen black-and-white photos of her sitting on our verandah, holding a baby, with the creases in her face wrapped in a smile.
>
> I've been told that she used to sit next to me while I slept and

watch over me. Bibi wanted to be the first person I saw every time I woke up, hoping that I'd grow up to be just like her.

Bibi loved being with us, but she couldn't live in Australia. When she went down to the beach, she kept thinking about how the waves were drawing the water back to the other side of the world.

She thought about her late mother and how she'd promised never to keep the doors on their house locked. So she moved back to Rurka, her small village in Punjab, before I was old enough to remember her.

When I was growing up, every time the phone rang late at night, my heart would stop and then start racing. A few times she was sick, and my dad had to fly to India to stay with her. Every year, I became more desperate to see her—especially after my grandfather died and she was alone. About five years ago, I went to live with her for a while in Rurka.

I remember driving up to her small concrete house and seeing her slowly walk out through the open blue doors. Bibi held on to the walls and was bent over, slightly shaking as she walked. At over eighty years old, she still had dark hair, with light streaks of grey. There was a small tattoo on the inside of her arm spelling out her name: Kartar Kaur. You could still see her nose piercing, although she no longer wore a ring.

When we hugged, she felt tiny and a little bit hard. She was still shaking and held on to both my arms, looking up at me. I think she might have been expecting to see a child. I held her as we walked back into the house together. Bibi sat down on her hand-woven bed and gently wrapped her shawl close around her. My parents were there and we were surrounded by a growing group of excited neighbours, who couldn't stop talking.

An old laminated photo of our family stood next to a radio on a large shelf above the bed, and the letter I'd written years ago was tucked away in a wooden cupboard. The ceiling stopped halfway across and daylight poured into the room.

I remember every morning Bibi woke up just as dawn was breaking, filled a copper jug with water and poured it on top of the reflection of the rising sun. She then spent most of every day lying on her bed and soaking up the sun. I spent a lot of time sitting next to her.

Sometimes we'd sit on the neighbour's doorstep together, and once she started telling me a long story. I understood small fragments—there was a prince sitting on top of a house ... and it ended happily ever after. I smiled and nodded as she told her story. Her face started to twinkle in the sunlight. Could this be love?

We spent days wrapped up together in this simple way. We didn't do much but that seemed to be all we needed. I wanted to stay in Rurka, but knew I had to go back home. I was missing our farm and the clean air.

Before flying back to Australia, I gave her another hug—much softer this time. When she hugged my dad, she clung to him and started to cry loudly. We didn't know what to do except hold on to the tears in our eyes. Then she suddenly stopped, stood up straight and told us to go and be happy.

A few months later, our phone rang. Bibi had died.

It still hurts to think about her, but the more I do, the less it hurts. Bibi will never be gone because I'll always have her in my memories, living next to the feelings built up inside from my childhood.

Melissa's sadness is almost tangible, and a testament to the fact that these days, with people travelling so much and moving to other parts of the world, the loss of the extended family continues its rippling effect through many communities.

Hope is a thing with feathers
That perches in the soul;
And sings the tune without words
And never stops at all.

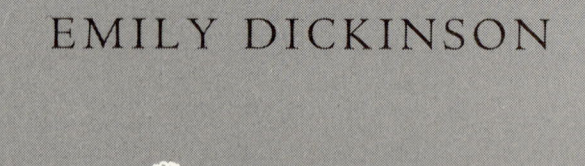

EMILY DICKINSON

7

A Mother's Day present

*I*t's a strange notion, Mother's Day. Our complicated beliefs and experiences around our mothers all culminating in one day of the year, which is, of course, supposed to be perfect. And of course, for children, their attempts at giving to their mums are not always so. I remember only too well one particular Mother's Day when my younger sister and I decided we would give our mother breakfast in bed, and I also decided that I would make her a little spring garden as a present. I found a shoebox, carefully filled it with lovely dark, damp earth from the garden, and placed in it crocuses and pansies and jonquils. I spent a lot of time making the design and the colours look beautiful and I was very pleased with the result.

My sister and I carefully carried up our burnt toast and cold tea offerings complete with my lovely little garden. Unfortunately, as we woke our sleeping mother and leant over her with her Mother's Day garden, the weight of the earth was too much for the shoebox, and it opened at the bottom, covering my mother, her bed and the breakfast with lovely dark, damp earth. Poor old Mum. She tried her hardest not to be too cross at me, but it wasn't easy for her—and she did look a sight covered in bits of flowers and dirt and toast and tea. I was very upset, of course, but the funny thing is that over the years, what I mostly remember was the thrill of making it and how pretty it was, and not the disaster at the end of it. I guess the moral of this story is never make a garden in a shoebox!

Of course it doesn't have to be Mother's Day for daughters to 'gift' their mothers—flowers, drawings, poems, hugs and kisses will all come your way if you are the mother of a little girl, and sometimes if you are lucky your daughter might write something like the beautiful tribute Zali Gecso penned for her mother.

I L♥VE MY MUMMY

My mum:
Inspires me
Protects me
Keeps me honest
Is my hero
Is the person I aspire to be
Teaches me right from wrong

A Mother's Day present

Is the coolest
Is perfectly beautiful
Is totally carefree
Is amazing
Gives everything she's got
Loves me/my family unconditionally
Stands up for her beliefs and mine
Is always there when I need her
Is a free giving spirit
Lives life
Will always do the right thing
Has reached wonderful achievements of which I'm SO proud
Will stay in my heart forever
Is the most open-minded and open-hearted person I know
Respects my choices
Always encourages me when I need a push
Cherishes me
Makes me feel safe
Is always spontaneously happy
Knows me better than anyone else
Wants only what's best for me
Has the most gorgeous heart
Is so generous
Will forever be important to me
Is so wonderfully weird and quirky
Has the most uplifting smile and spirit

THE WISDOM OF WOMEN

Gets me
Gives me advice when I need it
Shares laughs and giggles everyday
Holds me as if she'll never leave
Is a mummy I can trust
Is special
Passes on wisdom to me
Writes spiritual and heartfelt poetry
Takes care of me and my family
Loves nature
Has a keen eye for beauty
Sings random songs at random times
Volunteers in the community
Really listens
She is the mummy I will love to the moon and back, forever and always xx

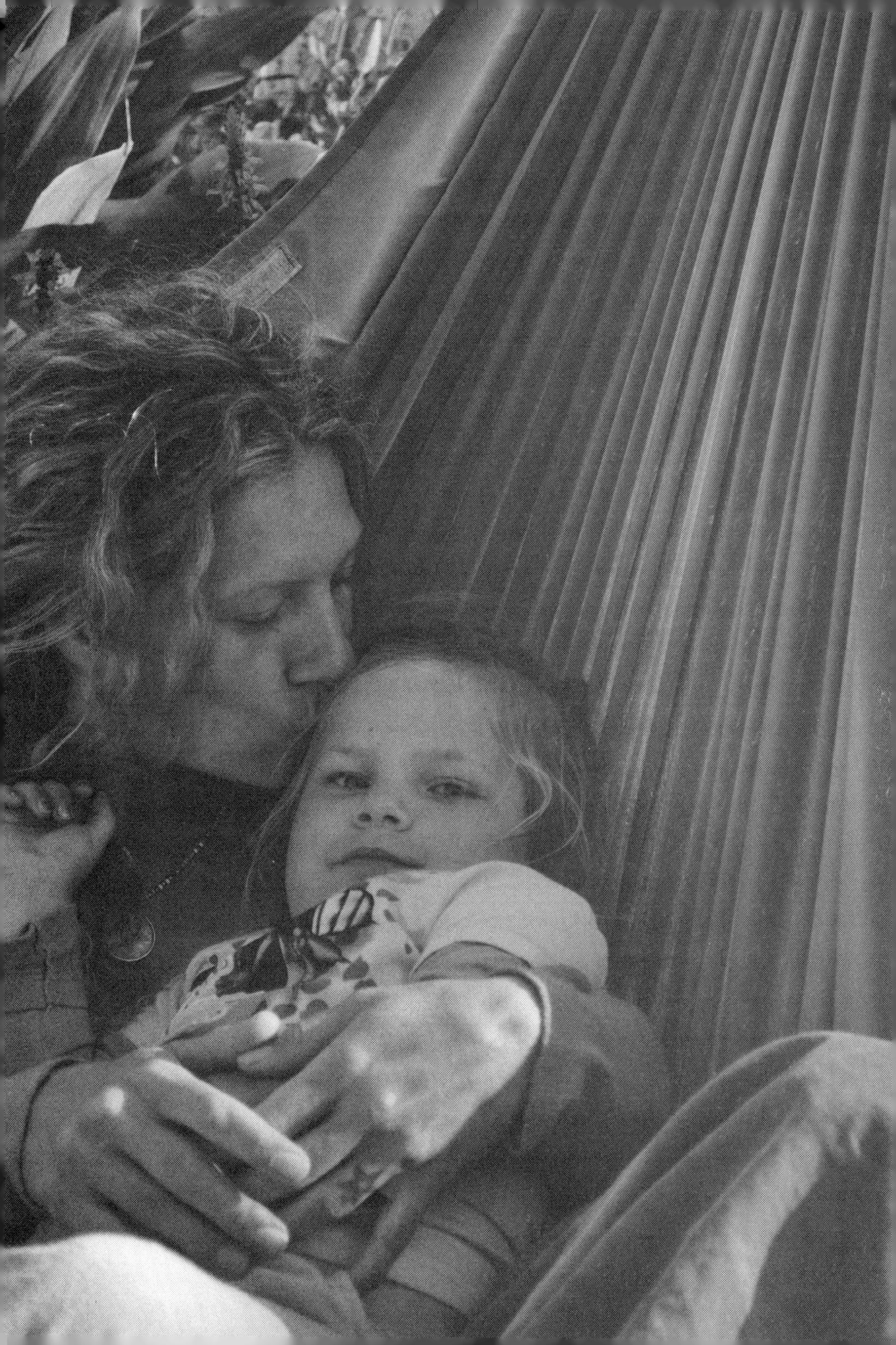

8

Mothers-in-law or the absence of them

Mothers-in-law and friendship aren't often found in the same sentence. I've never had a mother-in-law. My ex-husband's mother died many years before we were married, and my current partner's as well. When I was in my early twenties I was in a relationship with a man for five years, and his mother was a sweetie. That was the closest I have ever come to knowing a mother-in-law, and I loved the fact that she lived in a house with a beautiful garden, and made us home-cooked meals that she served on a lace tablecloth. She loved the fact that I had a passion for old china, so much so that she gave me some of hers, which I have and cherish still. In a way, Dot gave me the idea of what it was like to have a mother-in-law. I know that for some women this is a relationship fraught with difficulty, so perhaps in some ways I have been lucky, or so many of my friends would have me believe!

I think Sarah Taylor's story about her mother-in-law, Mrs Chen, describes beautifully an unfolding relationship, which in fact lasted longer than Sarah's relationship with her husband.

'The plane's landed. There it is, Air Singapore,' I said jumping up and down in front of the large windows high above the busy terminus.

'If only she'd been at the wedding. I know she didn't have the money and we couldn't pay.'

I brushed the auburn curls back from my face and smoothed down a tightly fitted green cotton dress. It matched my eyes and brought out the peaches in my cheeks. A sprinkle of nutmeg freckles spotted the bridge of my nose.

'Remember what I told you—no flinging your arms around her. You'll frighten her. A simple handshake is all that is acceptable,' said my new husband, Cheng. 'In my language we have no such word as love. She'll not understand. You'll put her off.'

'I want to hear you say "I love you." It isn't that hard. Come on, try.'

'It's not necessary. You know how I feel,' he said.

'If you don't tell me and hold my hand in public, I'm not sure.'

Cheng had always puzzled over the reason I hadn't chosen any of the boys I'd grown up with. Tall, tanned gods towered over him wherever he turned. But his father-in-law, my father, had picked away at these bronzed heroes, loathing the beer swilling, the endless talk of sport and the poor treatment of women. Even so, cigar fumes were often blown in Cheng's direction. He wouldn't be accepted either. The 'yellow peril' was still firmly in my father's store of prejudice.

The cabin doors opened and the giant steps made ready to ground the occupants. I pressed my nose up against the glass.

'I want to run and hug her and smother her with kisses.'

A tiny woman dressed for comfort in shiny flat shoes, a white blouse and a straight, dark skirt walked toward us, accompanied by her husband. Her black bonnet of hair fitted snugly around her unlined face, the hooded eyes hidden behind a heavy-framed pair of glasses. She kept pushing them back as they slid down her nose.

'She looks like her photo, only smaller, I'm going to scream if I have to wait any longer.'

Cheng's hand held mine as I skipped from foot to foot; my husband was unable to take his eyes off his mother, who was making steady progress toward us. I couldn't contain my excitement.

Cheng had fallen for his new country, the beautiful, uninhibited girls so physical with other people. You could work at a job you chose. You could say and do what you wanted. His mother may not have liked the possibilities his new country opened up. He'd been raised to fall for a girl with demure looks who never expressed what she truly thought, and to marry for the purpose of having a family and producing sons. Whether he found happiness was neither here nor there.

Wrapped in his arms in the quiet of our big bed I'd whisper, 'I adore your mama and papa. Only a great passion could have created my Cheng and sent you to me.'

I wanted to be forever bound to Mrs Chen as I kissed Cheng's smooth, honey-coloured skin. His gentleness was a constant surprise and nothing was too much trouble. I was the centre of his attention.

Mrs Chen couldn't believe the wide-open spaces as we travelled for miles without sighting a building or another person. Cheng translated her surprise as if he was seeing the country again for the first time. I babbled about the special places we would take her. Sacred rocks, rugged islands, beaches that stretched forever and forests where bears that aren't bears live.

I served a breakfast of rice and left-over vegetables, no longer wanting cereals with milk. I filled the teapot with jasmine leaves and topped up Mrs Chen's cup, breathing the sweet scent. The house was slowly giving away the perfumes of other brews. English Breakfast lay abandoned at the back of the cupboard.

'Today we have picnic,' I said separating the syllables. Mrs Chen's hand lay in mine as I tried to push all I wanted to say through her almond fingertips. I acted out laying a rug, eating with the sun shining overhead. Mrs Chen smiled and nodded. Scrubbing invisible plates in the air, she offered to do the dishes while I went in search of the barbeque tongs. The water gushed into the sink past the filling point. I peeped over the room divider and watched as Mrs Chen spread detergent generously onto a face washer and held the foaming plates under the steaming flow.

'Cheng, tell her to use the plug,' I said. 'We can't waste so much water.'

Mrs Chen slipped on the round river rocks as Cheng walked in her shadow. Catching his mother's arm, he steadied her. She perched herself on a flat surface close to the water and tucked her skirt around her ankles. She tried to shield her face with a lace hanky. The flies settled across her back and buzzed around her mouth as if extending their own welcome. The smoke from the fire enveloped her, and she coughed secretly behind her hand. This was the fifth day of above-average temperatures without a wisp of wind. The she-oaks stood tall and patient, waiting for a southerly to start them singing. Mrs Chen smiled, thin-lipped, and forced her glasses back into place.

Cheng handed her a paper plate with a blackened sausage smothered in red sauce sitting on a soggy piece of white bread. He mimicked the way for her to hold the offering in her fingers. He bent to show her how. I poured her a glass of wine. An insect swam across the surface and lay on its back with feet flailing in the air. Mrs Chen balanced the fruity pool between her feet and nibbled at the mess.

'Australians do this for fun?' she giggled to Cheng.

My face asked what they were laughing about.

'She'd like to take us to Yum Cha tomorrow in a restaurant. She says thank you for a lovely outside lunch.'

Such was my introduction to Chen Huey Fong, or Gwen, as she told her new Australian friends to call her. She was born in

China and began the long journey to Australia in 1939 as she fled from Chairman Mao's revolution. Being a teacher, she feared re-education camps and worse. Over three years she hid in farms and the shelter of the countryside. She married during this journey and gave birth to Cheng. Arriving in Hong Kong to the safety of a Red Cross camp, she gave birth to a daughter. The family continued to move. Borneo, Malaysia and Singapore were their homes until Cheng could bring them to Australia.

Mothers-in-law are often maligned, and we did have our problems as I attempted to live within another culture and she adapted to yet another home. But she loved me, even after Cheng and I divorced, and she embraced her new country with equal passion. She was a lively, vivacious person who showed little trace of the hardships she'd endured. Her wishes and dreams were forever put to one side in the struggle to simply survive. Sometimes they bubbled over and she'd dance dainty steps with a mischievous smile hidden behind a hand. I could see the girl that slumbers inside of us all as we mother and minister others.

Her husband had been a scholar, a man who had lived in his books and his head. Her 'block of wood' she'd called him; the need for a more animated partner had spilled over into nagging and arguments when they were alone.

Cheng was the kind of man she yearned for—he was so like her. Handsome, charming, the life of the party, and he adored women, sadly for me all women. She flirted with him and he could do no wrong. Her face lit up when he walked into the room, and they could talk for hours, laughing and teasing. He played to her longing for fun and a man who found her interesting.

She was scrupulously clean in herself and her home. The word 'sleek' comes to mind when I think of her, her clothes simple but immaculate. She religiously bathed her skin in Oil of Ulan and was never in the sun without a hat—she couldn't understand women baking on beaches.

One day she asked me, 'What happens to old Australian women that turns their hair pink or blue?' Any thread of grey was meticulously plucked from her own black crown.

She relished learning her new language and fellow students of all ages became her friends. I gave up trying to learn Mandarin.

I saw her for the last time a few weeks before her death, when she'd gone back to speaking only Chinese. I held her hands, so soft and unblemished, her face the same and without a wrinkle. She'd always hoped Cheng and I would get back together. She never forgot my birthday—a pretty card would arrive in the post complete with a red packet containing money. She was always pleased when I rang her.

I believe she willed herself to die; trying to maintain her enthusiasm as her body failed was too hard. She never returned to China, never saw her sister or extended family again. Cheng had told me of her belief that relatives who have died don't shut their eyes until all the people they love come back.

And now she lives in my daughter, her tiny feet so perfectly replicated, her kind nature and her sweetness of temperament. The grandmother's stamp is so dominant I have to search for where I appear—maybe the red tinge or the slight curl in the dark cascade of hair, or the luscious bow of the lips passed from my mother to me and from my grandmother to her.

In those fleeting moments when I think of my certain passage from this world to the next I imagine a long line of these beautiful women waiting for me, this thought my balm as I travel the slow, bittersweet journey into their arms. Mrs Chen and my mother will look up at the same moment and smile.

Life does not have to be perfect to be wonderful.

ANNETTE FUNICELLO

9

The kindness of strangers

*I*t's an odd thing in life that sometimes help seems to come from somewhere or someone entirely unexpected. In my lifetime that help has often seemed to have had a slightly otherworldly aspect to it, like a brief encounter with a human or heavenly angel. We remember unexpected kindness, don't we?

I remember one visit back to England with my then six-year-old son. We were at Heathrow for our return trip home and he had fallen asleep. I had a hire car to return, a sound-asleep child and far too many bags. I had absolutely no idea how I was going to manage everything, when suddenly a man appeared at my window. 'Do you need help?' he asked, and I smiled up at him. 'I do,' I said. In one whisk of a lamb's tail he found a trolley, packed the luggage and wheeled it to the car centre for me so I could carry Sam. He took me inside and made sure that I found a seat. 'Travel well,' he said. I thanked him and shook his hand and off he went.

Often, of course, the help that comes is from woman to woman. Over the course of my lifetime women have often helped me, and I hope I have helped them. A gift of unexpected money, food provided when you have a new baby and are overwhelmed, a massage, a coffee and a conversation, advice, support, gifts, even just an unexpected telephone call. Some of these have come from women I didn't even know well, and some from women I had never met before—and how amazing is that? Not to say, of course, that my wonderful circle of women friends and family haven't given me all of that and more, but how extraordinary it is that someone who hardly knows you can extend a hand to you at exactly the time you need it?

Divine providence, perhaps? The sisterhood at work? A connecting telepathic thread between the women of the world? Who knows?

In the end, all that matters is that kindness exists out there in the universe in amazing ways, small and large. Jeweller and writer Tryphena McShane discovered such kindness when she was in the middle of a financial crisis that meant having to sell the family car.

> Many years ago when I was a young woman with a baby on my hip and another in my belly, desperately trying to hold my family together, a stranger appeared in my life who for thirty-seven years now has had a profound impact on me.

The kindness of strangers

My husband was studying at college. We had next to no money—only what I earned from my job at the vet's surgery across the road. Things were so desperate we needed to sell our little Daihatsu four-wheel drive. This was our only means of transport in the outlying bush suburb we lived in. With a very low heart I put an advertisement in the paper.

No sooner had the paper come out than a woman phoned asking to come around to see the vehicle. She had a little weekender nearby and needed a four-wheel drive to get her teenage kids, and herself, in and out of the land.

For some reason we hit it off the moment she arrived. She was over twenty years older than me, but I found it so easy to share my colourful, and well-travelled, twenty-two years of life history with her! I explained we had to sell the car because of financial difficulties. Some months earlier we had found ourselves in the path of one of Sydney's worst bushfires, which had also stolen a number of people's lives. Losing almost everything we owned, including my silversmithing equipment and jewellery, meant we were struggling.

To me as a migrant, the fire had been a terrifying introduction to the raw power of Australia's primal forces. I was already living on precarious ground, attempting to resurrect my life, and I now also had babies dependent upon me. I shared with this woman my family's history as refugees from the ravages of unstable African politics, telling of how my lawyer father, along with his Ghanaian partners, took cases against a corrupt government in Ghana, West Africa—a first for that country. On winning the cases he became a target. Determined to deport him even though the High Court ruled this illegal, the government had a magistrate order him to be thrown into Ussher Fort, one of the old slave jails. Eventually the whole family was thrown out of the country, which had been our home for over seventeen years, and since I was two years old.

I explained that my family had arrived in Australia three years earlier with only £10 between us. And that after my husband and I had set out to establish our tiny rented home on the outskirts of Sydney, a bushfire had appeared, a plume of smoke in the distance. By the time we had driven down a bush track to see what was on fire, it had already raged past us towards where we lived. In a terrifying inferno it was eating up all in its path in a breathless rage.

Racing home, I bundled our cat, the next-door neighbour's animals and thirteen-year-old daughter, who was home alone, in the vehicle alongside my baby daughter. Leaving the area as fast as humanly possible, I only stopped to collect an eighty-year-old woman, whose garden I had worked in, who lived in the path of the fire.

My husband stayed behind to release the water from our neighbour's above-ground swimming pool, which saved their home but not our belongings, all of which had been stored in our studio shed, which was razed to the ground. I was being taught important lessons about impermanence. And I was also shown that it is our relationships that matter above all else. These, if true, can never be destroyed.

After sharing a few cups of tea with me, the woman left, saying she would think about the car and let me know if she wanted it.

A few hours later she called back to say she wouldn't be buying the vehicle, but that she did have something else she wanted to say to me. She had decided she was going to give me a loan so we wouldn't need to sell our car.

I was completely blown away. How could a total stranger be offering me money to help us out like this? In that moment all my preconceived ideas of life were totally rearranged. I learned about the generosity of strangers and the unexpected links that can forge lifetime bonds between people. My connection to this incredible woman, Anne Deveson, has allowed me to experience first-hand what true resilience looks like.

Although Anne is in fact one of Australia's most respected journalists, as well as a filmmaker and author, it is her person-to-person humanity that is exceptional. She has tackled difficult social issues as a Human Rights Commissioner and has won UN peace awards for films. But it is her profoundly honest account of her beautiful and vibrant eldest son Jonathon's struggle with schizophrenia and his ultimate death, in *Tell Me I'm Here*, that is her most heart-wrenching gift of all.

When I first met Anne I knew nothing of this exceptional woman. But over the years I have been blessed to have travelled in her company, watching her demonstrate the most extraordinary personal resilience, traversing many devastating personal losses. To me, the cruellest and most unfair thing has been to witness this brave single mother nursing her dying lover, the brilliant American philosopher Robert Theobold, so soon after they had met and fallen so deeply in love.

When my father was dying at home, Anne visited him regularly, having become a close family friend. When he died she worked with us to write a brilliant obituary for this man, who had meant so much to us all.

Although Anne was awarded the Order of Australia, honouring her public work, in truth this will never touch on the true essence of this real, grittily honest woman. Her quiet personal generosity, so often invisible to the world, has impacted many lives, and I feel humbled to have been gifted such a truly wonderfully wise friend.

Those of us who have been privileged to know Anne are profoundly aware of what a special woman she is, and Tryphenya's story did not surprise me at all. Sometimes, of course, the kindness of strangers comes in smaller ways, but they are no less important to us at when we are under pressure, lost or confused, as Ally Redding, a mother of three, discovered when she was struggling with the hospital system.

'You'll probably get lost ...' What is going on? I was told the same thing yesterday. I vaguely remembered a few instructions like 'past the blue lift, left, past the starlight room, take the pink lift ... but you'll probably get lost.'

I was still in shock from the news I'd received less than twenty-four hours earlier. I had taken my two-year-old son to our local doctor with what I thought was an umbilical hernia. An ultrasound revealed something far more sinister; they suspected hepatoblastoma, a very large tumour of the liver. I sat in the cafe of the medical centre dazed

The kindness of strangers

and crying, unable to move and face the cruel truth. A paediatric oncologist called to tell me he would see us the following day at nine o'clock.

Standing in the foyer of the Royal Children's Hospital in Melbourne—my baby boy in his pram, my mum and sister by my side—we must have looked like country hicks on our first trip to the big smoke. A woman appeared in front of us and asked if we needed help. I told her where we needed to go and she responded cheerfully 'You'll probably get lost, I'll take you.' She guided us through the maze of corridors and saw us safely to the pink lifts.

It is now five years since my son was treated with chemotherapy and surgery to cure his cancer. I often think of that lovely lady. I assumed she worked at the hospital but I never saw her again. I know she was warm and friendly but cannot describe her appearance. From that point on, whenever I was at the hospital, I felt it was my mission to help anyone who appeared lost, scared or overwhelmed.

I am sure that it would be surprising to those who have helped us in our lives if they realised how strongly we remember that help, no matter how small. Perhaps if we all understood what a difference the tiniest amount of help can make, we would spend more time doing it!

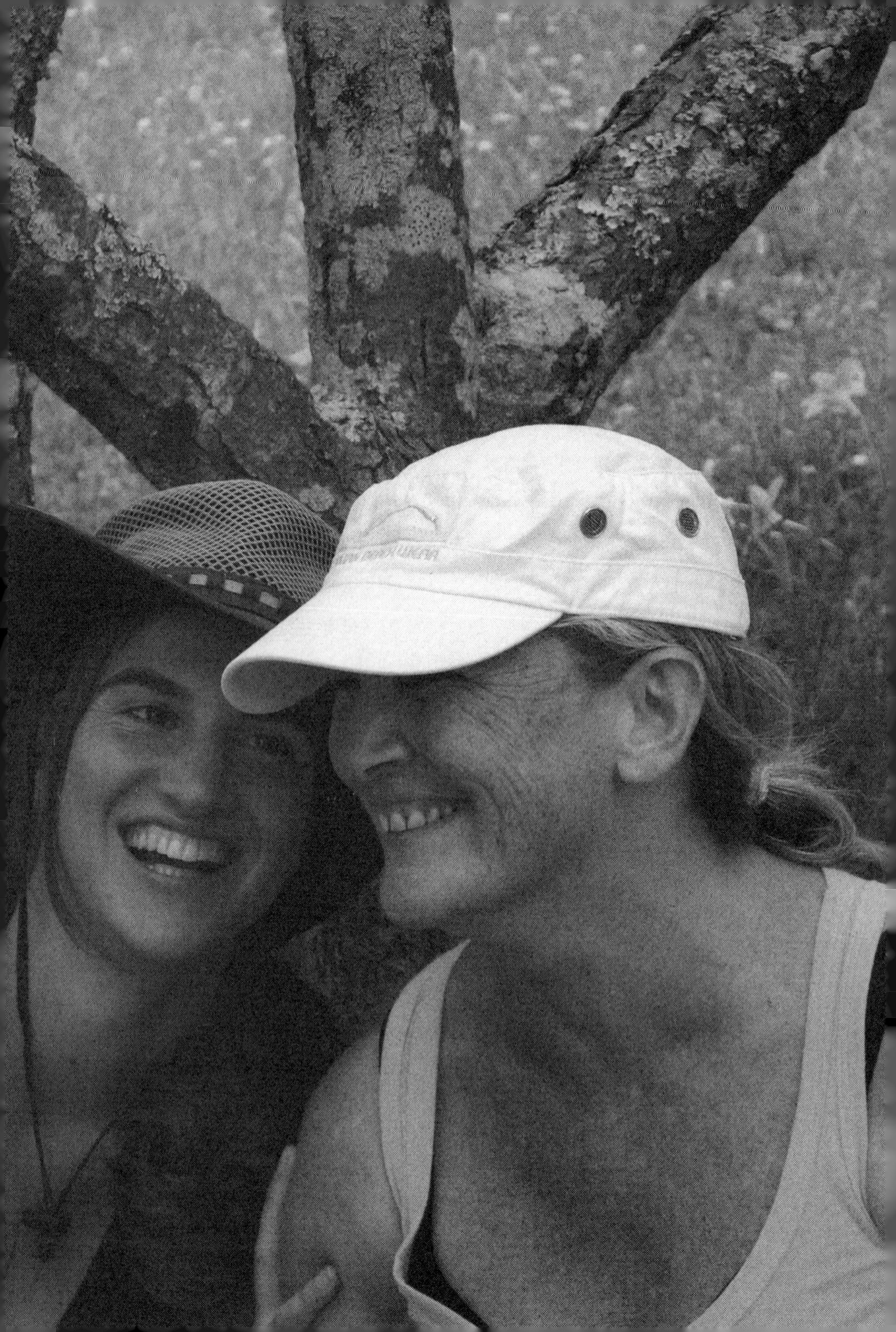

10

Who are we?

Perhaps one of the reasons we often underestimate our impact on the lives of others is that we spend so much time struggling with the issue of *who* we actually are! It often appears to me that a woman's sense of identity is perhaps not as strong as a man's, and her sense of needing to nurture others can overwhelm her own journey to find out who she is and why she is on this earth, this lifetime around.

I remember many years ago going to see the wonderful Spalding Gray give one of his devastating monologues, and he was recounting how he had asked for stories from the audience one time when he was performing in Amsterdam. A woman, he said, had stood up and said to him, 'I just want you to tell all the women out there—it is not your fault if it rains at a picnic.' It was not at all what he was expecting, and when he told the story we all laughed, but he used it as a brilliant segue into a speech about women, and why we often think things are our fault, or our responsibility.

I laughed a lot when he told us this, because one of my favourite occupations with children is to pack a picnic, and there is always that sense of personal failure if it rains, or if it's too windy or—heaven forbid—if I've forgotten the chocolate.

Finding out who we truly are—what we stand for, what we believe in—and accepting ourselves as good people with a purpose, even if we have not yet discovered that purpose, is the journey of a lifetime. Here, Susanna Freymark, a journalist and writer, tells us about the shame of her divorce.

Shame, as an emotion, can take on biblical proportions, but in writing, shame can be the compass to a story.

During a course about short story fiction writing at university my lecturer, Tegan Bennett Daylight, encouraged us to write about a point in our lives where we felt shame. I chose two moments: one where I had pretended to be something I wasn't, and another where I had told a big, fat lie.

Oh, such juicy stuff for a writer. But writing the words and reliving the secret moments in a fictional setting was exposing.

The first moment was one where, for two years, I hid my divorce from my parents.

I justified my decision because my father was ill—dying in fact. What better excuse could I have?

The truth was, I was too scared to tell them.

I was caught up in their potential disapproval and the tut-tutting of my mother.

Whenever she mentioned someone who was divorced she would lower her voice—softer than a whisper—and say the word very slowly. D-I-V-O-R-C-E.

She would brag about how in our family we'd had never had a D-I-V-O-R-C-E.

My pretence extended to cleaning my ex's house and having family meals with my parents when they visited. It was an elaborate facade; I'd even bring objects from my house so it looked like I still lived there.

This shameful lie has now been turned into a short story called *The Visit*.

In the next piece, Virginia Satir, a well-known psychotherapist and author who died in 1988, gives us a clarion call to stand up for ourselves and to accept who we truly are.

I am Me. In all the world, there is no one else exactly like me. Everything that comes out of me is authentically mine, because I alone chose it. I own everything about me: my body, my feelings, my mouth, my voice, all my actions, whether they be to others or myself. I own my fantasies, my dreams, my hopes, my fears. I own my triumphs and successes, all my failures and mistakes. Because I own all of me, I can become intimately acquainted with me. By so doing, I can love me and be friendly with all my parts. I know there are aspects about myself that puzzle me, and other aspects that I do not know—but as long as I am friendly and loving to myself, I can courageously and hopefully look for solutions to the puzzles and ways to find out more about me. However I look and sound, whatever I say and do, and whatever I think and feel at a given moment in time is authentically me. If later some parts of how I looked, sounded, thought and felt turn out to be unfitting, I can discard that which is unfitting, keep the rest, and invent something new for that which I discarded. I can see, hear, feel, think, say and do. I have the tools to survive, to be close to others, to be productive and to make sense and order out of the world of people and things outside of me. I own me, and therefore, I can engineer me. I am me, and I am okay.

Virginia Satir was a pioneer in the field of family therapy, starting the first ever family therapy program in the United States. She was also one of the first people to recognise the strength of networking, founding two groups to help people suffering from similar issues to their own. She put forward the notion of the presenting issue hiding the real problem, and also how low self-esteem could damage relationships. She believed in the strength of a supportive family, and her piece contains important pointers about how we begin to feel when we start to truly understand ourselves as human beings. For most of us on life's journey towards a greater understanding of ourselves, if it is not our family we turn to then it is our women friends. They shore us up when we feel wobbly, toast us when we have a breakthrough moment, and encourage us all the time to be the best we can be.

*We don't need to covet another woman's path or life.
It's so much more self-fulfilling to celebrate another
woman's abilities.*

TORI AMOS

11

Sometimes we just don't feel quite right

We have those days when nothing seems right—we believe we don't look right and we certainly don't feel right.

It's tough for all of us with the amount of celebrity-watching that goes on. We tend to bypass the bad news that so many seemingly successful actors and singers are in rehab or have been charged with drug offences, stealing or drunk driving. Somehow what we still see is the red carpet version of the same women—tall, glamorous, successful and, oh yes, thin!

What can we do when gloom, doom, hormones, self-loathing and criticism all pile into the pot of soup that we then have to try and transform into joy, peace, self-acceptance, unconditional love and lack of judgement? Easier said than done, as Linda Walker describes.

> I'm feeling a little fat tonight. As I'm a good five foot nine and only just hit double digits on the clothing size labels, I see the irony of this and am disappointed in myself to even have the nerve to sit here and feel this way. Because in my heart I know I am nowhere near fat. Yet I can't help it, it must just be a bad hair day ...
>
> It got me thinking about how as females we are just never quite happy with our outward appearance. The 'enough' monster rules our lives—we believe we're never quite thin enough, pretty enough, smart enough or good enough. I could point to all of my girlfriends one by one and you would see that there is something attractive and intriguing about all of them. Some may be perceived by outward appearances as conventionally prettier than others, but not one of them is unattractive.
>
> All the women I know have lovely hair, skin or eyes or a lovely smile. They all have personalities that make you want to get to know them more. They include tall and short and everything from a size 6 to 22. All have something about them that has attracted the attention of others at various points in their lives. They are, in short, lovely. However, the sad fact is I don't know one of them who hasn't looked at herself on a regular basis and been unhappy with what she sees. I don't think I could pinpoint one female I know who doesn't view her reflection in the mirror and hear the 'enough' monster in her head.

I wonder what makes us think this way? I can look at my friends some days and be surprised anew by how attractive some of them are. I have seen men turn their heads as these women pass, yet I know that earlier in the same evening, before venturing out, my friends have agonised over how they look or wished for some small change in their face or body.

I would not be the only one to have been told by the love in my life how beautiful and wonderful I am. I wonder how many of us really believe it? How many of us bypass this comment—perhaps even thinking that our partner is saying only what we want to hear?

I have watched my sister struggle with her weight and diets over the years and yet she has no idea how gorgeous she is. She is tall and womanly, with luscious locks and a winning smile. She has a husband who adores her and sees in her the woman I think she struggles to see in the mirror. Sometimes I wish I could tell her this, yet even if I did I fear that, like most of our sex, she wouldn't believe it.

My sister used to bravely joke to people that I got the skinny genes, and maybe I did just get lucky in that department. But her looks and personality far outshine mine, and for all those brains and beauty, the 'enough' monster seems to lurk in her head as well. I don't think I can continue to blame men for this 'enough' business either. The more I observe, the more I recognise that men are far less self-conscious of their own bodies, and less noticing of ours than we give them credit for. In fact, none of the men I know hold any fear about stripping off at the beach, while we sit covered in a towel worrying about the couple of extra kilos we are wearing on our hips. They don't seem to notice the extra padding or the blemishes on our skin as much as as we notice them ourselves. We, meanwhile, are so busy fretting about these small things we probably stop ourselves from having fun. I've been guilty in the past of knocking back a game of volleyball on the beach for fear of how I would look bouncing around in a bikini. What a waste of a sunny day on the beach, because I chose to hide myself in the water or under a shirt!

I'm quite sad I'm feeling fat and unattractive tonight, because I know full well it's all in my own head. I hope one day I manage to rid myself of this 'enough' monster I carry around, and I hope any woman reading this can rid herself of this too.

Until then, just keep knowing, I think you're all fabulous—okay?

Clare Wishart, a mother and writer, remembers the enormous anxiety girls feel around their body image and the labelling attached.

There is a children's song that German children sing when they wave goodbye to everybody. And it really is Every Body. They move their hands in appropriate actions as they sing the words: 'Tall people, short people, fat people, thin people'. As an Anglo-Saxon, I always wince when I hear 'fat people'. It seems so crude, so blunt. I want to cover the kids' ears from such descriptions. They are too young to start the war on their bodies in a society of too much.

I had my first brush with anorexia at school. A new girl came from the United States in Year 10. She was gaunt and pale, but had a nice laugh and was quick to share a joke. She wore oversized jumpers and had bleeding cuticles from where she picked them constantly. In those senior years, I started to think negatively about my weight. I always criticised my 'child-bearing hips'.

Those 'child-bearing hips' are what reconciled me to my body— those child-bearing hips and a wonderful childbirth educator whose classes prepared me in ways I never thought possible. After twenty-four hours of labour and an epidural for my firstborn, I lay in the bath in the hospital positively revelling in what my body had just done. I had such respect for its creative power. It had nourished a child and then given birth. Incredible. The way I looked at myself completely changed. I was now a mother. I had something in common with women all over the world. With my second child it was a labour of fifty-five minutes and an obstetrician who said it was a perfect delivery. His words stayed with me: 'Just after washing up the dishes and home before bed!' With that, I knew my body was a gift.

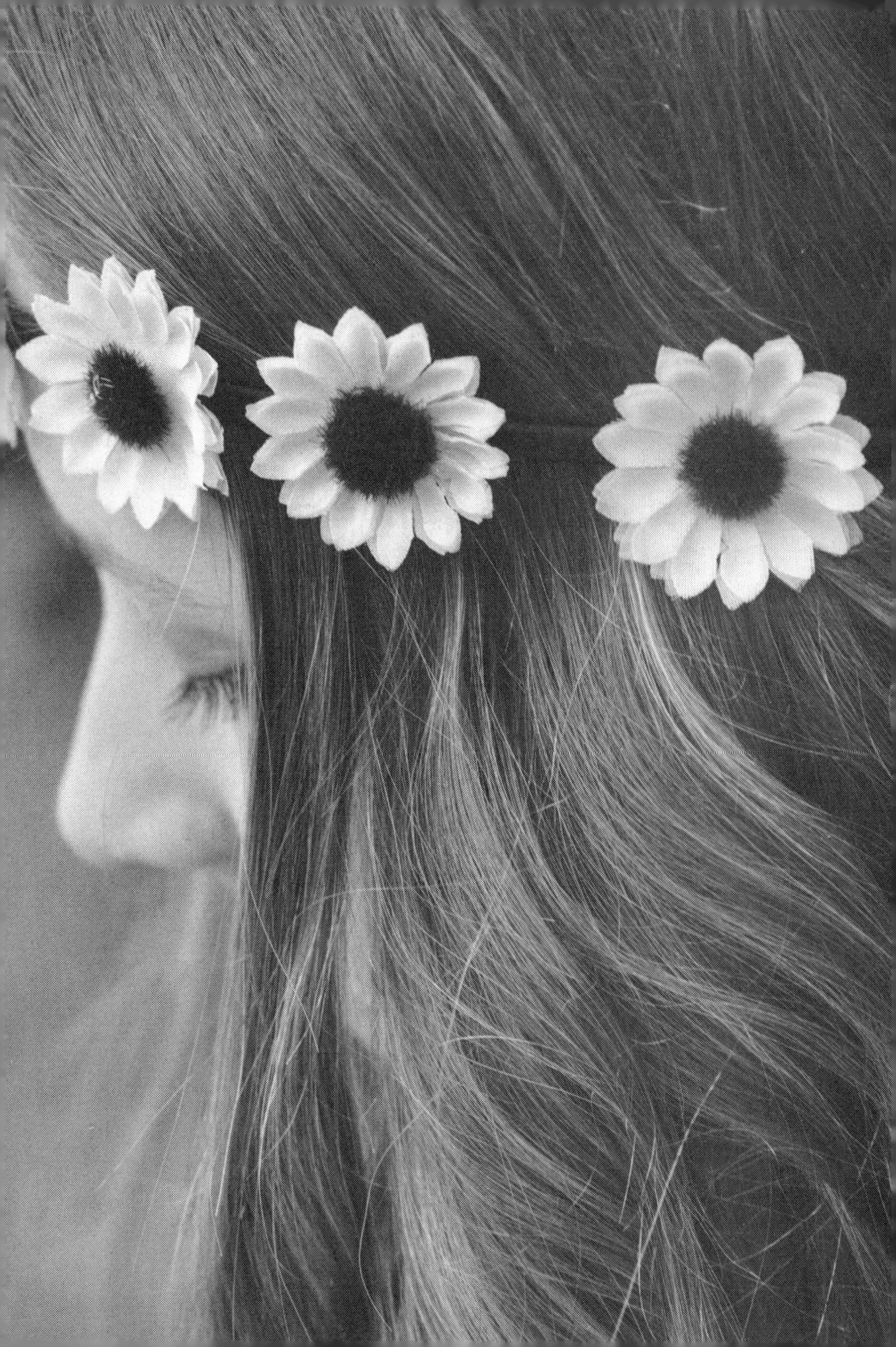

12

The dark word

There is a dark side to being born a woman into this world.

There's a word for what can happen to us. Abuse. It's a short, simple word, and it does not really sum up the dreadful connotations it contains within it, and the many and varied guises under which abuse can take place.

To even think about abuse takes enormous emotional energy, and to feel the emotions the memories contain is extremely painful—but in the long run, to not feel them is worse! Perhaps by sharing stories we can liberate the pain, and also know that we are not alone.

I had a father who was emotionally and physically abusive. The line stopped somewhere just before incest. I did not ever feel safe as his daughter, and that lack of safety is something I carry with me to this day.

One way I dealt with what happened to me as a teenager was to be wild myself—with an alcoholic mother, an abusive father and a chaotic home life, I spent as many nights as I could away, out and sleeping around. It wasn't a healthy lifestyle, and I'm not proud of it, but I guess I was doing the best I could at the time. I think that often when we come to terms with the effect abuse has had on our lives, we need to forgive not just the abusers, but ourselves. We carry shame and humiliation deep inside us, when really we were just doing the best we could to get through.

This is not to say, of course, that men and boys are not abused—we know they are, but I think the physical vulnerability of girls and women, the perceived notion even to this day that we are somehow fair game, makes us still the target of abusive behaviour by those who are stronger or wield more power in our lives.

Abuse is not an easy subject to write about.

I remember once reading a fictional short story I had written about a woman who had been abused by her father. She was a librarian and as an adult had married a man who in turn abused their children. It was not a true story, other than lending this woman some aspects of my feelings around my childhood. But after I had read it in public, one woman came up to me in tears. 'Thank you for telling your story,' she said. 'It comforts me to know that I am not alone.'

I was about to tell her that it was made-up, a short story, not factual, when suddenly I realised that she needed to believe that it was true, that someone could write about these things, and so I simply said 'thank you' and gave her a hug.

I would like to thank Fay Knight, a journalist and writer who works for Vision Australia, for being strong enough to share her story of abuse with us.

Back when I was just twenty, I was raped twice.

I didn't name it then. Although I had works by Susan Brownmiller and Kate Millett and many others on my bookshelf and had read them, I was too busy to connect my experiences to what they were saying. And then too sick.

The first time was at a party in a terrace house in Coogee. It was the mid-seventies and the theme was rock stars and groupies. Most of the people there were my friends from art college and their friends.

I had been flirting with a boy who had a girlfriend, although she was not there. I was feeling guilty about it but simultaneously enjoying his attentions. I was drinking, but not drunk. In between being way too close to this boy I was drifting off to talk to other friends, but would be drawn back to him, unsure but wanting it to continue. But on one excursion down the narrow hallway, my pathway was blocked by one of my college-mates' friends. He was good-looking and muscular in the way of a man who has surfed since he was a boy. I had met him earlier in the night.

He grabbed me and kissed me. He was drunk, but he was my friend's friend and I didn't want to make a scene. As the kiss ended I

The dark word

tried to pull away, but I couldn't: he had hold of my wrist. He pushed me through the adjacent doorway into the bathroom and onto the urine-splashed floor. He was on top of me and the door was held closed by his heels. It was a very small bathroom and my head was under the toilet bowl.

I tried to get up but he was heavy and pulling at my pants and his. You want to, you want to, you want to, he kept saying, blocking out no no no.

But I didn't scream. It was my friend's party. This was his friend. I didn't want to make a scene.

Open up, open up! He grabbed a bottle of shampoo from the edge of the bath and squirted some between my legs and pushed into me. The light bulb above me had no shade and was very bright. It left a shadow in my eyes.

He pulled up his jeans and left and I got up and sat on the toilet and washed myself. I checked my hair and face in the mirror, went back to the party, said goodbye and went home.

Almost a year later, at the end of a skiing trip to New Zealand, the girlfriend I had shared rooms with wanted the last night to be with the boy she'd met on the trip. Most of the group was from college, but to make up the numbers to get the group discount there were a few outsiders who came along. Friends of friends.

It was my first trip overseas. I had been really sick with asthma and thought that I wasn't well enough to travel, let alone ski, but I didn't want to lose my money.

The stoicism I'd learned from having asthma from an early age barely got me through this trip. Breathing was a battle, even with the drugs. Some mornings I would wake hot and feverish, despite the freezing conditions; other days I would shiver uncontrollably, unable to get warm. I was light-headed and my skiing instructor asked me what drugs I was taking and could he have some.

On the last night on our way north to Christchurch we arrived late at an old hotel; everywhere else was booked. We all joined the local policeman for a drink at the bar as he was leaving the next day, then I went to bed, utterly exhausted and struggling to breathe. One of the other boys on the trip, whom I barely knew, had taken the other bed in my room.

I woke struggling to breathe because he was on top of me in bed, pushing up my nightgown and into me. I could barely gasp, let alone yell, and I couldn't push him off me. Fortunately he was quick. I was still trying to get back to sleep when there was shouting and bashing on the doors in the corridor. The policeman wanted all of us back into the bar to continue celebrating with him. I stumbled down in my nightgown, sipped a drink and slunk back to my room.

A few days later back in Australia I was admitted to hospital. It was tuberculosis.

Recovering from it took eighteen months, during which time I continued at college while sleeping at least fourteen hours a day. I graduated and life moved on.

Two decades later I was sitting in a charming country bed and breakfast, chatting to the owner for a magazine story I was working

The dark word

on, when we were unexpectedly interrupted by a young woman who had appeared in the sunlit doorway, pushing a bicycle. She wanted to enquire about booking the house for a cycling group in the next university break.

My hostess invited her in to join us for tea and homemade cake. She accepted gratefully and introduced herself. She worked at a major university in student welfare services. We asked what that involved. Often serious things, she said. Like rape. Young women students were quite vulnerable.

I know, I said. I was raped twice when I was a student. I described both occasions, very briefly. Then I stopped, shocked at myself.

The young woman was not shocked, but my hostess was.

It was OK, I said quickly. I was lucky. I wasn't hurt. I was on the pill so I didn't get pregnant. But I've always felt guilty about it, that I didn't do anything. I just pretended it didn't happen. I felt it was a bit Oscar Wilde; once was unfortunate, but twice was positively careless.

I was suddenly close to tears.

The young woman leaned closer to me and asked: Did you ever think that you did the best thing you could for yourself at the time? If you had reported it to the police then, she went on to say, it would have been very disruptive to your life. It would have dragged on for months with very little likelihood of a conviction, but meanwhile you would have had to cope alone with all the dramas, and the second time you were also seriously ill. What you did was the best thing you could have done then. *The best thing*.

I sat there, blinking, sipping my cold tea while the conversation moved onto holiday bookings. I had done the best thing I could have done at the time. I was twenty again, but it was a better feeling. I had cared for myself in a difficult time.

This young woman had given me the gift of her attention, empathy and experience at a time in my life when I was again struggling, this time as a single parent. Her insight gave me a whole new way of seeing myself. I had not realised until I'd spoken that I'd waited two decades to be comforted.

The wonderful thing about Fay is that she did not allow this experience to shut her down. Always warm and caring, she has expressed beauty, through her work and life for many years, and brought that beauty, through the pages of the magazines she has worked for, into other women's lives.

Another one of our contributors, who wished to remain anonymous, had a very different experience. She somehow managed to navigate her way out of what might have been a dangerous experience, and in so doing found that she became stronger. She learned she could rely on herself.

Strangely, my close brush with sexual abuse turned out to be an empowering experience. When I was sixteen, I was approached by my stepfather while I was in the shower and my mother was out shopping for a dinner party. His intent was clear. My survival instinct was to latch onto his one moment of hesitation and tell him very clearly to leave me alone. I understand I was very lucky that I was able to talk my way out of it. I was terrified of telling my mother.

The dark word

I had never liked him, and I was sure she would believe him over me and think I was trying to cause trouble, or worse, that I had initiated it.

When I finally raised the courage to tell her a few agonising days later, she believed me immediately, was amazingly supportive, walked straight out of her marriage and out of the family home and never looked back. It was the one unforgivable thing that could have given her the courage to leave a very manipulative man and a bad marriage. She became the strong, empowered woman that I remembered from years past, and I in turn became an empowered teenage girl who learned the value of female support. My mother and I moved into a new home together and developed a beautiful relationship that is still thriving twenty years later.

This woman was lucky, and there is no doubt that at that time in her life her mother's support would have made all the difference between her ability to cope or not cope with what had happened.

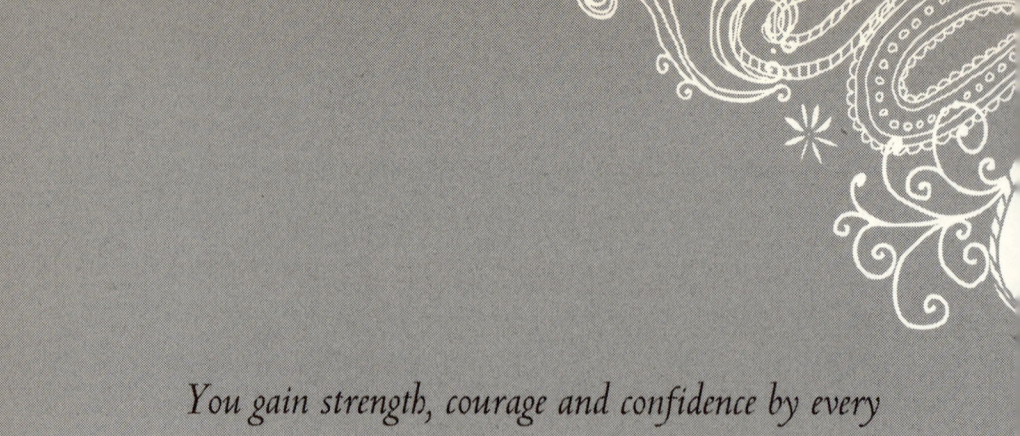

You gain strength, courage and confidence by every experience in which you really stop to look fear in the face. You are able to say to yourself, 'I lived through this horror. I can take the next thing that comes along.' You must do the thing you think you cannot do.

ELEANOR ROOSEVELT

13

Things are not always what they seem

Abuse unfortunately comes in many forms—it does not have to be physical to damage your self-esteem, or to wound you. Perhaps one of the least talked about aspects of abuse is how it can gradually increase over a long period of time, so that the person suffering the abuse becomes unsure of what is actually happening. The transformation of an apparently happy relationship into an abusive one is tragic, and it takes great strength to recognise what has happened, and to leave such a situation, as one of our writers found.

Like many women suffering an insidious form of abuse, she was in an abusive marriage for many years. It was made difficult for her to leave, and in doing so she had to temporarily lose the love of her sons.

I must have counted each grain of sand as I traced and retraced my steps for kilometres along my favourite place, the beach, as I contemplated the rest of my life. I walked for months on a beautiful, desolate piece of paradise—the beach of my home town at the time, a small tight-knit beachside community.

Life had been wonderful for me for many years after marrying my childhood sweetheart and delighting in the joy of watching my five sons grow into fine, healthy and happy young men. My husband and I had been the best of friends and each other's rock of strength for many, many years. I was only fifteen when we got together and he was seventeen—babies really, but we were hopelessly in love and couldn't imagine life without each other.

Over time things changed dramatically. After our fifth son was born we moved to a 140-acre bush block (and I mean bush block) isolated from neighbours and quite a way to town.

We commenced building our dream home, but by the time we were at the stage to connect the plumbing our money had run out. I showered all five boys with a camp shower outside for quite a while, obtaining hot water by boiling the kettle. We had a 'drop dunny' (a hole-in-the-ground toilet) for a number of years, no heating inside the house, no floor coverings over the concrete floor and no oven; my only way of cooking meat was with a frying pan or a barbecue.

There wasn't a garbage service so we had to travel 20 kilometres to the nearest rubbish tip. Death adders prevailed as well as the usual black and brown snakes. I don't know how many times my children were close to being bitten. I was constantly in fear!

My husband hadn't had any employment for many years so he started going away to work. He would travel to another state for six weeks at a time and leave me with the five boys. Every now and then we would get flooded and again I would be in constant fear. The six-week work period didn't get us anywhere, as when he returned home he was unemployed again.

I desperately wanted to move from the nightmare I was in! Eventually we moved to a beautiful beachside community on the mid-north coast and I thought life would finally be sunny, and the dark cloud that hovered over me would be removed forever. But my husband had lost all motivation to work, even though he was a skilled tradesman. He didn't look for work for around four years, and when I decided it was time for us both to gain employment and got a job myself, he went for an interview, got the job but didn't take it.

I was doing everything for many years: cooking, cleaning, washing and getting the boys off to school. He would stay in bed each morning until after the boys went to school, with a cup of coffee that I had made him. By then I had lost all respect for him and only felt a sisterly affection toward him. The passion and admiration had gone.

I began walking regularly on the beach and thinking of the consequences of telling him I didn't want to be with him anymore, and what it would do to the family, but I was exhausted and felt like

I was dying inside. When I eventually told him he took it really badly. He produced a gun and kept me prisoner within our home for a number of weeks. I escaped one day and he followed me, so I went back. The abuse kept happening and I left again. He produced a gun again, although he had told me he had disposed of it. I left again, this time only just getting out of there with a bag of clothes.

He wouldn't leave the home and he tried to turn my boys against me. He became a manipulator and a brainwasher. The damage he did to my boys is unforgiveable. He told me he didn't really want the boys—although I know he loves them—but he was doing it to destroy me.

To this day I will never get over missing out on the time with my sons! I also struggle with my own guilt, even though I know I had no option other than to go. I had to be far away from him, so I couldn't even visit my sons for a long while.

My family has been my saviour. I was left like a little girl who was unable to look after herself for quite a while—I didn't even remember how to cook. My mum was there for me every minute along the way to my recovery. She is an earth angel and a very strong woman.

Once I recovered and began living life without fear, my strength returned and I decided it was OK to follow my passions and live life to the fullest. Women are not just here for everyone else. We must remember it is our life too. We regain our personal power when we are living life in truth, as we truly are. I love life and I love people, and when it comes to the end of my days I want to say to myself that I lived life with passion and love.

I still feel pain every day thinking about the time I missed with my beautiful boys, but as they have grown they understand more and more of the truth.

There's no doubt in my mind that wisdom is born out of pain, loss and the consequential suffering of a life never to be the same again. Love like you've never loved before. Love each and every mineral, plant, animal and fellow human. Love is what it's all about. Heaven is right here, right now.

What a wonderful ending to this woman's story—that she has become strong enough to embrace her passions and her love of life.

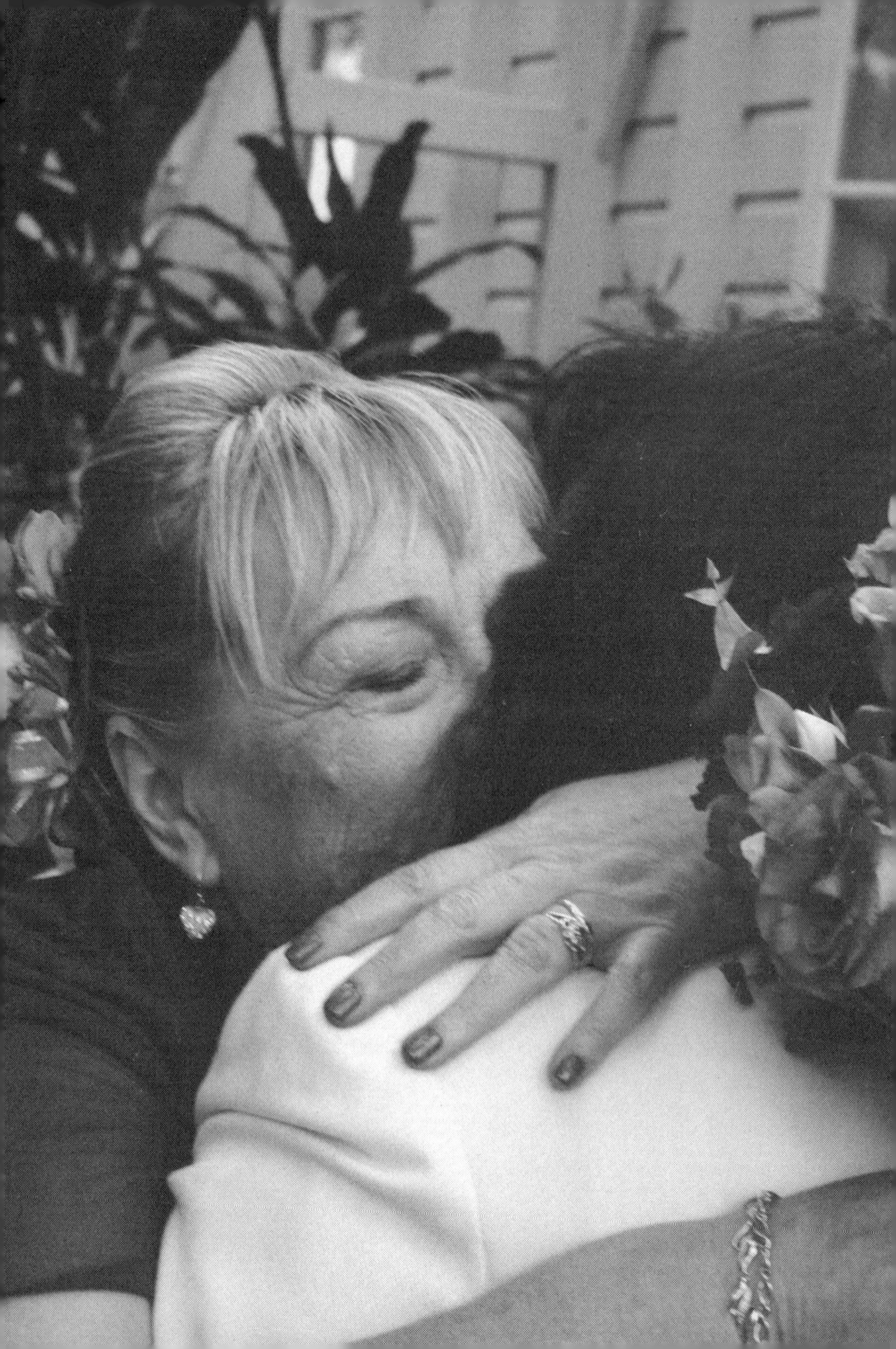

14

Which comes first?

I have often wondered which bits of my behaviour, or the bits of my behaviour I would rather not have, are a result of growing up in an alcoholic and abusive family situation, and which are simply a result of being me! Even with all the therapy in the world I think this is an almost impossible question to answer, as unanswerable as why some people can overcome addictions, tragedies and traumas, and others can't.

As I've got older I've begun to believe that watching my mother sink into a permanent state of depression has left me vulnerable to it. I know that this is not how people think of me, and most—even some of my close friends—would find it odd to think that I can live in deep, dark places for substantial periods of time, but I do, and can, and I've learned to be vigilant about it. All of us, I'm sure, get the 'what's the point?' voice from time to time, but it's a warning sign, and seeking out help is vital.

For me, alcohol has never been a problem—although many other things have—but for many sufferers this is a terrible addiction. Growing up in an abusive atmosphere has had repercussions throughout my life. However, I was lucky enough to find people early on who were able to join the dots for me so that at least the pattern made sense. Marian Clarke was not so lucky— she did not see how in her case repeated abuse may have led to self-abuse.

> I always felt different from other people, as if I didn't fit the mould. Perhaps that's why I was a good candidate for alcoholism. I can't blame my parents for my drinking, as I came from a happy home and secured a scholarship to an elite school, where I did well. I was repeatedly sexually abused when, like lots of London kids, I was sent off to the country to escape the bombing, but whether or not that impacted me I'm not sure.
>
> I had my first drink when I was eighteen. Dad took me to his local to show off his daughter. He bought me an advocaat, which tasted awful. But curiously, even my first drink left me in an altered state. I was a naturally shy person, but a drink made me bold.
>
> Apart from that one time, I really didn't drink. My boyfriend and I used to go and watch TV at a friend's house (TV was very new then). They used to make drinks for us; Pimms No.1 was in vogue. As I hated the alcohol, I'd only eat the fruit in the drink, and when no-one was looking, I'd tip the rest in a pot plant.

I didn't drink until much later, when I was about thirty. Even then I hated the taste, but loved the effect. I worked with a lively group of girls, and we used to go out and drink after work. My husband was away working, so nights out with the girls filled in the time. My friends all thought me funny when I had a few drinks and lost my shyness. I enjoyed the fact that they liked me like this, so I continued to drink and have fun. That's how I saw it: just having a bit of fun with the girls.

I suspect that's the attraction of drinking for a lot of people. Life's less challenging when you've had a few drinks. You have the confidence to say and do things you might not otherwise find. Sometimes I would stay out all night and not remember a thing the next day. I never gave any thought to my safety, or what my lifestyle was doing to me. I was lucky—I always got home safely.

I had a great job. I was a secretary to a director of a large company. When I found out he was an alcoholic, I would look at him and think 'Poor man. How awful for him,' never realising I was next in line. Over time I wasn't just drinking on nights out, I was drinking at home. This made things more difficult, because I didn't drive and so I had to find ways to get to the bottle shop. Then there was the problem of hiding the empty bottles at home. But like all alcoholics I was very resourceful and found ways to overcome this.

My husband was involved in films. At one stage he made a documentary on multiple sclerosis. When I saw the documentary it really shook me, as I had several similar symptoms. I often felt shaky and strange, but I still didn't really twig to what was going on for me.

My husband was an angel. He would put me to bed at night when I couldn't walk and loved me still. Life for me was a blur. Somehow I was still holding down a job, but things were getting worse.

Finally a friend told my husband I had drinking issues, and I was dragged off kicking and screaming to AA. It works for so many people, but of course I had to be different. So I used to have a few drinks before I went to a meeting, without my husband knowing, not realising that ultimately I was the main person I was fooling. The end result was horrible pains at two o'clock one morning. My poor husband had just about had enough. So we went to the hospital and eventually I was admitted. By this time I was like a skeleton and vomiting every day.

I remained in hospital for five of the hardest months of my life, which included a whole raft of tests and horrid treatments. I can't begin to describe the pain of withdrawal, or the awful hallucinations I'd get from time to time, which would leave most horror movies for dead. There were times when I thought I was losing my mind. When I was discharged, I had a new set of challenges. I had to go home and not drink. My husband was working, so I had the days to get through on my own.

I still had a friend from the hospital, now one of my dearest friends. She still weeps when she talks of the time when I had DTs and went berserk. I really had been so ill, but somehow I survived and didn't want to drink. But I yearned for the tranquillisers I'd taken indiscriminately with the drink. Looking back, it's a wonder I survived. I had really suffered the torture of the damned, yet I didn't want to go back to the hospital for more treatment.

The road back to sobriety was long and painful. Although I had friends and a wonderful husband and was eating again, I had to get better for myself. I got a job eventually at the hospital and made a slow return to health.

All these years later it's hard to believe this happened to me. While I wish I hadn't taken this path, my life is rich with many happy experiences and the love of good friends. Bad things happen sometimes, but it's what we do with them that matters. My experiences have made it much easier to empathise with people in difficult circumstances. It's been a privilege to talk with others struggling with their drinking issues, and to give them encouragement, because if I can stop drinking anyone can.

When I look at the binge-drinking culture so prevalent now, it saddens me. There's nothing empowering about this lifestyle. It's not glamorous. It's not even fun, really. It gives women a false sense of security, and leaves them vulnerable. As I've discovered, there's a thousand better, more beautiful ways to feel confident and good about yourself.

Marian sums up perfectly the insidious progression of an addiction, be it to alcohol, drugs, gambling or unhealthy behaviours of any kind—even something seemingly innocuous like shopping. We've all read of celebrities accused of shoplifting and wonder why these people feel the need to steal. But of course none of us know the journey that takes someone to any form of antisocial behaviour. I think the exposure I had to alcoholism in my family, not just my mother's but many other family members, caused me to be quite intolerant when I was young. I simply thought people should 'get over' things, but I hope as I've become older I've become more compassionate. We simply cannot walk in someone else's shoes, or understand another person's psychological make-up. Remaining non-judgemental, open and forgiving is the path to grace, of that I am sure.

Nobody can go back and start a new beginning, but anyone can start today and make a new ending.

MARIA ROBINSON

15

Learning that love is enough

Life is often a bewildering and difficult experience for all of us, but it is made much more complex for those who find that they perhaps do not fit the supposed picture of 'normality'. Yantra, whose stories on her mother, Faith Reid, and her friend Parampara are also in this book, found that in a society based on heterosexual relationships, families and children, the glorified fantasy of the life women should lead dies hard even when you have been in a relationship for a long time. She describes her journey towards the altar after she and her long-term partner, Suzanne, decided to get married.

Early one morning in late summer, the phone rang.

It was an unexpected interstate call with a challenging and unusual request. Would I do an interview on ABC Radio about my impending same-sex marriage? At the time, we were living in a volatile climate of terror and division. The day before my interview, George Bush had announced his intention to ban all gay marriages, and John Howard had obediently echoed him. But that weekend in Melbourne, the Midsumma Festival had celebrated over three hundred people declaring their love in the biggest ever same-sex group marriage.

And there I was, safe in my sleepy morning reverie, in a little terrace house with a white picket fence, climbing roses, a dog called Gilbert—and a fiancée named Suzanne Jones. Nothing could seem more normal to me, and yet ...

On Christmas Eve 2003, Suzanne and I had decided to celebrate our love and have a marriage ceremony.

I had always wanted to get married, and I felt that at last my dream was coming true. However, little did I realise that the slings and arrows of outrageous prejudice still lived deep inside my mortal coils. I became painfully aware of a part of my personal world that held on to vast secret mythologies of princes and princesses, brides and grooms. This was the stuff of fairytales and fantasies, yet it formed an undeniably deep and substantial strata of my underworld. Some part of me was still enmeshed with notions of what is supposed to be normality—the union of a man and woman.

The ceremony of marriage is one of the major rites of passage in our society. I knew on a deep and intrinsic level that my time had come to take this profound journey, but with this intention of same-sex marriage, I was catapulted into previously forbidden areas of my self, diving into undiscovered realms.

Even though I had spent the majority of my past twenty years in same-sex relationships (interspersed with brief and intense affairs with the opposite sex), I started to realise that there was a deep chasm forming between the long-held projected fantasy I cherished of marriage (i.e., heterosexual) and what I was about to embark on.

In a night of anguish and torment, I lost myself between the white and black notes of my haven that is the piano.

And I finally found two diametrically opposed women standing in bridal gowns. One, whom I will call Mrs Jenny Jones, was waiting at the altar for her prince, her knight in shining armour, her saviour—her man. And down that aisle was a path strewn with flowers leading to a home with a golden labrador and three children, to grandparents, public acceptance, private schools, tuckshops and mothers' meetings—a bright and rosy nuclear family.

On the other side stood me now, a woman in love with another woman, so sure that she is my miracle, that she is the best thing that has ever happened to me, that this is the right thing; so sure that we are soulmates, that this feels like my destiny, that there are no questions left—no questions, yet a raging battlefield inside me that chose to open fire with full force once the marriage plans were being made. Never before had my inner schism been so obvious.

So there we were, wedding fever was beginning, the invitations had been sent, the celebrant booked, catering, music, outfits—there were lists for miles.

And there I was, hovering between fear and love. I was scared. I could see all the challenges, the public outcry, the controversial debates, the pain, the humiliation and the prejudice.

And then I would see the truth of the purity of our lives together here and now; I would look to the reality of what I experience in our lives together. The magic of knowing that you can be alone with someone and, not uttering a word, answer each other's questions with just a look. The inspiration to be a better person and more loving to friends and family, sourced from the strength of your love. When you are challenged to uphold the truth and fight for your individual right to love, and you are left no choice but to learn how to accept and love yourself without shame, this is the true discovery.

In a society that is driven by a predominantly heterosexual culture, it garners a certain strength to be true to yourself and honour love rather than shame it. To be able to go deeper than the stares that fix you at an airport when you are departing from your lover and your heart is breaking and yet the dignity of your privacy remains with just a tightly held hand and a deep embrace—these things stick in the soul. All of these things made our wedding on 14 March 2004 not just a wedding but a courageous act of power and a statement of integrity, love and honour. Honouring that we are all different and unique, that we go beyond the titles of gay or straight, recognising that we are precious entities whose frailties and strengths are equal pillars supporting the temples of our souls.

What became of Mrs Jenny Jones? She still lives here, inside me now, but the battle is over, won by the power of self-inquiry and the love and support of my beloved partner Suzanne and my friends and family. Mrs Jenny Jones understands that times have changed and things look a little different to how they looked when she first came into being (probably when I was about seven years old watching a Doris Day movie).

My life has not turned out how I thought it would, or how my mother thought it would, yet both our mothers were at our wedding, in places of honour, surrounded by forty others of our friends and family, loving us, honouring us, supporting us and celebrating our love. Our parents are happy that we are happy.

At the pivotal moment of the ceremony where we exchanged our vows, I understood the power of ritual. I finally realised why I always wanted to get married. To say yes to love, to be opened up, split asunder by the power and intention of the word 'yes'—yes to love, yes to individuality, yes to the future of tolerance, yes to finding a new way for us all to live in this world and accept each other no matter what our differences and beliefs.

Yes, I do believe we can make a difference on this planet through our own deeply personal commitment to love and honesty.

I think that many women go through the fear of marriage—no matter to whom. In fact, strong evidence suggests that the fear is part of the journey! It's how you undertake it and with what understanding that can create a long-term, lasting relationship of the kind that Yantra and Suzanne enjoy.

Pure love is a willingness to give without a thought of receiving anything in return.

PEACE PILGRIM

16

Women who inspire us

The women who inspire or help us on our journeys stand out like shining beacons—at least they certainly did for me when inspiration and support went missing from my childhood.

I will never forget my drama teacher at high school, Jan Russell. Not only did she encourage my love of public speaking, poetry and drama; she very quickly took on board what was happening at home, and often drove me back home from school so that I could stay at rehearsals.

Jan later extended the same support and kindness to my younger sisters and became a family friend. She and I stayed in contact for many years—I still have a fine-bone china mug she gave to my son on one of our visits to England, and I think of her every time I use it.

Teachers were often my inspiration. As a fourteen-year-old I came down with a long bout of glandular fever. This resulted in almost a year off school, which coincided with a move to London from the country, me deciding that going out with a drug dealer was a good idea, and my parents descending even further into a morass of debts and crisis.

Finally, they put me into a tutorial college run by the formidable Miss Dixon and Miss Wolfe. Their teaching methods I couldn't recommend, but there were two teachers there, the art teacher and the English teacher (whose name I still remember—Miss Bell) who were staggered that my formal learning had sunk to such depths, and proceeded to drag me out of the belief I had created for myself that I was stupid and no good at anything.

It was entirely due to them that I rediscovered my brain and managed in two years to acquit myself reasonably in my Leaving exams. They also, and god bless both of them, instilled in me a love of writing and art, which have become touchstones in my life.

Elaine Harris, a radio host, also writes about the importance of education, and how it changed both her and her husband's lives.

I little thought that my husband's career change and Bachelor of Education studies would have such a profound effect upon both our lives, bringing new friends to us both, increased knowledge and, more recently, eye-opening depths of understanding and belated gratitude. We have always proofread one another's work, so I have learned about child development, education theories, ethics, methods, goals and strategies. I have often waxed lyrical about Miss Turner, the sixth-form English teacher responsible for bringing Shakespeare alive for me, demonstrating the flamboyance of language by example and introducing me to the powerful beauty of Milton's verse. It is only recently, however, through my partner's final teaching practice, that I have begun to realise why my primary school teachers did what they did and just how superb they were.

One teacher in particular springs to mind. Due to a reorganisation of my small boarding school, I spent two years in her class. We saw much of her outside lessons too, even when she was no longer our teacher, and it was she who read to us while doing evening duty on Tuesdays and Thursdays. She was a consummate storyteller and read aloud with spellbinding expression and impeccable timing. We covered the first section of *Jane Eyre* before I was ten and she finished the first instalment of *A Christmas Carol* just as Marley's ghost arrives outside Scrooge's door.

This teacher celebrated our successes but rarely if ever underlined our failures or highlighted our mediocrity. She did not scold when I spilled some of my pancake batter while walking from her flat to the main school; she didn't eject me from the Tuesday knitting club even when she had to finish my dishcloth before the school open day, and made no comment when I was the last to complete my cane basket. We both knew that I would never equal classmate Danny's success in maths, yet she never failed to foster my love of words, music, drama and books.

We acted out scenes from some of the books she read to us, made papier-mache igloos when learning about the real thing, assembled paper chains while listening to stories, and discussed constantly the meanings behind those stories and BBC school radio programs. I can honestly say I did not once fear or dread entering her classroom.

It is her demonstration of the meanings of words that I recall with such clarity. During a telling of 'Dick Whittington and His Cat' she asked if we knew the meaning of the word 'thrice'. No-one did. Leaping up and matching actions to words she showed us: 'I go to the door not once, not twice but ...' Then we understood!

Dear Miss Lamb, Evelyn, we both knew I loved you; that was a given. 'My girls', you called us. The bond was still intact when we met at a choir reunion several years after I left the school. Sadly, I never had the grace to say thank you. Let me do so now, publicly and in print, hoping the intent will reach you wherever you are. The lessons you taught and the knowledge you imparted rarely felt like lessons at all, yet still hold true today and are now being handed on. What better way to say thank you!

I also have a friend to say thank you to because over the years she has been very much a mentor to me, even if she may not realise it! When I went to the tutorial college after my bout with glandular fever, Zoe was there. We both came from interestingly dysfunctional families, as did most of the girls there I guess, but our dysfunctions neatly meshed and we became close friends. Over the years, however, our paths diverged. She became a young mum, I moved to Australia, and gradually we lost touch.

Fast-forward twenty years, and I was sitting on Bondi Beach with my partner and his three children when I was struck by the familiar look of someone sitting next to us, also with children. She seemed so like my friend Zoe, and yet I wasn't quite sure, and somehow I imagined that if she had moved to Australia, I would have heard, wouldn't I?

In confusion, I decided to go for a walk and think about whether to approach her. Nowadays my temerity seems quite odd, I would just burl up and ask her straight out—but some shyness prevented me.

When I came back I was none the wiser, other than the fact that she held her cigarette in a particular sort of way that so reminded me of Zoe. As I sat there wondering what to do, she came up to me: 'Didn't you used to be Candy Baker?' she asked. I laughed. 'I still am,' I replied, 'and you must be Zoe.'

Twenty years disappeared and a friendship was reformed that has since survived her moving back to England and then settling permanently in Australia a few years ago. I admire enormously her intellect, hard work and ability to juggle her commitments and look after those around her, and I think her description of inspiring women below is a poetic offering on the gifts our friends give us.

> I have been thinking about the question of who has inspired me, or inspires me now, and found that, unsurprisingly, it is all the women I know. Each one, at different times, has reminded me to fill my lungs, sing, laugh, sob, shout and howl into the waves of life. Drowning or swimming; riding the crest or dashed on the rocks; mixed and scraped by the sand or frolicking light as foam—up they get. Juggling

jobs, kids and torn-open hearts, they wrap the weave of their lives around themselves, make packed lunches, check for nits, create and bring to life new and refashioned dreams. They shift in an instant from deep in the abyss of despair and grief to the day-to-day of what can be done here, now, in this moment.

This is not to say that only women have this extraordinary responsive and reflective capacity. I see it all around me, but as a woman I know in my blood and bone what it takes to pull the heart's gaze back to the little things that also make a life. I feel that what we most admire in others is what we experience of their capacity to act and be in the midst of those moments when circumstances overwhelm, when the gap between what can be done and what it would take to give life to a dream or bring it back from death is so huge that denial, despair and surrender or rabid fury seem the only way to keep some semblance of a coherent effective self.

The temptation to resort to blaming, cruel acts and pointless comparisons can be acute. Sometimes there is a ravening hunger for a fitting blood sacrifice to stop the fates in their tracks or mark the agony of unbearable loss, but in that moment of murderous rage and tearing grief, somehow the grace and strength emerges to keep from acting on it and put one foot in front of the other, walking the detail of the every day.

I believe we are only as strong as we must be—there is no excess capacity. I would not wish harsh events or the death of dreams on anyone, and confess to offering anything if only life could be a little kinder. Nonetheless, I celebrate, wonder at, and take breath from the extraordinary expressions of strength found in the facing, and living with, both the extremes of human experience and the domestic details of survival.

My heart fills with gratitude when I recall the kindness and support I have received from my sisters and friends over the years, when life has seemed too hard and sad. Hours on the phone, late night talks, walks, swims, jokes and little gifts have soothed my heart and coaxed me to look up from my sorrows. Without their kind attention and companionship I would have wandered, wailing, for so much longer. I am also grateful for the gift of time that has made it possible for my mother and I to transform our relationship into a deep and loving friendship.

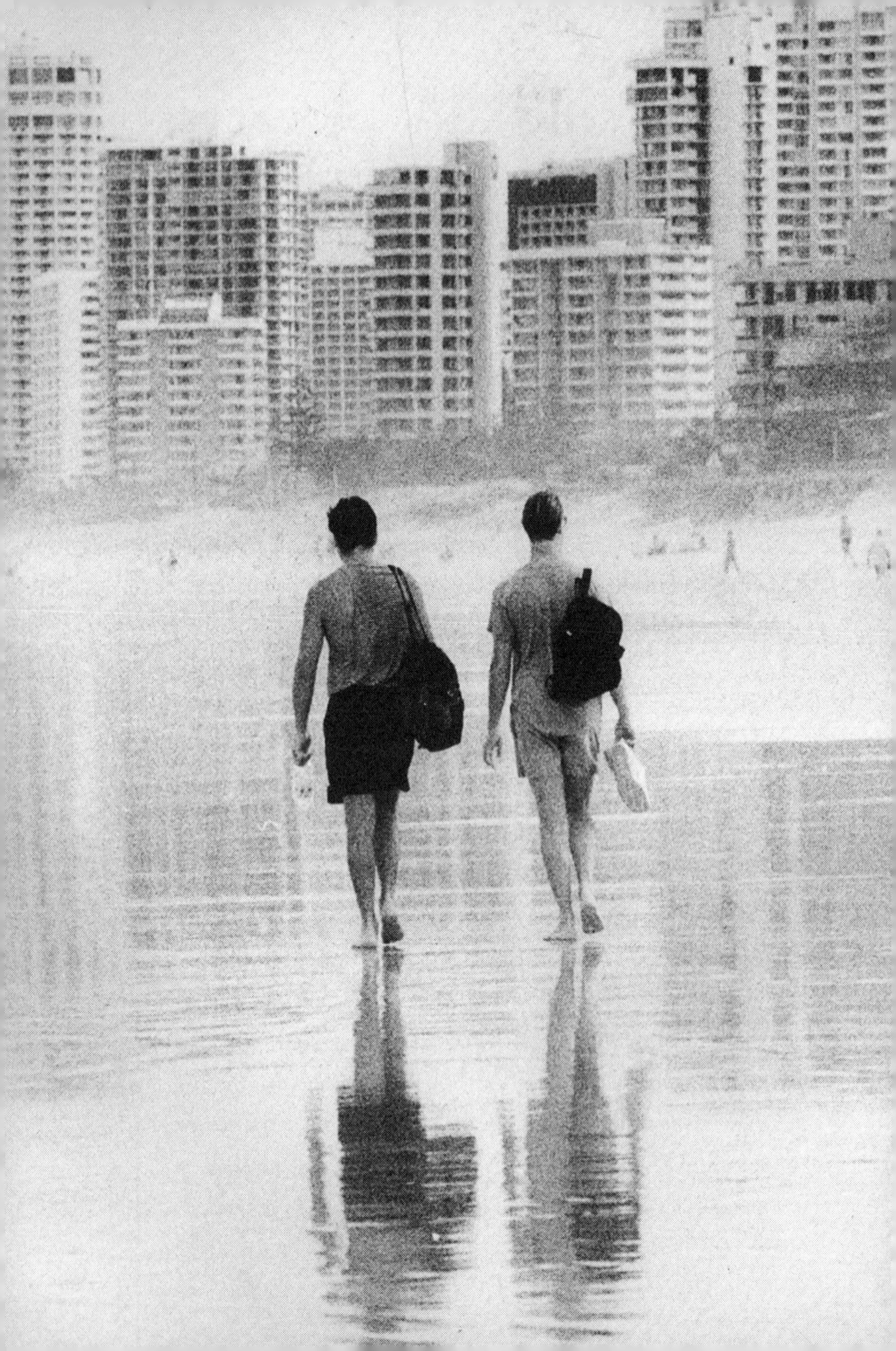

17

A mother's instinct

I remember perfectly the moment I really became a mother. It wasn't when my son was born, or even in the first few weeks. It was the moment I decided to ignore the nursing clinic's advice and put my starving baby on a bottle of formula.

I guess as new mums all we have to go on—and I had no mum with me to tell me otherwise—is the advice of those around us. It seemed odd to me right from the start that my baby seemed only to want to suckle all the time, and that he cried as soon as he was put down, but hey, what did I know?

He wouldn't sleep more than forty minutes. He'd cry and cry, and I'd attach him to the bosom, which would placate him for a little minute; then I'd put him down again, and again he would cry.

Everybody—the nurses in the hospital where we had to stay for a few days due to a difficult birth, my own midwife, and the clinic I saw once I went home all told me that I should eat, rest, and make 'lots of milk for my baby'.

When, after a whole month, he had still not regained his birth weight, the sister still got cross with me! She told me to go home, go to bed, drink beer (!) and eat chocolate. The sheer absurdity of the advice given without even asking what my home life was like, or even if I drank beer or ate chocolate, was astonishing. And as it was, with three stepchildren, a rather large and mad dog, two homes and the book I was then writing, the idea of staying in bed, even if I wanted to—which I didn't—was ridiculous.

It was at this point that I suddenly felt myself propelled into a different consciousness. I thanked her, walked out of there, straight into the chemist next door, bought formula and a bottle, took it home, made it and gave it to my baby. I think he thought he had died and gone to heaven! He sat on my lap like a little nodding Buddha, a tiny dribble of milk from the corner of his mouth, and a beatific smile on his face. He then went to sleep for three whole hours.

There have been many times in my life since that moment when I have intuitively known that my instinct as a mother was right.

Simone Smith, a TV producer, was extremely lucky that her mother followed her instinct, as she tells in the following story.

My life began when I was three years old, sitting on the sand with my mum. We were at the beach and I was wearing a one-piece

A mother's instinct

frangipani-print swimsuit, and my chubby arms and legs were crumbed with sand. We had built a sandcastle and were decorating our handiwork with seaweed and shells. Apparently we were always painting and creating beautiful things together, but this was the first time it actually registered, my earliest memory.

For Mum, my life started many years prior. Mum and Dad had travelled to India, their last stop on their three-month worldwide honeymoon. They were at a temple, one of many on their trip, but this one was different as it was a wish temple. On one side the entire wall was marble and was carved so intricately that from afar it looked as though it was made of lace. Dotted all through the marble were scraps of red fabric cut into ribbon-like slithers. Mum bought a ribbon from a beautifully dressed old Indian woman in a tangerine sari. Through hand gestures, she indicated to Mum to tie the ribbon to the wall, shut her eyes and focus intently on something she desired.

Mum, ever the optimist, tied her ribbon to the wall and wished for a child, a healthy baby girl. Dad, ever the realist, believes he saw the old woman untie the ribbon and resell it to a backpacker as they were leaving the temple. But regardless of whether the wishes were recycled or not, five weeks later back in Australia Mum discovered she was pregnant and was adamant it was the girl she so desperately wished for in India with her holy red ribbon.

Thrilled with the news, Mum and Dad started preparing their modest one-bedroom flat for the arrival of their first child. Mum strongly believed in the benefits of a good diet and homeopathy, and transformed her body into a temple—her very own wish temple—by eating organic foods and taking herbal medicines to increase her wellbeing. Despite it being the first for Mum, the pregnancy was uneventful.

The birth, however, was not. I simply refused to be born, turning myself upside down every time the doctor tried to position me head-first. Mum believes I was content in there and wasn't ready to face the world just yet, but the doctors told her they were worried it was due to something else. Without properly consulting Mum, the doctors decided to perform a caesarean. Once born I was rushed away, and Mum's intense dislike of doctors began.

'What was it?' Mum questioned the nurse. 'A boy or a girl?'

'A girl, she's a girl.'

That was it. That was all Mum was told. She had only glimpsed the top of my head over the curtain covering her from the waist down as I was carried out of the room.

'Well, where is she? Is she OK? I want to see her!'

'In due time, lovey. You just relax and we'll fix you up first, OK?'

'No! I want to see my daughter! Where did they take her?'

Two hours later, Mum's doctor finally returned. There was a tall, lanky man following closely behind him.

'Ann, this is Dr Jekyll.'

From that moment on, Mum would refer to the two doctors as Dr Jekyll and Mr Hyde.

'We believe your daughter has cranial deformation and needs

an operation to insert metal shunts in her skull to prevent her head from expanding.'

'What?'

'Cranial deformation ...'

'You've got to be joking!'

'I understand you've had an eventful forty-eight hours but ...'

'Eventful! Look, I just want to see her. Where is she?'

'We're preparing her for surgery. Now if you just let Dr Hyde here explain ...'

'You're what?! Where's my husband?'

'Mrs Smith, please don't raise your voice. It isn't necessary—we are just trying to help.'

'Help?! You know what would help: if you let me see my daughter. This is insane!'

'Mrs Smith, please. This isn't good for you getting worked up like this. Your husband has been informed and ...'

'Get me my husband now!'

My mother can only be described as cherub-like. She has short, white blonde hair, blue eyes, a 'cute as a button' nose and an overall demeanor about her that just makes you relax when she is around. She is always smiling and always thinking of others. She is a great judge of character and can sniff out a phoney from a mile away, but behind her cute, chirpy exterior lies a strong-willed, intelligent and passionate woman who will not stand by if she senses an injustice is taking place. This side rarely shows itself unless provoked, and it often startles those who don't know her. It really is a unique and powerful combination, the sweet looks and the fiery, intelligent personality.

'I want to see my daughter, now!' She bellowed. 'Please.'

After another thirty minutes, the doctors finally brought me into my mother's room so that she could meet me for the very first time. She took one look at me with my large head and then looked up at my father.

'She's Scottish, Dr Jekyll,' Mum said. 'My husband is Scottish and, guess what, so his father. My daughter is therefore Scottish. Other than an uncanny ability to play the bagpipes, the Scots are also known for their rather well formed craniums. Just look at my husband. You will not be cutting open my daughter's skull.'

Mum and Dad laughed for a good ten minutes after Dr Jekyll and Dr Hyde slipped out of the room. To think they wanted to put metal shunts in their daughter's perfectly formed, albeit rather large skull had enraged them. But that wasn't the end of the doctors.

Around my third month, Mum was bathing me and noticed something wasn't right. My father was away on business, as he often was, and so the next day she begrudgingly took me to see Dr Hyde.

'I think there is something wrong with my daughter's legs.'

'Her legs?'

'Yes, one leg seems longer than the other.'

Dr Hyde took one look at me from behind his desk and laughed.

'Mrs Smith, there is nothing wrong with your daughter.' Smirking, he continued: 'Perhaps those Scottish ancestors of yours are also prone to having one leg longer than the other so they can stand sideways on those steep Scottish highlands.'

Mum was outraged and made an appointment to see another doctor at the hospital the next day. He also sent her away after barely looking at me. Three consultations later and Mum finally got in to see a female doctor who not only listened to what Mum had to say but gave her a referral for an x-ray on the grounds of a suspected dislocated hip.

The doctor explained that when diagnosed early enough, sufferers of dislocated hips must spend eight months in plaster from their ankles to their upper waist, with their legs elevated in stirrups for the first six months. A small hole is cut out at the back of the plaster to enable them to go to the toilet. But if left undiagnosed and not treated, sufferers' hips fuse in a dislocated position and they must spend their entire life wearing one normal shoe and one shoe with a platform of an inch or two. They are unable to walk without the aid of these special shoes, cannot run, and certainly cannot dance or play sport.

The x-ray showed that I had dislocated hips, causing one leg to sit out of the joint and making one leg longer than the other. Mum was right.

Those eight months, I am told, were excruciating for all involved. I cried day and night while in hospital rigged up to what looked like a medieval torture device. The nurses were amazing but the ward was severely understaffed. Rigged up the way I was, I wasn't able to be held or cuddled, so Mum and Dad would often find themselves nursing other babies while they sat and watched over me.

After a few weeks at the hospital, Dad became feverish and quickly came down with meningitis. It was severe. He believes he caught it from one of the sick babies he was nursing while visiting me. He was bedridden for four-and-a-half weeks. Poor Mum was torn between nursing him at home and visiting me in hospital. If she hadn't been such an incredibly strong woman, she simply wouldn't have got through this. None of us would have. Her life became about everyone else and yet she carried on with that angelic smile on her face.

Of course, Dad eventually recovered and after a few weeks returned to work. He wasn't able to visit me at the hospital any more, which must have been hard for both him and Mum. Looking back, I am thankful that I can't remember this period of my life, the beginning. Although I do think about it often and wonder if, in my mother's situation, I would have coped as well as she did. Not a day goes by that I am not thankful for my mum's wisdom and determination to see that I was properly examined, diagnosed and treated.

Although my first memory with Mum on the beach is very special to me, it's my second memory that is so special to Mum. It was a few weeks later and I had been out of hospital for over a year. I came stumbling into the kitchen where Mum was listening to the radio and cooking dinner. I had make-up smeared all over my face and I was wearing her oversized high heels. I fell out of the heels and began to bop and sway, dancing like the cheeky three-year-old I was. Mum put down the spatula and knelt on the kitchen floor next to me and we danced together.

A mother's instinct

It had taken years of heartache and tears but my mother's wish had finally come true. She had got her healthy baby girl. As I get older and continue to run, skip and dance my way through life, my only wish is that I grow up to be as strong and beautiful a woman as she is.

Never give up, for that is just the place and time that the tide will turn.

HARRIET BEECHER STOWE

18

A road less travelled

I wonder if it is possible for those of us who have conceived easily to understand what the journey is like for those women who either can't conceive or have great trouble conceiving. Even with all the empathy in the world we cannot walk that particular journey.

The story below is particularly poignant to me, because the woman in question is my younger sister, Charlie. I remember as if it was yesterday how happy we all were when Brian and Charlie met and were married, and how obvious it was to all of us that they would in due course become parents, and how great they would be at it.

And yet it was not to be. At the same time, I was busy with the baby that had unexpectedly arrived for me when I was forty-five. Two sisters, two such different stories. I have always had such admiration for Charlie, and even more so now she has been brave enough to record the journey of her disappointment.

> You think you have mourned and travelled through the corridors of disappointment, that your life has moved on. Only to find yourself on the sofa, in the garden, having a cup of tea, and you realise that tears are falling softly from your eyes, old wounds starting to seep; the things that have been put to rest get remembered and disappointment seeps through the very cells of your being into the crevasses of your heart where grief resides.
>
> We all deal with loss and grief differently; my husband sort of just stopped being fully in the world, went into a cave and took years to come out. I seem to have lived at half-mast for many years, not completely aware that I was doing that until we both started to move on. When disappointment arrives again from time to time, I feel it for a lesser amount of time and yet it is momentarily intensified.
>
> It was not until I was twenty-five that I truly wanted a baby. I was happy being young and healing my inner child, working on becoming a whole human being. In fact I often prayed not to be pregnant when my period was late, because I knew I was not ready.
>
> Then the biological clock ticked—OH MY DID IT TICK. Unfortunately I was with a man who did not want children, and coming from a broken home and having witnessed people having children without their partner's consent, or without partners, I thought to myself,

A road less travelled

'I have time, there is no way I am bringing a child into the world when its father does not want it.' That partnership inevitably broke up.

The years rolled on and the ships passed in the night or stayed docked for some months and then moved on. I did not allow myself to become pregnant; I just thought that one day it would happen. I held some deep-seated belief that I should not get pregnant unless I was in a long-term relationship.

I watched as many friends had children. It was not necessarily easy for them—pain seems to be associated with parenthood in some form or another, yet the primal urge to procreate just kept on going. I longed to be a mum.

When I was thirty-seven I met an amazing man, we fell in love, we danced and romanced and I kept faith with my long-held belief of being sure of the man and his intention for children and having to make sure he was trustworthy. I would not get pregnant until we knew more about each other. We got married a year after meeting and finally I could let go of fear and all would be well.

We tried to fall pregnant, but oh, the disappointment every time my period arrived.

We did not go straight to IVF—we went to a clinic for natural fertility first. We trusted these people to send us to IVF as soon as was necessary—as they said they would—and so in both blind faith and the desire not to put that many chemicals in my body we stayed far too long.

At forty I did fall pregnant. I was never sure if that was due to the natural fertility clinic or just that I had visited my sister in Wimbledon,

England, where we went for a walk in a park and saw more push chairs and young parents than I had ever witnessed before in one place. She said it was something about the water and that people had been coming there for centuries to aid pregnancy. Nine weeks later I miscarried. It took me just under a year to recover from that. Too long, some would say, as the biological clock kept ticking. Not the French: they believe that it takes the full nine months for the body to complete the journey of birth whether you carry the foetus to full term or not.

I was starting to feel it was too late and that my time had passed. My husband had wanted children since he was seventeen and he was now forty-five. We decided (after some long and painful conversations) to do IVF, and I made a rash promise to us both that I would try three times.

I have absolutely no idea how women go through this process eight to ten times.

On our first visit the staff called me geriatric. I had fought to keep my womb many years before, had prepared myself to lose it and then woken to find they had not removed the place where miracles are made; yet here I was being told my womb was geriatric and not to get my hopes up.

The first cycle of IVF, I struggled with staying not too far away from my normal personality. I struggled not to snap and say shitty things I did not believe to the man I love wholeheartedly. He struggled to hold the space for the difference. We struggled with how hard I found it to give myself injections and yet somehow could not let him do it.

A road less travelled

There are many, many things you both have to have done to you, and many hoops you have to jump through for IVF, yet mostly it is the woman who has to have the checklist ticked. Then, of course, having journeyed through all these things you get to the egg collection and replacement of eggs, a horrible and invasive procedure that replaces something that should be natural. It is, however, still an amazingly hopeful time. So you can imagine my shock when I was told the very first time I had the egg collection that I had no eggs: it was very rare, although not unheard of, they said, to have no eggs.

I was debilitated by this news. It took some time but in the end we decided that although it was horrible we would continue with the plan and go again. The experience became less positive and somehow more private and possibly devastating.

I saw an acupuncturist for three months prior and during the treatment. It helped settle the anxiety and I believe it is down to his help that this time I had six healthy eggs. This time we fell pregnant, we were not so quick to tell people, to believe the baby was in the bag, but it was so secretly exciting and hope was everywhere between us.

This time on our second ultrasound we were told there was no heartbeat. I remember I had gone alone, saying to my husband, 'Why not? It's early days and nothing could have gone wrong yet.' I had to phone him and tell him—it was so hard to hear the breath being pulled out of his lungs.

This one had been such a gargantuan effort it had taken more than the wind out of my sails. My faith in Great Sprit was shattered, my lifelong belief in angels was gone. It seemed my vision quests in the garden, my walks and talks to myself, to my higher self and to my angels had come to nothing. This shattering has taken longer to heal then almost anything else. In fact I am not sure if it is completely healed or if it ever will be.

You don't just stand to lose the child or the journey of parenthood when you walk down the IVF road. There is so much more to it—so much unseen and unknown that we risk.

Another year passed and I knew as one does sometimes that it was not going to happen, that I was not going to be a mum. I told my husband and he quite rightly challenged my knowing, and why shouldn't he? It's hard to truly know something to the very core of your being and ask someone to trust you when they stand to lose so much. Why should they believe you? Why should they take your word for it when you have nothing tangible to give them or show them but just a deep, deep knowing?

And so I tried again. It still makes me cry, the third try, doing something to myself I did not want to do that I knew was not going to get me what I so desired. Some would say that what I needed was positive thought, that I jinxed the whole thing, that had I been able not to be so negative ... What I know is there's a place for positive thought, there's a place for being a realist, but this place had nothing to do with either of these mindsets, this place was from deep within my womanhood and she said 'It ain't happening honey, take your hat and go home.' But I did not take my hat and go home. Funny what love and hope will make us do.

It did not make it easier knowing the outcome, because there was always the outside chance I was wrong, or so I told myself. But it did not happen for us that time either. I had eggs but they did not take and so that was that. Or so this fast-paced world would like us to believe. But it was not over because the disappointment (as a dear friend says, a highly underrated emotion) just invaded and infiltrated our very beings. We had to start to rebuild our life. We had to get through disappointment and blame. Blame that takes a long time to truly understand, deep in our subconscious, that it takes both the sperm and the egg; that it takes the age of both mother and father; that it takes the health of the womb and a huge amount of magic to even make it to the first base of pregnancy, let alone what it takes to safely navigate the full term. Blame is a big one—it takes some pushing, some negotiation and yet more pain to work through it. We were up for the journey, up for tears, ready for the resolution; sometimes this attitude is exhausting but the honesty it brings helps mend and build health in the end.

For years after the IVF I had the desire to create something, to build something from scratch, perhaps start a business that I could watch grow, create an energy with its own personality, which, with luck, would get its own wings and fly. I still have this desire but recently I realised I had put all my dreams into the same bucket as the baby dream—all the colours and hues of my daydream of being a mum had got mixed up and muddled up and I had just dressed them in the clothes of a business. How insidious this desire for procreation can be; you think you are over it only to find it hiding somewhere unseen! I have safely removed these new dreams from that bucket and have started to see if the business of opening a business is in fact what I want for its own sake and not to replace something I lost along the way.

I am one of the lucky people though, because I did not lose my marriage or my love for my husband. The rebuilding of us as partners has been long and hard, but I believe we are stronger now than before and have negotiated many streams and valleys, as do people with children—so, not so different in the long run.

As for my friends, all the way through this journey we call life women find each other—and if we are lucky some of them stay with us for years and get to know us inside and out. They can be a mirror for us when we have strayed too far from ourselves, and they can pull us back. I remember that during this five-year journey the women I am lucky to be surrounded by were always there, whether it was to make me laugh, to tell me to get a grip or just make me a cuppa and listen as I tried to explain my feelings.

One day a friend called and I remember telling her I had been sitting in the kitchen staring at the floor for ages: 'I'm not sure what's wrong with me, really—I just didn't know how to move.' She gently told me that depression will do that to you and it was OK to sit there just as long as I needed to—but if I stayed there too long she'd come and get me and take me for a walk. Until then it was OK not to think for myself.

Another friend asked me if I had a plan B, and—this has always stayed with me—I was so shocked because I had my plan A but no, no plan B. When she said you might need one, I thought, yes, indeed we might.

No-one in my circle of friends had travelled the IVF road, which was hard for me and for them. Since then, however, some have been down the road themselves. One dear friend said recently that if another person told her she did not know what it was like to be a parent she was going to scream. So we did—we sat in her car and had a good scream.

Women have that age-old gift of chatting, even if we don't really get how important it is and how amazing the webs of our lives and the stories we tell each other can be until years later when perhaps our world falls apart for some reason. Then it is these people who hold your story and remember who you are so that you can walk back to yourself, somewhat changed but essentially yourself. I sometimes wonder what men do as they don't seem to chat like we do; maybe that is why when they lose their way it takes them so long to come home. No-one holds their threads as our women friends hold ours.

Through writing this I am reminded that angels come in all sorts of forms and although at that time I had lost my connection with my spiritual understanding of that energy essence, I was in fact always surrounded by angels in the physical form.

A very wise woman told me that it would take at least twelve years to get to regain my equilibrium. I am on year six and I think she may have been right.

My darling sister travelled a hard road, but on the way she has collected so many children who adore her—and not just family members. I hope she feels proud of the love and support she gives them, and everybody in her life. I know I do.

Of course, having children—or not—is an unfolding journey, one that Bella Vendramini is still experiencing.

> I'm not sure I want to have kids of my own yet. It's too soon to tell. Last weekend my boyfriend and I took my nieces and his kids to the country for the first time. I watched as they played together, their tiny hands pushing shoes onto tiny feet. High exuberant bounces on the trampoline. Smeary faces from mud pies. I felt such an unexpected and overwhelming love for that ragtag bunch. Their quips and tiny voices, their small personalities forming right in front of us. They felt like my kids. I knew it then; they don't need to be mine for me to experience that lioness love. Kids, I discovered, are universal—belonging, in the moment, to any open heart. Beautiful innocent creatures with muddy faces and twinkling eyes, ready to be loved completely.

Last in this chapter is the heartwarming story of lecturer and broadcaster Jenny Palmer, who was about to give up on having a baby when she happened to listen to an interview with Dorothy Green, whose books still sell today.

> Dorothy Green is one of those relatively unsung heroines of the Australian literary world—a woman who combined both passion

A road less travelled

and razor-like reason in the analysis of texts she illuminated in the course of her teaching career. Social justice was pivotal to her beliefs, and her views on the status of women brought her to the notice of many of us not fortunate enough to know her as a teacher.

The right to abortion, Dorothy Green believed, was mandatory. And so she came to express her view too on the antithetical argument about the right to life embodied in the practice of in vitro fertilization and the freezing of embryos.

I was listening to her one Saturday afternoon as I did my usual weekend chores in the kitchen—the apple cake, the casserole and curry, the ironing—tasks made lighter by the flow of talk from the ABC radio station for which I worked. I had interviewed Dorothy recently and was riveted now as she attacked this subject in her usual incisive manner.

Dorothy had children: I did not.

Only the previous year and for reasons I won't explain here—it's too complicated—I had sobbed at the loss of three pairs of such embryos, already named when I peered into the microscope to see my babies in their most primitive form, just little knots of cells about to be lodged in the wall of my uterus.

It was February, June and November when they were injected there, each time following a period on pills designed to goad my ovaries into overdrive and swell them to the size of golf balls; a period when every drop of urine must be collected. I had taken the precious containers with me to work and parked them discreetly in a paper bag on a corner shelf in the women's toilet. Not a drop must be missed. And then, twenty-four hours before my eggs were to be lifted away from their ovarian nest, a massive injection had been plunged into the big thigh muscle of my right leg to ensure they stayed put, waiting for the doctor to collect them and introduce them to their father's sperm in a test tube.

Others have written of the indignities associated with this oh-so-public process of conception. They were borne more easily through humour, but in my case also through the company of my female doctor, who had a taste for champagne! We toasted each successful implant well into the night after she had finished that particular round of playing stork.

Three times we congratulated ourselves and three times we treated the empty ward to a Sally Bowles–like gutsy rendition of 'Maybe this time, maybe this time . . .' But my doctor was not there in May, August and January when my bloody little clumps of baby left my body. These were lonely affairs. And after three times there could be no more.

I would have no baby. I was probably just too old. Instead I would have a new job in a different city. A new life of my own.

But now into my new life came Dorothy's words, swirling through my kitchen, crisp as the wintry air as they denounced the extravagant waste of medical resources on a tiny minority of people who were not even ill, questioning the ethics of these experiments in conception and ringing with absolute knowing of the longing we objects of the in vitro process felt to be just like her: not an intellectual of prodigious knowledge and talent, but a mother. My reflection in the kitchen window crumpled and I heard myself howling like a lost child, in a frenzy not of fear but of grief.

Later, when the curry was made and the casserole and the cake removed from the oven, there was comfort for me in their mingled aromas. And a strange calm came over me. In the wake of Dorothy's words I had made a decision. I would not give up trying for a baby after all. But I would not go the way of needles and prodding and pills. I would try the antithesis of this contentious scientific approach to motherhood. I would consult a white witch—as she might have been known in the dim and distant past.

A woman friend recommended a herbalist. I have not been able to trace this woman since the time she listened to my story, looked into my eyes and gave me a bottle of tonic she said would do the trick. I told no-one I had seen her, not my husband, not a soul. And I sipped my tonic in secret.

Summer was brewing and we went to a beach for a short break—a wonderful wide sweeping beach north of Sydney where the mist hung over the rolling surf and made rainbows with the November morning sunlight. I walked in the shallows with my dogs as the sun came up over the horizon and glazed the sand with gold where the water rushed away to meet it. I had been at peace in my sometimes troubled marriage that week and my husband unusually amorous. And as the sun rose this humid summer morning I felt it. Like a bird singing. A little current of energy beneath my brown belly.

A few weeks later, after a job in Melbourne, it was confirmed. I was pregnant. Was the tonic responsible?

But there was a more urgent question—would we make the distance together, this new little knot of cells and I?

I was convinced that I was about to have a son. I asked not to be told if this was true after the long wait that followed the risky tests I needed to endure. My husband and I were so sure he was a boy, we called him Tom.

He and I walked to work together. We discussed the day to come, and on the way home we shared the ups and downs and wondered what to cook for tea. I sang him songs my father taught me and in the evening if I had no work to do we sat with his father and read while he watched TV. We listened to music. We floated in the ocean. And he turned upside down as I stood on my head in the yoga sessions that were an essential part of my life. We would be friends forever, I told him, even though he was a boy and must love his father in a special way. But I would always be there for him as long as I lived. It was important for him to know this.

I would imagine squeezing his small hand as we walked through Paddington, down the hill through Five Ways and Darlinghurst, to my office in William Street. And again on the way home, looking in at the illuminated rooms in the pretty terrace houses we passed until we came to our own house and the dogs who would be his pets and love him too.

I had no sickness, no aches and pains, just an unbelievable contentment.

In August, my fortieth birthday having passed four months before, a daughter emerged. She arrived with almost indecent ease.

A girl! No needles, no pills, a minimum of prodding. We called her Maggie—little pearl.

She is now twenty-four, and not so little anymore. Yet I still think of Dorothy Green, who is dead now but whose books live on, and the white witch I never found again, and who is still perhaps prescribing potions out there somewhere. Two clever, caring women, like so many who have touched me over my lifetime with words that have challenged my brain and knowledge that has healed me.

These two women have a particular place in my heart because without them my greatest joy would not have eventuated. I have a daughter who loves me, who is my friend, who makes me laugh and comforts me when I am sad. Who drinks wine with me and makes me delicious cakes and curry and casseroles. Who leaves my kitchen—for she still lives at home when she is not travelling overseas to study or enjoy herself—fragrant with mingled aromas as well as covered in an unholy mess of unwashed pots and pans. And whose dresses I still iron with ridiculous pleasure.

I have a daughter. I am blessed.

*I really don't think life is about the I-could-have-beens.
Life is only the I-tried-to-do. I don't mind the failure but
I can't imagine that I'd forgive myself if I didn't try.*

NIKKI GIOVANNI

19

Home cooking

Perhaps one of the pleasures of being an adult is how the smell of a home-cooked meal can whisk you back to being a child. That is, of course, if your mother was a cook. I was lucky, mine was, although my father always claimed credit for her cooking and said that when he had met her she couldn't even boil an egg, a fact she didn't dispute. I think I was lucky that his exotic childhood in Bulgaria had given him a taste for dishes not yet known in the fifties in England, and my mother perfected the art of 'normal' English dishes, roast chicken and apple crumble, legs of lamb and gooseberry fool, roast beef and Yorkshire pudding. Yum.

Of course it's also true that food can be used or even abused in a family. Childhood dietary habits are hard to break. (White bread with dark chocolate in the middle, white bread oozing with cold dripping—you get the picture.) Sometimes food can be used as bribery—not something to nourish and protect but something to force and cajole, as writer and journalist Susanna Freymark writes in her story about her mother's secret recipe.

She holds out the photo in its expensive brown frame.

'I put this by Dad's hospital bed, you know, when he started forgetting things.'

She's proud of this, and getting the frame at a reduced price was a bonus.

'I thought it would comfort him to see the family,' she adds.

It's a kind thing to do when a man is dying. I take the photo from her hands. Peter, the eldest, stands at the back, his lanky arms hanging by his side like strands of seaweed. Monika stares straight ahead, while Sylvia, the peacemaker of the family, flashes her wide smile. Mum, so much smaller than the rest, stands next to Dad, who towers above her. The illness is there in Dad's eyes but not his body—not yet. The picture was taken at a posh restaurant we went to before Dad became too sick to go to posh restaurants.

I count the people in the photo. Five. I count again to make sure. My mother is busy tidying the shelves behind me. They're already so neat but she finds something to clean.

'I'm not in the photo,' I state as plainly as I can.

She stops rearranging the clean shelf and looks at the picture.

Home cooking

'Yes, you are,' she insists.

I pass her the frame and she peers at her family huddled together in the car park outside the restaurant. She keeps staring at the picture as if somehow I will emerge.

'Look, five people,' I move closer and my voice rises, 'one, two, three, four, five.'

She stares harder.

'I'm not in it,' I say again.

She puts the photo back on the shelf and sighs. I wait for her to say something, but she moves across the study to rearrange more books and ornaments.

A large, square photo of my father's face sits in a glass frame on the desk. It's the same picture that sat on his coffin at the funeral service; now it lives here in front of the computer where he spent most of his afternoons. I'm puzzled by my mother's choice—how could she choose this photo? It's not deliberate, I know that—she's been under a lot of stress with years of Dad's illness and she's tired. But she's always been tired. After four children, she ran out of mothering and left my sisters to pick up the pieces. Monika resented it the most, her seething anger towards me thinly veiled on the few occasions the family came together.

'You were so spoilt,' she would declare after copious amounts of scotch.

I never found an answer for her accusations and felt anything but spoilt. My mother was busy, she had a house to clean and beautiful cakes to make. She was known across the neighbourhood for her baking skills.

Sweet blueberry crumble, crunchy apple tart, cheesecake, buttercream sponge, moist banana loaf; they all tasted delicious. She liked nothing better than to retrieve her best white tablecloth from the linen cupboard in preparation for a spread. Never just one cake—guests were treated to a feast of three or four.

Yet when these feasts were over, everyone looked satisfied except my mother. The guests admired her cakes and stroked the fine china cups, but when she cleaned up after they'd gone she complained with a bitterness in her voice as sharp as the lemon icing on the carrot cake.

'Who does Sophie think she is, and what about Annie? No wonder her husband isn't interested in her the way she dresses.'

I would sing inside my head to blot out the words; they were like poison spreading over the cake crumbs sitting on the empty plates. As soon as I could, I would sneak outside and throw the ball to Rex at the far end of our big backyard.

'How could you forget me?' I say out loud. I don't want to hide in the corners of the backyard. She ignores the difficult question and heads into the kitchen.

'I'll make your favourite tonight,' she announces. 'You know, the fluffy omelette you like.'

This is all I'm going to get. A special dinner and inane chatter about the neighbours and friends who have let her down, dressed inappropriately or offended her by not mowing their front lawns when she thought they should.

I take another look at the photo. Nup, not there. I turn and look

Home cooking

at the photo of my father's face. We used to pretend to fight for the biggest slice of my mother's latest baking creation or we stole pieces when she wasn't looking.

'Don't tell your mother,' he'd say in jest.

Her eyes shone when Dad and I argued over the last piece of apple strudel. She'd cut it in half and give Dad the bigger slice. He piled whipped cream on top and I copied him. We never seemed too full for more cake. Since Dad had died I'd lost my appetite for cakes. When afternoon tea was served, I took a small slice and spent most of the time moving the cake around the plate until it looked misshapen enough to not draw attention to my lack of enthusiasm.

While Mum and Monika ate and gossiped, I put on my iPod and blotted them out. They said I was rude.

'I can't hear you,' I called through strains of the Rolling Stones.

They tut-tutted and I turned up the volume. Monika nodded as Mum talked about the fat woman she'd seen at the mall and how disgusting the woman looked in shorts. I turned up the volume until their voices disappeared into the background.

I started to visit less, even though it was only two hours drive north on the Pacific Highway. When my mother rang I pretended I was busy and could only talk for a moment. Her rant about the lady at the shops who gave her the wrong change was cut short.

'I have to go Mum, the kids are calling.'

I edited myself so much around my mother that I forgot how to be her daughter. She offered me recipes. Secret cake recipes, written in spidery scrawl in notebooks tied together with brown string. Do you want to know how to make the chocolate biscuit cake? Aaah, the chocolate biscuit cake, the one with rum in it. For years we had begged her for the recipe.

That'd be great Mum, I lie. Next time I come up, that'd be great.

It was a long time between visits. Sylvia, the middle sister who lived two states away, phoned and asked when I had seen Mum.

'She says you've been busy,' said Sylvia.

I have, I replied, and asked about the kids, her job and their next skiing trip.

When Monika starts to call, it becomes tricky. Her accusations target my neglect and how I've never cared about Mum. She raves at me while I rearrange the fridge magnets. This family I belong to holds no nourishment for me; it's a pretence. I want to tell Monika that but there's little point. Her idea of family bonding is shopping. She showers my mother with expensive perfumes and designer shoes. She bought Mum a dress for $780 to wear to Dad's funeral. Mum took it out of the wardrobe and showed me when I visited, it's Chanel, she said every time. Love, according to my mother, is measured in gifts; the more costly the item, the more love it holds. My homemade presents and photos of the kids were stashed at the back of the shelf, or put in my mother's drawer of unwanted gifts. My bond to this family that owns me thins. I give up on the presents and the cakes.

Months pass and the visits to my mother's house are less frequent. It's every second month now and my excuses become

Home cooking

more feeble. Our lives are distant, and even though I hear repeats of the stories about her neighbours and the shocking things they've done, I don't hear the words any more.

'Okay,' I cut her off mid-sentence, 'I have to go, lots to do, Mum.'

The distance becomes comfortable and we slip into half-yearly visits and monthly telephone conversations. I rely on my sisters to occupy my mother's loneliness as I struggle to be a good enough daughter by proxy.

On a bright Saturday morning, Nina is at a loose end, her usual social life has become unhinged and she's looking to me for entertainment.

'Hey Mum, let's make a cake.'

She's excited and pulls old greasy tins out of a forgotten cupboard in the kitchen. The noise of metal on metal jars me and Nina senses my impatience.

'I can do it on my own you know—but then you can't eat any,' she says.

Relenting, I take the butter from the fridge so it can soften before its beating. Nina lines up jars of sultanas, chocolate bits and sugar. She has a natural instinct for the ingredients but is unsure of the correct amounts.

'Let's ask Granny, she knows a lot about cakes,' she says.

I cringe.

Nina jumps across the kitchen and grabs the phone. There is excitement in her voice as she tells Granny about our domestic adventure. She barely leaves room for her grandmother to reply and is breathless when she gets off the phone and relays the instructions. She gathers the mixing bowl and sifts the flour as she tells me some of Granny's special secrets. I cream the butter and sugar while Nina adds the choc chips. We work together like this with my mother's baking wisdom between us. I laugh at how Nina interprets the advice and how she adds extra chocolate to the mixture.

'Did Granny say to do that?' I say.

'No, but she didn't say don't do it,' Nina says.

I laugh and together we pour, we mix, and then grease the tin before putting our masterpiece into an over-hot oven. It's a lumpy looking cake but neither of us, with our flushed cheeks from the warm kitchen, seems to care. The phone rings and I pick it up. It's my mother.

'Yes, the cake is in,' I say. 'It doesn't quite look like yours,' I add.

'You never were much of a cook,' my mother says.

This is true.

'No, I wasn't,' my voice is passive. There are no words left. A slow silence hangs across the telephone like an empty washing line.

'Mum.'

'Uh-huh,' she says.

'Mum,' I repeat, 'I have to go.'

I lower the phone and feel how tender my fingers are against the hard plastic. I rest the handset in its cradle and stand right where I am and watch my only daughter peer into the oven.

Home cooking

When the cake is cooked, we use bright blue food dye and make the most magnificent icing ever and smear it over the the top of the cake. I make tea and we sit at the long wooden table in the middle of the kitchen and sip our tea and eat warm blue cake. We lick the crumbs off the plate before we reach for a second piece.

Personally I think recipes are made to be altered. Surely that is half the fun! Liz Porter remembers her mother's much more casual approach to cooking, a sort of 'what if?' approach rather than a measured amount of this and that.

> Mum never prided herself on her cooking, although I always enjoyed the simple meals she turned out after getting home from work. It is her famous orange butter cake that lives on—always a hit despite the fact that it was made according to her 'who can be bothered doing that?' kitchen rule. This meant that she never 'creamed' butter and sugar but simply melted the butter and dumped the sugar on top. Nor did she ever sift flour.
>
> Working as a biochemist in a hospital pathology department, Mum was very precise about measurements and procedures at work. But at home she tended to do the kind of cooking that relied on instinct and confidence. And because she felt she didn't have to prove herself in the domestic goddess department, we always felt free to laugh at the occasional failure. Why not? She always did. She was laughing hardest of us all on the occasion when she attempted a pavlova and opened the oven to reveal a flat squishy browned meringue (it tasted

good, we assured her, but it looked awful). Clearly, she had applied the 'who can be bothered' principle to a close reading of the recipe rules about cool oven temperatures for pavlovas. She never tried pav again, retreating to her trifles and puddings—equally fabulous but more flexible in their rules of preparation.

Sarah Taylor will never forget a dish her mother used to cook.

My mother's chicken and almonds was to die for. Cooking after a busy day teaching excitable adolescents was 'her time'. With a glass of whiskey and the burble of the radio reporting the day's shenanigans in politics, she'd lose herself in the steady coming-together of the recipe. We were forbidden to speak to her until she called 'dinner's ready'.

The secret was the almonds, browned in the oven and sprinkled with a little salt.

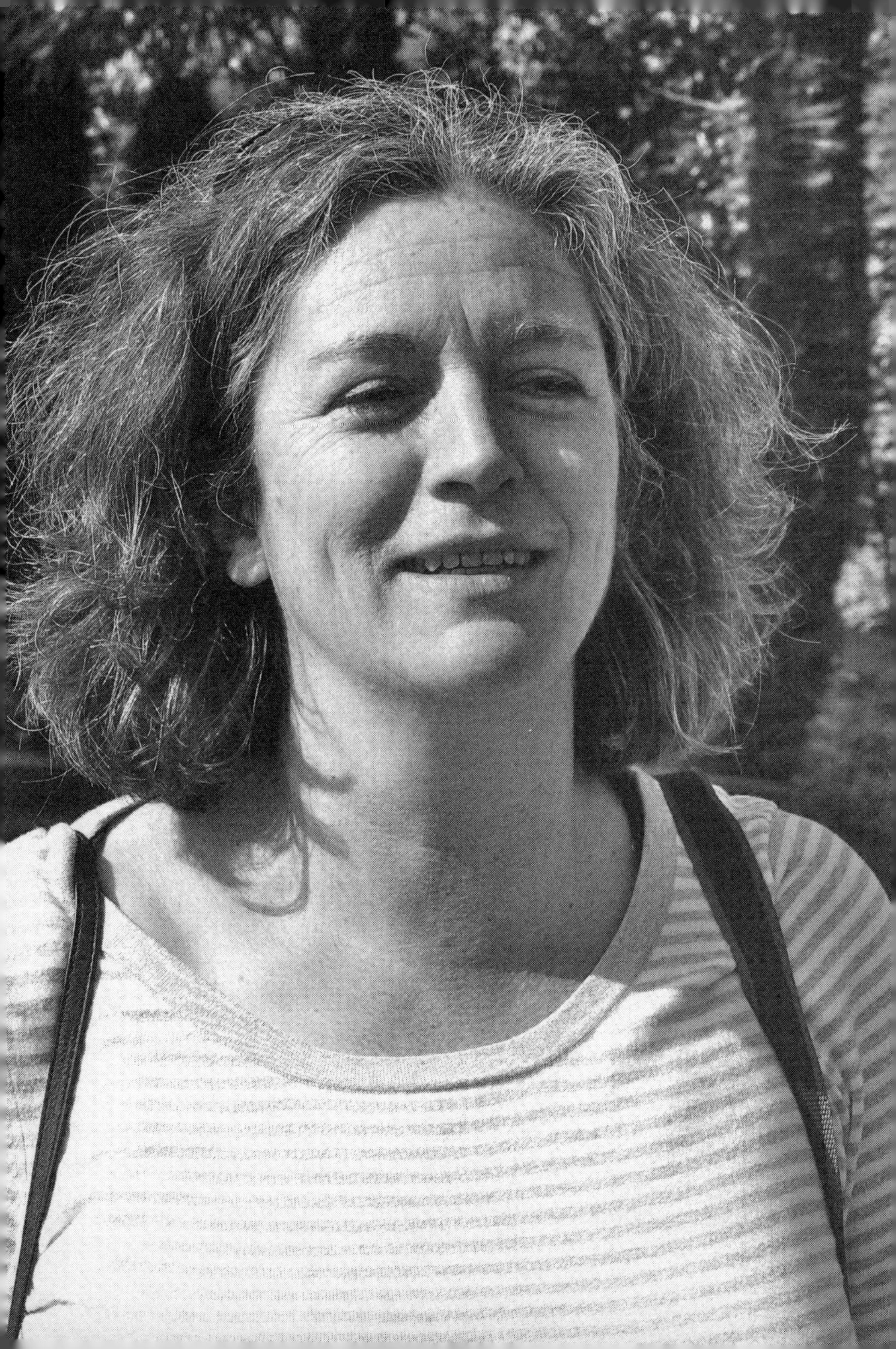

20

The creative touch

At the same time that life has never moved more quickly, with technology changing how we communicate almost daily, there has also recently been a move back towards a slower time. Slow cooking has become the rage; knitting is seeing a resurgence. The very tools that have sped up our lives are also allowing us to research the ways in which women of the past practised their domestic arts, as publisher and author Maggie Hamilton describes.

I'm so glad we're rediscovering how profoundly soulful creativity can be, especially as so much of what we have and wear has been mass-produced with little thought or love. Sometimes we lose confidence in our ability to create, believing that if we don't produce a prize-winning work of art or fiction then it has no meaning. But the thing is, our creative impulses don't have to be lofty to be meaningful. They give us the opportunity to find new and exhilarating ways to feed our spirit and the spirits of those around us. This was one of the many secrets women of past generations knew well. They understood how healing the quiet moments spent with needle and lacework and other domestic arts could be when their men were away at war, their children were finally to bed and the silence of their home embraced them.

There are many ways the women of the past reach out to us, whispering their wisdom, reminding us of what feeds us. My mother has some samplers in her possession made by young women in the family well over a hundred years ago. What makes them so precious is not just their age but the fact that they were the first tentative steps these young women were taking in their self-expression. These are not great works of art. The needlework is far from perfect, but they have a wonderful authenticity about them that we struggle to attain. We're so caught up in having to produce something perfect, we miss the whole point of being quietly creative—of losing ourselves in something that may only be meaningful to us. It's taken me a long time to remember that first and foremost my creativity is to delight myself. Should someone else take joy in it, then that is a bonus. When we can approach the womanly arts in this way, something rather magical happens. Freed from the need to perform, we find ourselves delighting others with what we do without even meaning to, and so the delight grows. I remember hearing some time back how after a shocker of a day at the United Nations Madeleine Albright came home and knitted a hat for her grandchild, and in the process her equilibrium was restored.

There's no end to the ways these timeless arts can feed us. As well as being a professor and mum, my sister Cynthia fills quiet moments with baking, knitting and needlework. More recently she has begun to make jam and marmalade, and to collect beautiful jars for her jam. She relishes the intimacy and nurture these moments bring, as they give her the opportunity to inject a little more intimacy into her own busy life and the lives of those she cares deeply about.

'For me it's important to experience the rhythms of daily life outside work, even in the midst of busy family life,' she tells me. 'These include quite simple things such as making jam, which then becomes part of my early morning ritual of tea and toast, and gives me cause for reflection. As I use the jam I made earlier in the summer, I remember how I gathered the raspberries or chose the plums, or found a particular jar, or varied the recipe in some way. The pleasure of those experiences stays with me and provides some balance with the often unpredictable demands of daily life. In the same way, when I make the jam, I think forward to all the mornings when I will enjoy the fruits of my labour, and to the colour and pleasure it brings. I suppose in a way it serves as an anchor, to keep my life more centred in processes that are important for my overall sense of wellbeing and groundedness.'

Who would have thought such a simple act could be so profound? If there was one thing I would wish for the women I love, it would be to rediscover an art that was almost lost to us.

I would venture to guess that Anon, who wrote so many poems without signing them, was often a woman.

VIRGINIA WOOLF

21

Becoming a mum at forty-five

At exactly the time that my younger sister, eight years younger than me, met Mr Right and began to think about the baby they were sure they would have, I was secure in the knowledge that I had been a mum once and that I was not going to do it again. I had a big city job, my writing career, stepchildren, a marriage, my then eight-year-old son Sam and no intention at the age of forty-four of getting pregnant again.

But Anna was waiting in the wings and had other plans, and thus it was that for the second time in my life I wondered why I had this strange stomach virus that only seemed to happen in the morning—

only this time I worked it out a bit quicker. 'My god,' I thought. 'I'm pregnant!'

I was subjected to the usual barrage of tests, and this time we decided to find out the sex of the baby—so we knew, early on, this would be our little girl. We even knew she would be called Anna, and her middle name would be my mum's—Julia.

One of the reasons I wanted to write this piece was to dispel any notion that being pregnant at forty-four and having a child at forty-five is in anyway peculiar, or that you need to coddle yourself.

I don't think I've ever been healthier—or hungrier! I ate like a horse, and rode right up until I was seven months pregnant. At that time I would take Sam to a ranch every couple of months, and Fred, who ran the horses there, had become friends with both of us. He wasn't very keen on me riding once the bump had become fairly obvious. On the last ride I could only just get my stomach in the stock saddle. Fred insisted that I agree not to canter. So I stayed at the back of the ride where he couldn't see me, so I could enjoy my last few canters!

I was healthy, happy and incredibly busy. On the day the contractions began I had to go to my publisher's office and see the ideas for the cover for my novel, *The Hidden*, which was due to be published only a few months later. My husband drove me, and I decided that perhaps it was time to call it a day work-wise since it seemed the birth would be imminent.

Twenty-four hours later, however, there was still a lot of pain but nothing going on, so we went into hospital and I decided to be induced. It turned out to be accidentally perfect timing food-wise. I had a cooked breakfast at home, much to the consternation of my friend, Christine, and my husband, both of whom I could see thought that eating quite so much food when you are about to have a baby was, well, somewhat unseemly. We arrived at the hospital, the nurse did the induction business, and we had morning tea while we waited for the contractions to begin. I had sandwiches during the birth. I remember the nurse wasn't keen on me having lunch. 'You're having a baby!' she said, almost crossly.

'So?' I replied.

'You'll be sick.'

'No I won't, and anyway I'm hungry.'

So that was that—sandwiches came and were consumed, Anna was born, and by 5 p.m. I was in a hospital room tucked up with a roast turkey dinner! One of the saddest things for me about no longer being pregnant was that I didn't have an excuse to eat all day.

Anna was a perfect baby right from the start. And unlike her brother, who had taken almost a year to sleep through the night, she slept through from the age of six weeks.

So would I recommend having a baby that late in life?

Well, yes and no.

Yes, because if you want a baby and you are able to have one, there is no reason not to.

However, and it is a big one, there are things you have to take into account.

For instance, I was plunged into menopause when Anna was only one and it was unbelievably extreme. Made more extreme by having a baby at that age? I don't know, but maybe.

Also, Anna's wonderful sleeping habits disappeared at the age of eighteen months, not to return again until she was ten. Sleep deprivation is one thing when you are in your twenties or even thirties. It's another in your mid-forties to fifties—take it from me, I know!

You are going to be an old mum by the time she starts school—fifty for goodness sake! You will be the age of some of the grandmothers taking their grandchildren to school. And of course a by-product of my age and her father's is that Anna has no grandparents, a fact that makes her very sad.

On the plus side—it keeps you young (I think!). I'm up to date with kids' books, music, fashion and trends. (At least I think I am, although I am sure the eleven-year-old trendies I am now surrounded by would disagree.)

When my younger sister was unable to conceive, after many tries at IVF, I felt guilty that for me it had been so easy. I told my sister that if I were younger, I would have had another baby—for her, and I meant it. She has been a wonderful and caring auntie, not just to my children, but to my sister's children, and an honorary aunt or godmother to many other friends' children—full of love, play, advice and dance moves than never fail to amaze them.

For me not a day goes by where I don't thank the Universe for the presence of my Golden Girl in my life. I was lucky and I know it.

What a lovely offering this beautiful, personal poem from mother and volunteer Lynn Gecso is; all about being the pride of being the mother of a daughter and watching her 'girlchild' grow up. Lynn's two beautiful and creative daughters are both featured in this book as well.

RITE OF PASSAGE

Girlchild I have watched you grow
into the woman I love and know
I bestow upon you Blessings and love
May Angels watch you from above

In your heart may you always hold dear
friends and loved ones both far and near
May you always stand in your Light
May you see the world as a glorious sight

Coming to the end of this chapter reinforces for me how blessed we are when we fall pregnant and how important it is to be aware, right from the start of our pregnancies, about the amazing journey we are undertaking. Those months when we are expecting our baby bundles are some of the most exciting of our lives—before the exhaustion and the reality set in! Kerry wrote this lovely letter to her then unborn daughter, and I think it is a beautiful summation of the feelings we have when we are growing a new life within.

A Letter to Baby

11th September 2003

My darling Baby,

I've been awake since four am. It is now five thirty and I'm sitting at the table with a cup of tea, the kitchen light on and our boys (your brother Marty and Dad) are both still sleeping. I feel incredibly protective of you all. Expecting you in the next few days or weeks seems to be driving everything that I do and the way that I do it.

I am totally focused on you and Marty and Dad. I can feel us all pulling in together and it's lovely. I've never been so happy or felt so blessed in my life and yet at the same time I could cry at anything. So I am now ...

I am nervous about the approaching birth and yet so incredibly excited about getting it under way so that we can all meet you, hold you, kiss you and love you to bits.

So I am sitting here making lists. Being driven to consider and organise so that I am ready for you, although none of it matters except your safe arrival into our world.

I am trying to imagine the person that you are but it's all fictional except that I know I will adore and admire you. Look at you with love. That's inevitable.

It's getting lighter outside, birds are whistling and calling. A day of preparations ahead. A sunny day is forecast. We're a step closer together.

Love Mum

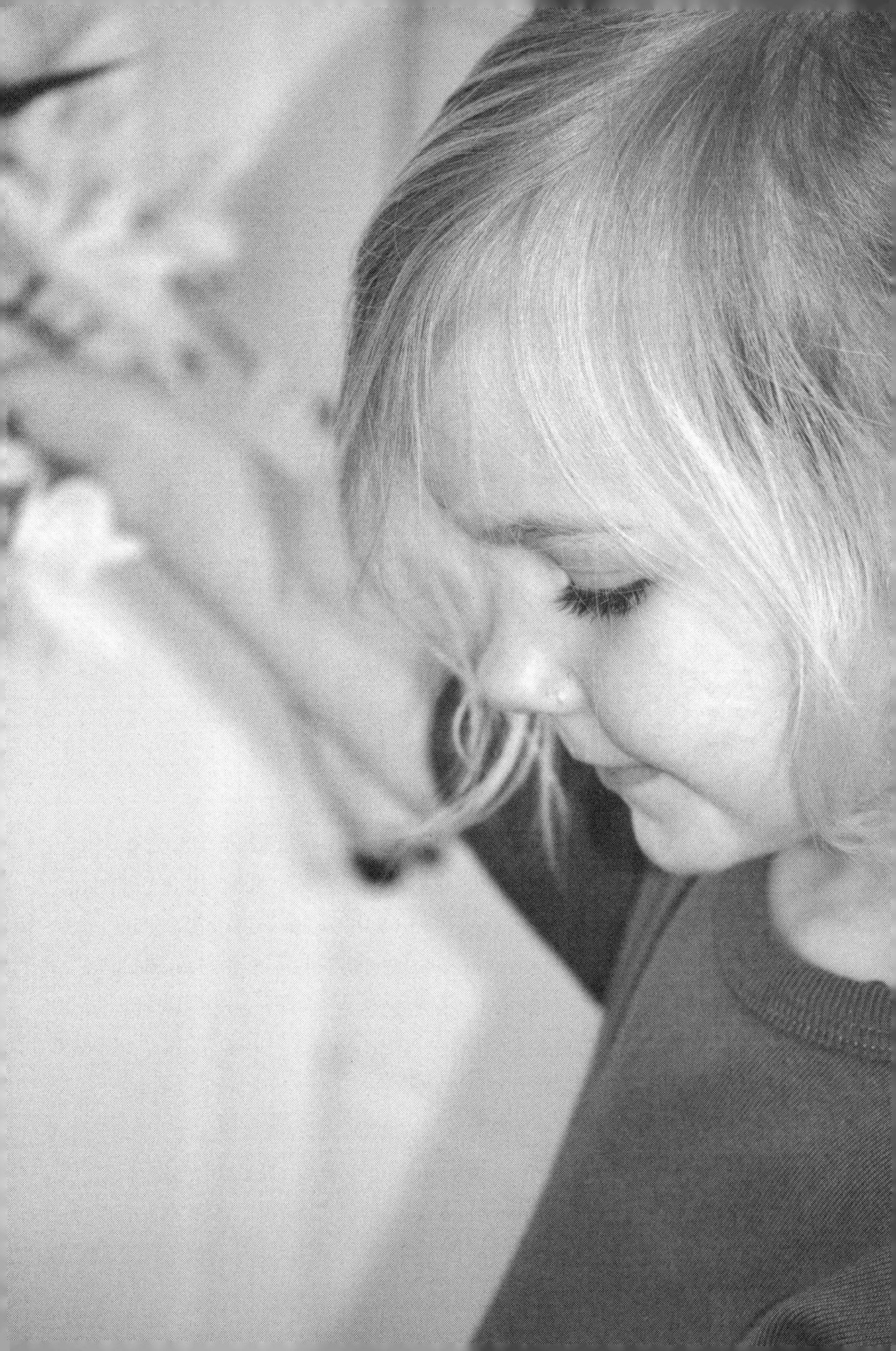

22

Magic mothering

Kim Falconer is a speculative fiction author whose books star amazingly strong female characters. Kim allows female relationships in all their forms to blossom in her books, and one of my favourites is the relationship between Nell and her pregnant daughter Rosette. This small extract from *Strange Attractors* is taken when they are waiting in a magic corridor—a portal that will take them (hopefully!) to their desired destination.

Nellion Paree felt a waft of air in the corridors. It lifted the hair that framed her face the moment she'd let go of Rosette's hand. A spell?

Magic mothering

She glanced over at her daughter and the temple cat. They were making their way to the back of the portal and didn't seem to notice. 'Wait,' she called to them both. 'Did you feel that?'

Rosette rubbed her belly and yawned. 'I felt the baby kick. Are you saying you did too?'

'There was something else,' Nell said. 'Be mindful.'

Rosette's hand went to her sword hilt but her belt was empty. The temple cat's head came up.

'Where did you leave it?' Nell asked.

Rosette groaned. 'No idea. An' Lawrence will disown me.'

'Perhaps not under the circumstances. Never mind. You have a blade at the cottage.'

'I wish you'd warned me that late pregnancy was akin to amnesia.'

'I did.'

Rosette winced. 'Then I've forgotten that as well.'

Nell laughed to hide her shivers. In spite of her daughter's lack of concern, she felt certain someone had just been in the corridors. *Darlings?* she asked the Three Sisters. *Anything?*

They perched high on a ledge, flapping their wings before they folded them neatly into their backs. *All's well. Only our family be here.*

'I don't sense anyone,' Rosette confirmed. 'Nor does Drayco.'

'Nor do they.' Nell tilted her head towards the ravens before passing her hand over the plasma Entity.

'Just us.' The tiny zaps of electricity tickled her palm.

'Something's not right though.'

'Do you think we're being tracked?' Rosette asked.

'Is Makee about?'

'I think she's running the corridors like a scent hound.'

'I guess my timing's not the best.' Rosette slid to the ground, her hands holding her belly. 'What can I do from Dumarka?'

'Plenty,' Nell said, sitting beside her. 'First and foremost, you can have this baby. That's a complete enough task on its own.'

Rosette closed her eyes. 'I won't argue.'

Nell listened for her daughter's thoughts but her mind shield was tight. That in itself was not suspicious. She'd taught her to keep it that way. Whatever she and her familiar were saying to each other was private. She respected that. There was something, though—perhaps in the complacency and speed of Rosette's agreement to come to the cottage—that suggested trouble. Nell shook her head, remembering how she felt, late pregnant with her own daughter and uncertain of the spell. She had taken comfort in the safety and seclusion of Dumarka. It made sense that Rosette would too.

Stop worrying about it, Nell! she told herself. *If there is anyone lurking in the corridors, all the more reason to take the next step.*

'Are you nervous about seeing the Watcher?' Rosette asked. She hadn't opened her eyes but took her mother's hand and held it in her lap.

'I always feel some anticipation.'

'That's a new word for it.'

They both laughed.

Magic mothering

'Come.' Nell stood, helping her daughter to her feet. 'We're here.'

Drayco was up and sniffing at the edge of the portal.

Nell and Rosette followed, listening, feeling, sensing.

'Right time, right place? No battles, no temple?' Rosette asked.

'Feels so.' Nell led the way into the woods, her arms stretched wide in greeting. 'Winter's past.'

The air smelled of early spring, of sap running in the pines, daffodils and jonquils poking their yellow faces up from the loam, and white berry blossoms floating like stars on the breeze. The Three Sisters whizzed past, out of the corridor and skyward. They were high above them in seconds, circling over the treetops.

Home, Nellion! All clear and home beautiful. Come!

'Are we good?' Rosette asked, her face to the sun.

'Indeed!' Nell put her arm around her daughter.

'Home, shall we?'[1]

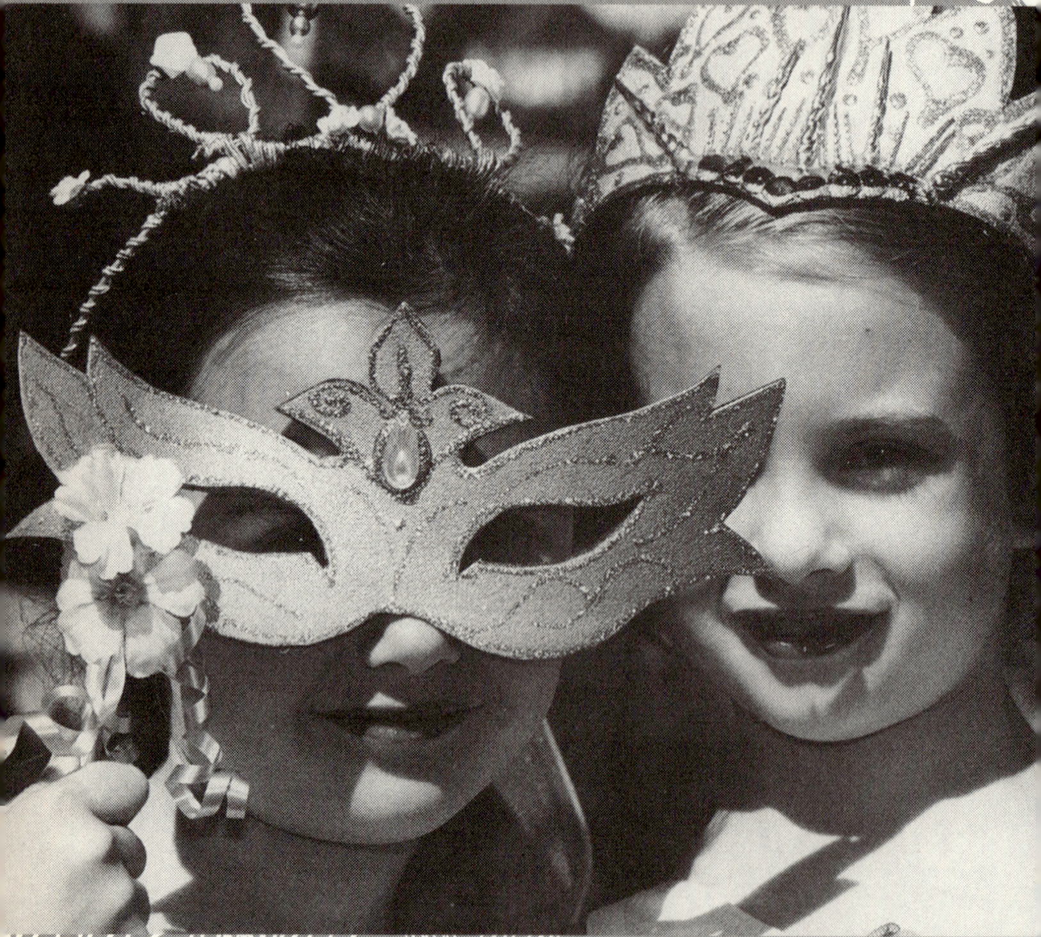

23

The call of mysticism

Transformational life coach Noelene Kelly was drawn to the mystical life from an early age, knowing even as an adolescent that she wanted to go into a convent. At twenty-one she joined a contemplative and active order, the Ursuline Order, founded in 1535 by Saint Angela Merici, and would have joined earlier if her mother hadn't objected. Noelene stayed with the church for thirty years, leaving when she was fifty-one.

'The leaving process began a few years before that,' she says. 'It evolved gradually. Of course I was always involved in the world, as a teacher and a principal. I did my Master's in Arts, and I gradually evolved from a traditional religious base to become more and more immersed in the mystical tradition.'

These days Noelene does healing and inner transformational work. In her story she writes about the women who have stood beside her on her journey and how they have been there for her even when she has lost her way.

Along my journey, I have at times strayed and lost my way. As I look back I realise that when I did stray, a beautiful Soul Sister was always there to shine her light so I could turn up my own light.

There is Veronica, a companion in the early days of my life as a nun, who in guiding me on a retreat gently asked, 'What image would you choose to describe your relationship with Spirit?' Straightaway the image of a strongly flowing river cut off from its source came to mind. It's only now that I more fully know that my soul's deepest grief lies in the experience of feeling disconnected from the love of this source!

Inspired is the word I choose for Veronica; as a teacher she touched beautiful soul notes in me, particularly in poetry classes. She is a visionary who later went on to establish a centre for spirituality and ecology.

There is Genny, another convent companion, who laughed and cried with me through the soul's dark night. We don't see each other so often these days and our paths have taken different turns. However, after so long on the journey together there remains only gratitude that a beautiful Earth Angel stood with and beside me.

Beauty is the word for Genny. She has tapped the beauty in her students; she has brought art and colour to the rituals she

The call of mysticism

has crafted. She enables others to see their own beauty while she creatively supports them in sensitive ways; she has lightened the load of countless fellow travellers; she has brought beauty's touch to life's significant moments and to the experience of death.

There is Jenny, whose surname is Trust. *Trust* is the word for Jenny and it seems no accident this quality is inscribed in her very name. Some would say that trust is the toughest challenge for us humans; that it is even harder than love to master. Seeing this quality so alive in Jenny is something I'll never forget. Even when she had no ready cash she invited us to her home, trusting that all would be provided for—and it was. She continues to heal through her inspired words.

There is a random acquaintance, Rose, who was giving me a massage one day and who 'saw', beyond the veil, the founder of the religious order to which I still belonged. Rose had no background in the Catholic Church and knew nothing consciously about the sixteenth century woman she was describing to me. This was a profound connection with the universal energy for me, and set me on my path of knowing that to reconnect with my soul on all levels I would need to leave the convent.

Integrity is the word I choose for Rose. She says it as it is; so straight from the heart. After that particular massage I began the slow, painful task of leaving the community that had loved, nurtured, stretched and challenged me for thirty years.

The task of finding my work and place out in the world happened seamlessly enough, as my experiences of running a school and other leadership roles equipped me well. It was the emotional dislocation that I found most harrowing, yet ultimately full of growth. As a nun I had had enormous opportunities for spiritual and intellectual growth. Outside the community, with the support of many Soul Sisters, I have found emotional clarity and tracked my patterns of fear and grief to their source. Little by little I am reclaiming my emotional being and allowing my heart to open fully. And finally I am learning how to honour and nurture my body. So the alignment I sought of body, mind, heart and soul is gradually coming to fruition. It seems I was destined to move out of institutional life. What a journey it has been, and I can only thank my Soul Sisters and my Spirit Sisters for being there to support this process!

I met Helen when my light was flagging on my path outside the convent, when I faced a familiar institutional challenge in my work. It was as though she could see beyond that moment into my soul's destiny. She connected me with many beautiful, powerful women in whose presence I found anew my soul's purpose. I never left the essence of the convent's mystical tradition and Helen connects me with work opportunities that enable me to carry that essence, renamed and rebranded, into the marketplace.

Goddess is my word for Helen. Her name means light. She carries an ancient wisdom and knowing and it seems she has come to raise the bar for women. She has come to honour the feminine essence and spirit, to raise it to its rightful pedestal in a world in need of its presence. Helen holds senior roles in corporations where she cleverly and sensitively brings both feminine and spiritual intelligence into workplaces. She is a powerful leader.

The call of mysticism

Recently, I met Khandro-la, a Tibetan mystic who led a Return to the Heart pilgrimage that I joined, to the centre of Australia, Uluru and surrounding country. She felt the call of the copper-coloured mountain when she was only eight years old in Tibet, which has its own special copper-coloured mountain where holy people have meditated for centuries. To be in her presence was so special. Her empathy for the land and its peoples seemed bottomless, and I was touched by the laments she spontaneously broke into for the devastation and desolation suffered by the land and its people.

Ecstatic is a word for Khandro-la. She is a Buddhist adept who brings the eastern mystical tradition to new life in both the West and the East. She is enlightened, creative, sassy and pure joy.

Through the love of these six and many others I am now firmly on my sacred path. I trust that in aligning my body, mind, heart and soul I am assisting the planet align and rebalance. I am open and ready for the next stages of this transitional moment, and joy is bubbling in my heart at its unfolding.

Just like a sunbeam can't separate itself from the sun, and a wave can't separate itself from the ocean, we can't separate ourselves from one another. We are all part of a vast sea of love, one indivisible divine mind.

MARIANNE WILLIAMSON

24

Soulfulness

We all need a little 'soul' in our lives, don't we? And yet, perhaps it is already there far more than we realise. If we stop to think about it for a minute, soulfulness, kindness and ritual are, if we are lucky, around us from our earliest memories. The smell of freshly baked cakes, the gifts brought by colleagues into workplaces, the little gestures and thoughts that in our busy lives pass more unnoticed than they should. Perhaps, if we watched, listened and paid attention, we might notice gestures around us all the time from those who care for us, or even notice them in the acts of one person to another.

In the following story Maggie Hamilton recalls how much she appreciates the fine details of life.

I'm always moved by the overwhelming kindness of the beautiful women in my life who constantly seek new ways to make life better, gentler and more enjoyable for those around them. It's a miracle to me how they always seem to know what is needed, how selflessly they infuse the day with a little more warmth and beauty. Their loving attention to detail nourishes me in ways other things cannot. It helps chase away my demons and gives me the courage to continue to get out of bed in the morning. It also helps me be more compassionate, more human. And it's also a wonderful counterbalance to a world that is so often seduced by splashy gestures and celebrity.

Often these small act of kindness appear in our lives at the perfect time.

At one stage I was blessed to work with Trish, who would pick a flower every morning on her way to work and leave it on my keyboard. I cannot tell you how often this simple act of love helped me through a difficult day at work.

Then there's Janet, who kept in her work drawer chocolate hearts that she'd place on someone's chair if they had done something special, or were in need of a little bit of love.

For years after work my diminutive mum would lug home huge boxes of peaches, plums and nectarines that she'd picked up at the markets. Then once all her other work was done she would bottle the fruit late into the night. Or she'd spend hours on the sewing machine making new clothes for my sister and me. And now whenever I go home to see my mother, even though she is well into her eighties she insists on making my favourite meals. In my bedroom there's always a delicious stack of books and magazines she knows I will love.

Then there was our lovely nextdoor neighbour Kate, a brilliant cook who would often ring at eight or nine at night, her voice full of excitement. After a busy day at work, she'd come home and been inspired to make a lemon cake, and wanted to give us a generous slice for supper.

I thank God for these special women and more in my life. I really cannot imagine a world without them. Who then would help inspire us, and work actively to dissolve our moments of sadness and quiet despair?

Maggie's description of the special women in her life reminds me of comforting words—words like women, home, hearth. These things speak of goodness, even if we know that often the visual image is only one aspect of a much more complex story. So too rooms in a house are evocative. They can vary from severely austere to floral and chintzy—each room speaking of a part of ourselves. When I think of my mother and rooms, I think of her in the first bedroom I knew in our London flat, where she had the most wonderful dressing table covered with silky material. It held all her jewellery, which was so fascinating to a small child, and her make-up, her hairbrush and combs, and her perfumes. Perhaps most of all I loved her face powder—dabbed on last of all, and leaving tiny little clouds of golden dust in the air.

Bernadette Curtin, an accomplished artist, writes about the importance of particular rooms to her, and ties them in with some of the paintings she most loves.

The kitchen

Dressed in her faded floral apron, which scrapes the floor, I help my grandmother mix dough for her celebrated scones. The mixture is laden into the scone moulds and then the privilege is offered and taken—to lick the spoon and scrape the large ceramic bowl clean. I enjoy the sweet creamy-floury sensation in my mouth. My grandmother wipes down the linoleum-covered table and then we walk out into her garden to pick fresh peas. She opens a pod and expounds their green glory. Her garden is an oasis in the small dusty town. For my grandmother, both cooking and gardening were rituals to be savoured.

The completeness of domestic tasks and their beauty in their own right is perfectly portrayed in Vermeer's paintings. The purposeful movement of his women and the order of domestic rituals are held in suspension in the milk being poured from a jug held by a woman in his painting *Maidservant Pouring Milk*, 1660–61. The maid is caught in a moment of stillness, concentrating on her action, her face and sturdy forearms lit by a cloudy window. On a table in the foreground rustic hunks of bread have been torn from a loaf. But it is the trickle of milk between the jug and the bowl, frozen in time for eternity, that commands attention.

The bathroom

On a South Australian summer morning my mother comes into the bathroom to put on her lipstick. She is wearing a pink dress and coats her lips to match. I tell her she looks pretty. She is the mother of six children and looks so fresh and feminine for a farmer's wife.

For how many hours did Pierre Bonnard's wife have to soak in the bath so that he could paint *Nude in the Bath* in 1936? He told a journalist that he spent six months on the painting and needed several more to complete it! The true Bonnard bathroom was rather grimy white, but in the painting the tiles are rendered as a fluid, shimmering pattern of light and colour, reflecting in the bathwater and illuminating the female form with glowing pinks and golds. The artist is giving the viewer an intimate and loving glimpse of his wife.

The bedroom

My sister and I are staying with my Auntie Marnie while my mother is in hospital giving birth to twins. We are sitting up in our beds in her spare room, our small bodies wriggling with pleasure inside her night-dresses. My sister is asking lots of questions. My auntie opens a wardrobe in front of our beds and brings out a magenta silk ball dress. She is a pianist and plays in a band at local and district dances.

We want more, and there are more dresses, with full skirts, petticoats, beaded bodices, fine shoulder straps, swathes of chiffon to be swept over bare shoulders, diamante clasps and tiny buttons in the same fabric. The magic wardrobe spills them out one by one. We are in raptures and can't wait to grow up.

In Manet's painting *Olympia*, 1863, the model has disrobed with the help of her servant, and reclines, gloriously nude, on her daybed. She looks directly at the viewer, totally at one with herself and languidly confident of her beautiful alabaster body. Was Manet in awe of his muse, staring him down, daring him to lose concentration in the act of painting?

The dining room
The floor is green linoleum and the air conditioner is humming. The room is bare apart from a large wooden table and a framed photo of a dolphin on the wall. The venetian blinds are half drawn to filter the intense sunlight.

A list of things that have collected on the dining table: snorkelling gear, a camera, some reading glasses, sunglasses, books half read, magazines on health and fitness, keys, a mobile, baseball caps, a teacher's lesson notes, some brochures on whale watching and snorkelling trips to the reef.

My sisters and I are holidaying at Coral Bay, near Exmouth in Western Australia. My husband was allowed to come with us, because, as my sister said, he is so 'amenable'.

We sit around this table after mealtimes, reminiscing about our childhoods on the farm and dramatising the experiences of our teenage years spent in boarding schools. We discuss our children, almost all of whom are all now adults, and our aged parents, who are living at home and need extra care.

And in between times, snorkelling in the clear turquoise water, the rhythmic gentle breathing, the lightness of the body suspended in salty water and the beauty of fish and coral formations under water melt away the worries and cares.

Even though the paint has peeled from the wall and the colours have faded and been repainted, the image of Magdaleena in Leonardo's painting *The Last Supper* can still be seen to be one of feminine grace. Leonardo has shown her to be an equal partner to Jesus, seated on his right hand. His right wrist and her left wrist (their lifelines) are touching. Note also their identical clothing and how close their feet are under the table. Leonardo was experimenting with egg tempera and oil paint on a dry plaster wall in the dining room at the Dominican convent of Santa Maria delle Grazie. Unfortunately, much detail in the work has been lost. In the image that survives, Magdaleena is leaning away from Jesus towards Peter. Next to her sits Judas, his face fuelled with the fury of his jealousy. Leonardo has painted a hand emerging from behind his back, holding a knife. The hand appears to be disembodied, as if it is an entity driving him to set Jesus up against the power-driven authorities. Is it possible that the wide V between Magdaleena and Jesus stands for Veritas? The truth that continues to be withheld from us? According to the scholars, Leonardo has composed the scene right after Jesus has announced his prophecy that 'one of you will betray me'. Nobody is eating at this table. All of the apostles seem to be in disarray, engaged in intrigue and debate. Only the two central figures, the man and the woman, the perfect balance of male and female, remain harmonious and still.

The living room

The black glossy Schimmel is open with a sheet of music placed ready to be played. But my friend Lyndy does not want to play. She has given up her music until she can find something truly soulful to play. Enough of emotion! Beethoven is so sad.

Her living room is the centre of her cottage, which is tucked beneath a mountain slope of rainforest in a valley in northern New South Wales. Near the entry to this room there are two rattan chairs with colourful cushions large enough to curl up in while she makes tea and checks on a nut cake baking in the oven. There is a pot-belly stove warming the room. Even in wintry weather the room glows, radiates light.

The young woman reclines against a carved chair in Matisse's painting *Odalisque with a Turkish Chair*, 1928. Her right hip is thrust upwards by the cushion underneath her hips, her right arm propping her head up so that she can look straight ahead. She wears Turkish harem pants, a wide cummerbund and a blue silk jacket. Her long hair is braided and around one ankle is a beaded bracelet. Behind her is a vibrant patterned screen that reinforces the exotic mood of both model and setting. Her posture suggests that she has just sat back from the chessboard on the carpet beside her. To balance the composition the artist has added a large blue-and-white ceramic vessel above the chessboard. The form echoes the female body. The whole effect is one of opulence, a decorative female object in a decorative room.

Matisse understood how a woman going about her daily rituals brings each room of a house to life. With her movements she leaves an imprint that echoes long after she has left the space.

Everyone has talent. What is rare is the courage to follow the talent to the dark place where it leads.

ERICA JONG

25

The many faces of motherhood

Because I was only thirteen when the relationship between my father and the woman who would become my stepmother became known and my younger half-sister was born, I was not then at an age or stage to appreciate my stepmother's gifts to all of us, and the strength of her love for my father and, by extension, for us. My love for Sally was a gradually unfolding love, something that blossomed with time as I could see how much happier and settled my father was with her, and as I learnt to appreciate her humour and patience with us all.

When my mother died more than twenty years later and I decided to write and read her eulogy, it was Sally I practised with, sitting on the wall at the bottom of our garden while she listened.

I asked her if she would take over if I was overcome and couldn't manage it, and she smiled. 'Of course,' she said, 'but you'll be fine—just look at me if you're feeling unsure—it will be alright, I promise.' And it was, partly because I knew she was there as a safety net, and I think for all of us, particularly for my father, that is what she was, our safety net.

My father and Sally were unable to come to my wedding many years ago, only a few years after my mother's death—she had just been diagnosed with cancer. At the time it seemed as if she would beat it, and she—so everyone has told me—handled all the treatments with grace and strength, but finally the cancer in her spine returned and she died only a short time after my son was born.

When my father told her, just before her death, that Sam had been born, she smiled and said 'one life entering the world as another life leaves …'

Of course, another way of mothering or being mothered is by adopting or having been adopted. For many people this is a positive experience—all the more so in recent years since open adoptions have become more normal. I think the need for people to know the tribe to whom they belong is essential, as scores of stolen-generation children in Australia would attest and as would all those who have longed for a simple answer to the question of where they came from.

Trish Landsberger, who works with families, grew up with a mother who was adopted. Her mum was the youngest of seven children and the only one adopted out. By the time her mother found out who her family was, only one of her sisters was still alive.

The many faces of motherhood

My mother was born in 1918 in rural Manchester, England, the youngest of seven children. Where she came in the family is, however, almost irrelevant, as Mum did not get to know any of her siblings or family until early 2000. By this time she had one remaining sister alive, and a host of nephews and nieces she had never known or seen grow up. In early 2000, Mum finally met her remaining sister, thanks to the internet and her persistent searching of adoption records.

Rural Manchester 1918, a working family, a father who had done a bunk—life was not easy. Two days after my mother's birth, her mother died. The six elder children carrying the newborn seventh set off along the country lanes to deliver themselves into the lives and safekeeping of their maternal grandparents. Several months later they were on the move again to paternal grandparents who could take them all, except for the baby—she was too young and too much for them.

At this point, my mother's journey took a very different course to her siblings. Mum was deposited with the local vicar and registered with the children's home, as there was nowhere else for her to go. And that was that—she was up for adoption.

By chance the vicar, through his clergy contacts, had heard of a family in Benson, in rural Oxfordshire, who wanted to adopt a baby. The family was of good bearing. He was the local builder, churchwarden and head of the tower—a church bellringer. She was a woman of good character who apparently could not have a child. Word was sent to the Oxfordshire family to prepare for the child, and word was sent to the Manchester family to clean and dress the baby well so that she looked her best for the viewing. No police or health checks: a viewing and a fancying was all that it took to be given a child. So she was cleaned and transported and viewed and accepted; she never returned to her Manchester family, and they never knew where she had gone.

Mum's life in Oxfordshire was safe but loveless. Her mother, it became apparent, had chosen not to have children naturally, as it was a messy business. However, she knew that local tongues would wag if she continued in a childless marriage. Adoption would fix the tongues and fill the gap, mess free!

Mum's early years in the village were lonely as most of the locals were not good enough in my grandmother's eyes to mix with her daughter. Mum's days were spent playing alone or in her father's carpentry workshop, and she was packed off to a Catholic boarding school as soon as was possible. The cold acceptance of the Sisters and their crisp, harsh ways coloured the preceding loveless years. Here, though, she was free to choose her friends and dream her dreams, among her chores and studies.

When her schooling was done, Mum went straight into the workforce as a nanny to a child of a family acquaintance—Mum's parents, she would tell me, did not have friends, just acquaintances. It was perhaps an odd position for a young woman who had grown up without love, affection or attachment, but she had been taught well by her mother and the 'caring' Sisters to administer whatever was necessary to keep a child clean and healthy while keeping

The many faces of motherhood

detached and avoiding any annoying emotions that could get in the way of a job well done.

From her life as a nanny, Mum moved onto training as a nurse. Her mother was not happy about this and showed a rare and unusual interest and concern. She insisted on going along to the interview and having a chat to the matron first. Had age got the better of her, and was she at last showing some concern for her adopted daughter? The truth of this clandestine visit became apparent several months later. Mum was feeling troubled, confused and lost about her life when she was summoned to the matron for a talk. The starchy medical matriarch, in the course of their conversation, pushed a paper toward Mum, and Mum sighted her birth certificate for the first time in her life—the truth was out.

At last things started to fall into place. The odd snippets of conversation she had heard over the years; the loveless relationship with her parents; her strong sense of not belonging. She was not a soul who did not deserve love, just a soul in the wrong place and with the wrong people. How things changed! Life took a turn. She made friends, partied hard, and after some years married my dear dad. Three children later and in-laws she loved, and Mum at last had her own family.

My mum inspires me. A woman who had such a loveless beginning was able to give so much love to us, her children. We never had a great deal materially, but we knew and felt love, safety and acceptance. She had the ability to make better any scraped knee or bumped head with warm enveloping cuddles and a well-stocked first-aid kit. The kitchen was always full of steam and good smells and a welcoming, encouraging mentor. We knew we were hers and she was ours; we had no worries apart from getting on with being kids and growing up in the fifties.

My job now finds me working daily with women who come from unsafe and chaotic childhoods, often mothered by women who come from the same damaged backgrounds. I support them on their journey to be reunited—reunified—with children who have been removed and are in foster care.

As I work with these women I am reminded of and inspired by my mum. She too was a woman who came from a childhood stripped of maternal nurturing, and she managed to pass onto her children an innate sense of safety, security, love, attachment, belonging, purpose and hope. What I have learned from Mum is that there is hope, it is worth trying, we can turn things around. Once Mum was loved and accepted and felt part of a family, she was able to shine. I can offer the women I work with respect and acceptance, and hope that they are able to find their shining mother souls inside and be inspired to turn their lives around for their children.

Thank you Mum for your ability, against great odds, to give to us love, safety and a strong sense of belonging. Precious gifts given by someone who was denied the same gifts in her early years.

I had a pact with my sister Charlie that if anything happened to me and my kids' dad that she would take them for me. Even though that time, at least for one of them, is now over, it's a pact that still stands. Perhaps the closest thing a child could have to its mother is the mother's sister. That was Mel Fleming's experience, which she recounts in this story about her Aunt Paulie.

When I received the request to write about great women for this book, my first thought was that I would write about the many women who aren't famous and go unnoticed—those mothers, grandmothers, nurses or carers who never receive media attention, awards or accolades. As I was thinking about this I realised that there was one special woman in my life who really fitted this picture: Aunty Pauline, or Paulie as she is affectionately known by our family.

Paulie began her working life as a missionary in Papua New Guinea, then worked as a house mistress in a boarding school and later as a child-care worker in a children's home.

At the time my mother was diagnosed with cancer, we were a family of five children, aged between five and fifteen. Paulie left her work and came to live with us, caring for her sister, our dying mother, and for all of us children; cooking, washing, cleaning—she did it all. Our mother passed away a few months later and Paulie stayed for a couple of years, fulfilling the mother role. Paulie effectively put her own life on hold to care for us. It was an act of pure selflessness, an act that was so significant, yet as children it was hard to grasp that fact.

Now that we have all grown, Paulie continues to play a large part in our lives as a support person and stand-in grandmother for eight grand-nieces and -nephews. She is always offering a place to stay, a meal or a loving hug whenever any of the family are passing through. She is a truly giving, loving, caring person. She deserves the very best. She has given us all so much and we are eternally grateful.

Paulie, we love you, appreciate you and thank you very, very much.

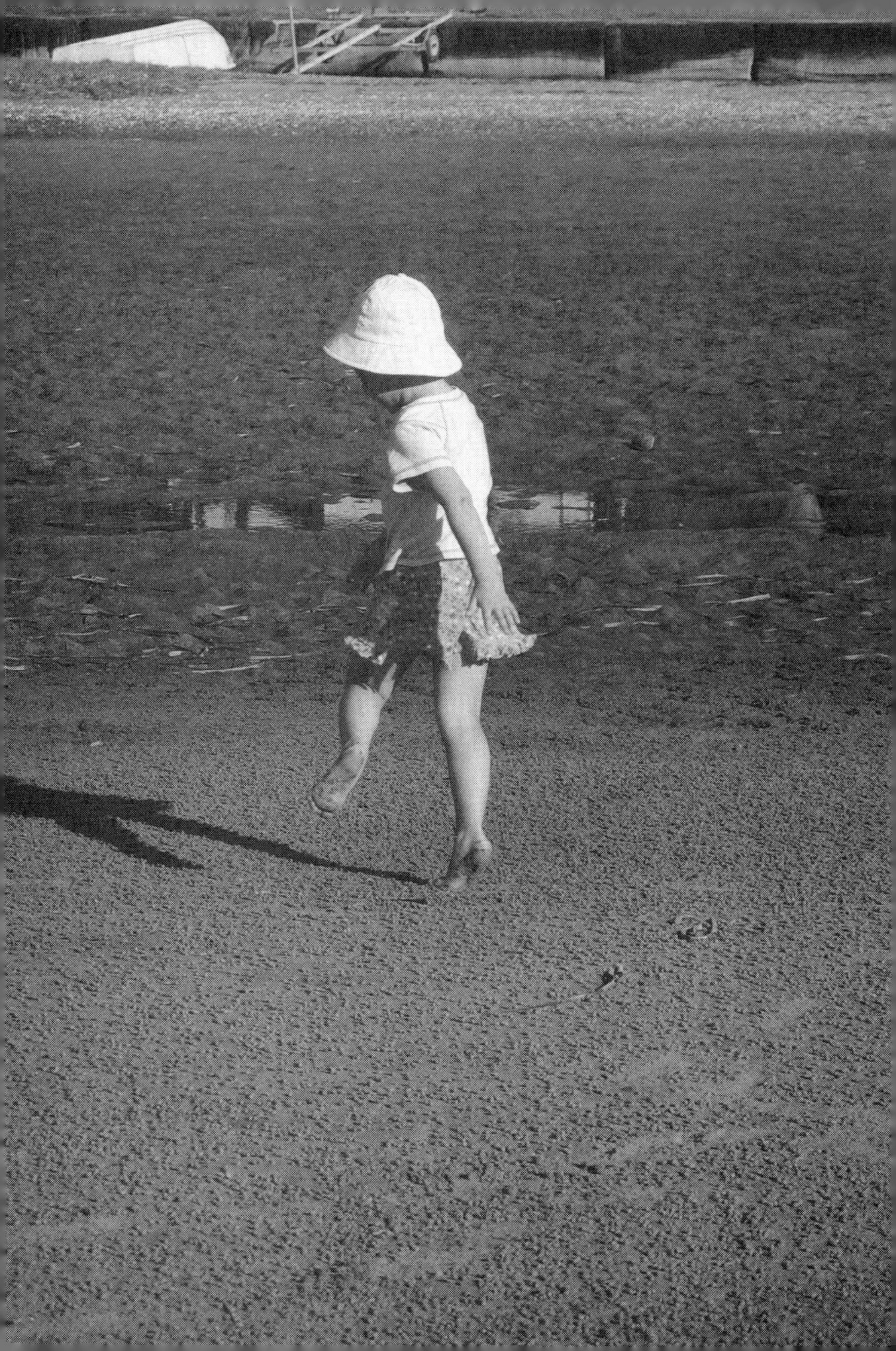

26

Sisterly love

I am very lucky to be the eldest of five daughters—four born to my mother and father, and one to my wonderful stepmother. We are scattered to the four winds, alas—two of us in Australia, one in the south of France, one in the far south of England and the youngest, Sarah, in Wiltshire. To Sarah fell the task of being the main carer for our father, who was in a nursing home until his recent death, so visiting him meant a constant juggle of jobs and family life for her, which was not easy.

Despite the fact that we all live so far away from each other, there is an amazingly strong bond between us—a bond that has grown as we've become older.

Sisterly love

Being in Australia, I've been in an odd position for the past few years, because it was once very much my place as the eldest to feel responsibility for my younger siblings. I've offered, I hope, ongoing support whenever I could.

Finding myself in a situation where I needed help over the past few years was not easy, and turning to my younger sister Charlie for support was incredibly hard for me. The love and support, financial and otherwise, that she and her lovely husband have given me has allowed me to carry on through some dark times and also given me the knowledge of what it is like to be supported emotionally as well.

We've shared a lot, my sisters and I, and I thank the universe for every one of them, every day. When sisters help sisters it is something very special, as journalist Louisa Deasey also knows.

About ten years ago I moved cities to try to get a job in a women's magazine. I interned for free during the day and waitressed every night. I was exhausted but excited. I got myself a flat but had no furniture—I slept on the floor in my sleeping bag and was waiting until I could save enough from waitressing to get all my furniture shipped up from Melbourne. Nights were pretty boring! Until then I'd been at university sharing with my sister, and one of our habits was to watch *Charmed* together on Tuesday evenings. No more *Charmed* for me on my nights off! All I could do was stare at a blank wall in my empty little flat.

One day I came home from work to find a TV in my living room. 'You can watch *Charmed* now Lou,' a note said. My sister had shipped it up, organised my cousins (who had a spare key) to let the delivery man in, and suddenly I had something nice to do in my flat when I wasn't working!

Another time when my sister and I were living in the same city, I went jogging and had a sense that I should stop at her house—even though at the time I was training for a half-marathon and it meant a deviation from the route I was meant to take. My intuition was right. When I got there my sister was in a terrible state; she was seriously unwell and pregnant at the time and hadn't been able to get anyone, including her husband, on the phone. She also had her two-year-old son at home with her, so I minded him while she went to hospital. Her illness turned out to be quite serious but treatable, and I was so relieved I had followed my instinct.

Other times we've had similar dreams, or she dreams something, calls me to tell me and we find I've dreamt the same thing. Sadly, our mum died recently, and then a number of other family members also passed away in close succession. Instead of calling me to tell me about our cousin, my sister, knowing how upset I would be, drove over in the middle of the night so I wouldn't hear the news alone. We got Thai takeaway and tried to watch a DVD (not very successfully).

A few months after our mum died I had been thinking of a poem about the sea, which oddly comforted me. I didn't know what the poem was called or where I'd seen it, I just kept thinking of a line from it and couldn't find it because I didn't know who had written it.

That week, my sister invited me over for dinner and gave me a poem she'd thought to write out for me. It was that very same poem. She also sent me flowers to comfort me over losing my cousin—even though it was her cousin too! She is my blood sister but I think she's a soul sister too.

If you are a sister, then you are either older or younger—and whichever way it falls for you, I hope it is everything that twelve-year-old Maya Gecso writes about her big sister Zali.

> My big sister Zali makes me laugh and feel happy. She helps me with my homework, and if I cry she is always there for me. Zali teaches me how to always be myself. We love to dance together and do crazy dress-ups. Zali shows me right from wrong and I love her to the moon and back!

Speaking or writing of sisters, it's an odd feeling to have asked your sister to write a piece on a woman who has been important to her and to discover it is about yourself! I so expected my younger sister to have written about her twin that it wasn't until I got to the middle of the story that I realised it was about me. To say I was overcome would be an understatement. It is a wonderful gesture of sisterly friendship, love and support, and I thank her for it.

I think one of the themes to come out of this book is how important sisters are to one another. This is not to say of course that close 'soul sister' friends are not just as important, or that if you happen to be an only child, or a child with no sisters, you will not discover the profound friendship and love that can exist between sisters, but perhaps the fact of sharing one's early years can never be repeated. Sisters are part of a family history, for better or for worse, and with the love, laughter support and friendship they provide they are a constant link between the past, the present and the future. This was my sister Charlie's present to me.

When I was asked if I would like to write a story for a book on women by women, I was thrilled, yet somehow daunted, when I started to think about all the women in my life who have meant so much to me, most of whom still share my life and my thoughts. The women in my life guide my decisions and allow the questions of my soul to have a place to be voiced. More often than not the questions find an answer or guidance—some sort of solace in our ever-challenging and changing roles.

Yet one story seems to want to be told. It is of two sisters—one eight years older then the other. The elder of the two always, from a very early age, made sure the younger one was fed and clothed, even when their mother was unable to do so. She seemed always to be there, even when thousands of miles way. It seemed that there was a never-ending support from an unnamed source. Of course with any journey in life there were times when there were misunderstandings, lack of acknowledgement, even perhaps blame and judgement, but as they have grown older those things have disappeared from the language and thoughts they have for each other.

Sisterly love

By some twist of fate, or was it in fact the foresight of another being, they ended up living twelve thousand miles away from home together in a land they now call home, leaving their other incredible siblings behind. Which in itself is a story of pain and longing that always had, and has to this day, enormous love, pull and pain. But that is not the story that is begging to be told in these pages.

It seems in my life I draw to me amazing women whose lives inspire me, whose strength inspires me, and it is my eldest sister's drive that has always bewildered me. From a young age I noticed she was somehow able to live her life and work and be the stepmother of three, yet still be concerned about me: 'We're having ham and salad for dinner with baked potatoes, butter and heaps of cheese [always my favourite]—are you coming? There's a place set if you can make it.'

I always knew this was code for: I'm concerned you're not eating enough and we haven't seen you for weeks—get yourself over here and be part of our family meal. It worked every time.

It seemed her role was one of mother more than sister.

Then one day when I was twenty-nine I got the call—she'd gone into labour.

It was here that it was noticed and noted by her husband that in the moments that are somehow both your most public and your most private, the moments of giving birth, the two sisters met each other in very different ways. Somehow in these moments the mother role shifted and all he could see was two women who loved each other and would walk as far as was needed together.

It is a fantastic journey we take with each other, from youth to young womanhood and into middle age and on. With each stage I am able to see what I might need to handle, to understand the risks that lay ahead, as my sister journeys the uncharted water in front of me.

Each step of the way there seems to be a drive for her, a forward searching—a quest she lives by to keep questioning, growing, changing and learning. These are the things that I wish to emulate and encourage in myself.

To follow your heart and to challenge yourself to live your dream has always been a huge conversation between my sister and me. Some years ago the chance to do this came her way and off she set in her most indomitable fashion. The journey has not been easy and yet with each step, with each turn that did not turn out the way we'd hoped, she found more information on how to be who you want to be and how to live your life with integrity.

It is this part of my amazing sister I would like to honour here, her never-ending drive to pull herself up, to pull through and then embark on the next bit of life. She inspires me to be true to myself, to be true to my womanhood, to honour the journey that is so uniquely female. To be as bold as a lion with dragon wings, and not to be caught in the crosswind.

We have, as many of us do, a lifetime of stories. Some are best untold; some have at last been put down on the side of the road; some are stories of encouragement, some of dismay, always with the bond of sisterhood.

Sisterly love

I find as I grow older the comfort of the 'elder' coming in to play. I have always wondered what that meant. When I was very young it meant the person who looked or felt like a grandmother; when I was an adolescent it meant someone who did not understand me—how could they? Now as I navigate middle age, it means someone who has walked before me with grace, age in fact playing only the part of coming first.

If you asked me what I most admire in my sister, I would have to say her generosity, courage and drive.

When Candy asked me if I would like to share a story for her book, and I said 'yes', I did not know it was to her I would be writing. Yet here is where I feel I want to honour her, to thank her for her parenting, her friendship and advice, to thank her for allowing me to in turn be her confidante, her friend and her younger sister.

To tell her that I love her and that she is most dear to me.

Bless you, my darling, and remember you are always in the heart—oh tucked so close there is no chance of escape—of your sister.

KATHERINE MANSFIELD

27
Old friends and changing times

Jane Camens and I first became friends thirty years ago when we were both working on a women's magazine. It was a friendship that has withstood the test of time, including Jane's relocation for fifteen years to Hong Kong and quite a few years spent in Europe or travelling elsewhere. Our friendship was initially formed through a mutual love of horses, but was quickly extended through a love of singing—at which she's much better than me—reading and writing, and generally chatting and communicating. I was thrilled when she returned from Hong Kong and decided to live near me in the country, and to perhaps both of our surprises we ended up thirty years later once more riding horses together and, less surprisingly, talking about books and writing.

In Jane's story, she writes about a different friendship, with Marian, and the complexities of a relationship when people don't change or grow.

I don't know what I look like any more, Marian said, turning away from the mirror, trying to catch my expression. She had lived alone in Paris for five years.

You see, she said while looking for her reflection in my eyes, there's no-one who knows me here. No-one knows who I *was*.

I can tell you who Marian is, or was. We'd known each other for almost twenty years. She was from Chicago via New York, and had come to live in Hong Kong to make a ton of money in stockbroking. She could be feisty, bossy, even rude. She was also classy and generous. In those days she had a harbour-view apartment in the Mid Levels that I helped paint magnolia, or perhaps we did it stark white. She would have wanted the softer colour gone. My own small apartment in Happy Valley looked straight into the windows of another residential building across the street. I didn't need a television as big as hers.

Something in Marian must have reflected in me. She found me, perhaps, less narrowly focused than most people she worked with. I'm not sure. She liked to come with me to the foreign correspondents' club and would take me just as often to the American Club's better gym and restaurants in Exchange Square.

She was still looking at me, deciding whether she could see

anything of herself in me, or whether we'd both changed too much.

After Hong Kong she'd fallen in love in Singapore. He was a much younger man, a gym junkie making good money as a model. Marian, the one who told everyone what to do, gave up stockbroking for him and became a personal fitness trainer. When he dumped her she left town, I think because there was a billboard in the MRT stations showing him in underpants. Imagine having to eyeball that every day!

I was living in England by the Christmas I went to stay with Marian in Paris. A man I'd met in Hong Kong had bought me a house in Norwich. I know, how lucky! But the trouble with being given a house is that when the man's wife finds out he's spent several hundred thousand pounds on someone else, he has to take the house away, doesn't he? And then one is left with no house, but an old friend with a rented apartment across the Channel.

You should use my night cream, Marian suggested. I'd gone soft around the edges; she, in the meantime, had toned her bitch muscles in gyms throughout Paris. How flabby mine had got, thinking there were priorities other than pumping iron. That's also what the French seemed to think, for Marian's personal training business had gone down the toilet.

That night cream. I remembered she had used the same cream years before. She had told me that if a lover came into your bathroom, which he would, he would know from a cabinet full of Dior products that you were a classy person. I never believed in the transformative powers of branded products and was amazed to find Marian's marble Parisian bathroom full of Dior, tastefully arranged, even though she could no longer meet her rent.

She had been lighting candles, she said, and saying prayers to Saint Jude, patron saint of hopeless causes. Marian was not religious, or hadn't been. She had asked everyone who was still speaking to her to lend her money. I'd given what I could afford, a few hundred dollars, on condition she never paid it back. Christmas was payback of sorts.

And so, although my man had left me, and Marian was about to lose her apartment and abandon her fantasy of remaking Parisians in her image, we celebrated Christmas at a restaurant with goose, minus the skin, and a good red wine which we enjoyed after a workout at one of her grunt gyms. And we toasted each other.

Here's to us, she said, holding up her glass. You're looking... not too bad. I can still make something of you.

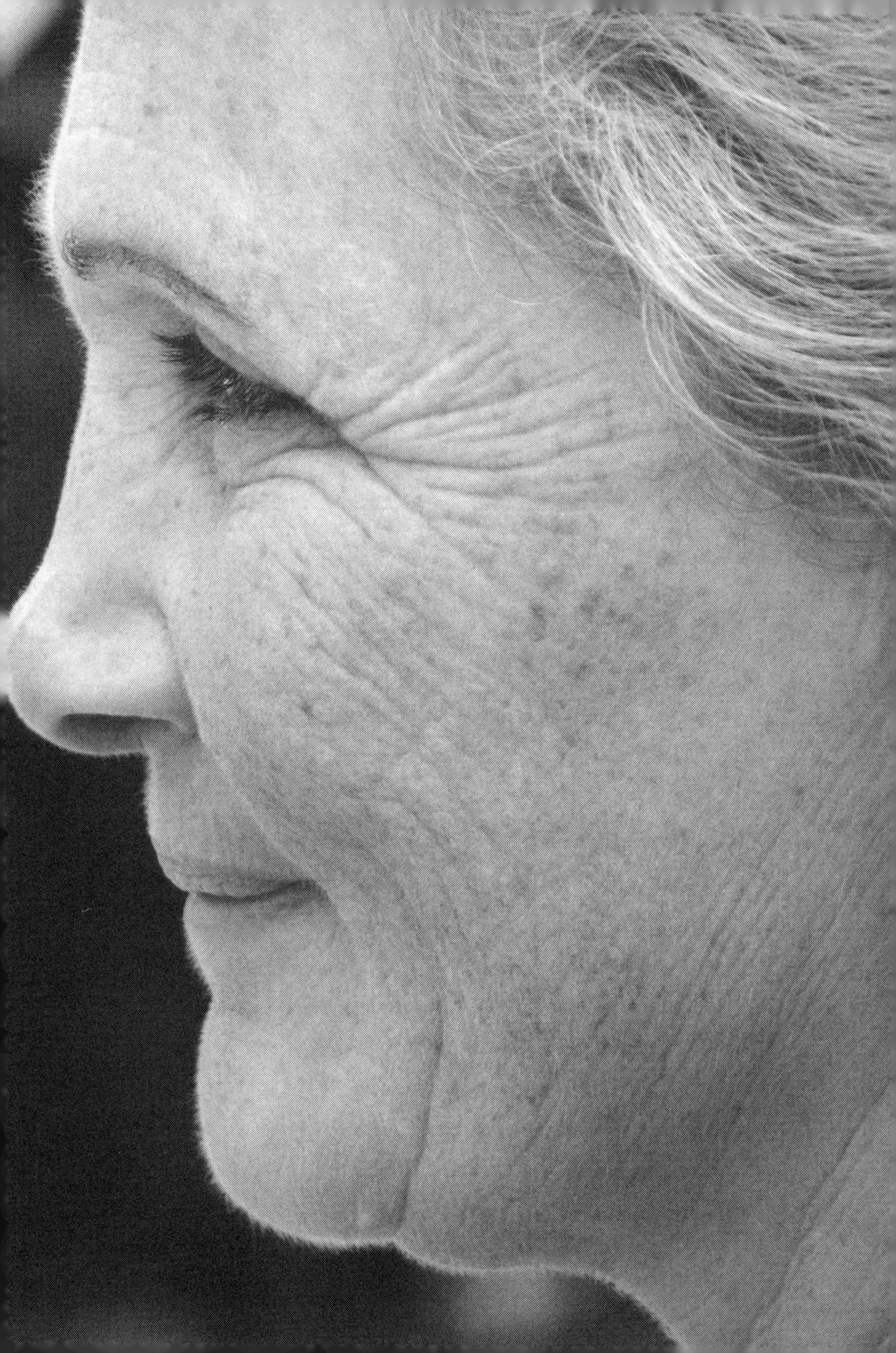

28

A woman's welcome and a nice cup of tea

I don't know about the rest of the world, but I do know that in England and Australia the Country Women's Association plays a pivotal part in retaining a sense of community.

I will never forget travelling around the east coast of Australia in the mid-seventies on a theatre tour and being toasted everywhere we went with wonderful morning and afternoon teas—scones, lamingtons, pikelets and, of course, pavlovas! All provided by the CWA.

In Australia the wonderful agricultural shows are in large part supported by them, and imagining a world without their produce, arts and crafts is to imagine something much less rich and diverse.

A woman's welcome and a nice cup of tea

In the story below, Cecilia Novy describes how her terror turned to delight when, as a young refugee, she was ordered off the train that was taking her to her new home.

The date was 1 March 1950. We had come a long way.

Days of waiting in wintry Trieste, crammed into a bare concrete building, one thousand of us, men, women and frightened children, had already increased our mistrust into an unknown future.

The passage on the refugee ship, a former troop transporter, had been arduous enough. We knew, though, that the journey would have to come to an end and hoped that the hunger pangs would soon be relieved.

Some of us had come from migrant centres near devastated European cities where people who had lost home and family could find asylum. Many had suffered in concentration camps or hideouts in cellars and attics, never knowing where their next meal was coming from or whether worse fate could play with their lives. Years spent in internment had affected body and soul.

Having disembarked in the early morning in Melbourne, we now sat in a rattling train, our few belongings at our feet, on the way to an unknown destination—our new home. With great interest we looked out on what seemed to us a flat desolate landscape with wilted, dry grasses, barely ankle-deep, where some cows tried in vain to find a few green shoots. Here and there clumps of strange, straggly trees gave shelter to sheep apparently lost without a shepherd. Very rarely in this enormous open void did we glimpse any farmhouses, and in vain we looked for villages.

Suddenly the train pulled into a station. The train guards rushed through the carriages, shouting: 'Out, all out!'

No explanation given: 'Out, all out!'

'What's going to happen to us here? Have we arrived at our destination? Are we going to be herded into another detention camp?' We turned to each other in confusion.

Hesitating and worried, we descended from the carriages. We stared in disbelief. Along the whole platform were tables set with food. We could hardly believe our eyes. On white tablecloths were set dishes with nice, fresh, clean sandwiches. We looked at plates with small white buns, pots with jam and cream.

Behind the tables stood ladies in prettily coloured aprons, smiling and nodding to us: 'Yes, this is for you! We made them ourselves. Eat as much as you can!'

Teapots and cups in hand, they asked: 'Milk and sugar?'

'Welcome to Australia!' one lady after another joined in, laughing at our surprised faces and tear-filled eyes.

Our hands were trembling as we held those fine porcelain cups, words of thanks on our lips, our hearts touched by this unexpected gesture of generosity.

We ate the new delicious dainties with much relish, laughing at our few struggling English words, trying to express our surprise and gratitude.

As I later found out, these ladies were from the Country Women's

A woman's welcome and a nice cup of tea

Association in Seymour. They welcomed the 'New Australians' on their journey to Bonegilla, the reception centre for thousands of immigrants from war-torn countries.

This was not just our introduction to scones and jam and cream, but our introduction to the generosity and kindness of so many Australians, giving us hope and trust in our common future.

All these years I have wondered how to thank these unknown citizens of Seymour—I know that the giving is its own true reward, and that they could see in our faces just how much we appreciated their generous gesture.

Who knows, all these years later some of the ladies may still remember their good deed.

Learn to get in touch with the silence within yourself and know that everything in life has purpose.

ELISABETH KÜBLER-ROSS

29

Losing the women we love

I know that I have been incredibly lucky with my friendships, my sisters and my children. We are still here. I've talked to women who have lost those beloved of them, and their grief when they talk about it, even after many years, is palpable.

I think when you do experience those kinds of losses that, even with the strongest spiritual beliefs, you need to give yourself the time you need to mourn, to come to terms with what's happened.

I believe that the body is simply a house for the soul, that we are all, if you like, energy, and when we leave our earthly body we still have just as strong a connection with those not-yet departed, and I hope this belief turns out to be true!

In the area where I live, Zenith Virago, who writes about the death of her friend Sylvia, is well known for her work with the dying. It was her experience with Sylvia that set her on the path towards her destiny.

> Sylvia was my dearest friend. She was many things to me—a mother figure, a sister and a spiritual companion. Sylvia was in her early fifties, in excellent health and happily married with two teenage daughters, eighteen-year-old Sarah and twenty-year-old Louise. They were a loving and close family.
>
> Early one morning while Richard, her husband, was out shopping, Sylvia was in the garden doing her daily yoga practice and Sarah was at the kitchen sink. Suddenly, Sarah saw that her mother was on the ground.
>
> As it transpired, Sylvia had suffered a massive brain haemorrhage and died almost immediately. In distress and panic they called the ambulance, hoping against hope that Sylvia could be revived. With the arrival of the paramedics came the invasive thump, thump of the machine in an attempt to try and restart her heart, but Sylvia was dead.
>
> Eventually her body was taken away and Richard and Sarah, although distraught, rang me to let me know. I was deeply shocked when I received the news, and my partner drove me straight to their house. It felt surreal and empty, a new and disorientating experience. As I looked out through the car windows and took in the world,

Losing the women we love

I somehow knew my life would never be the same. Although I was in shock, I was very aware of the moment. I wanted to experience it fully, with as much understanding of life and death as possible. This was a woman I loved, who had been a treasured mentor and with whom I had shared my heart. Her sudden death was a profoundly life-changing experience for me, but I had no idea then of just how much it would influence my life in the years to come.

Sylvia had a much-loved and wonderful family, all of whom were also friends. After her body had been taken away, they were left in shock and disbelief. They telephoned friends and family; Louise was overseas visiting her mother's family.

Later that afternoon, Richard and Sarah had to go to the hospital to identify Sylvia's body for the police, which is the usual procedure with sudden death. They asked me if I would like to go too so I could see Sylvia's body for myself. I thought that seeing her body would allow me to accept the reality of her death, and I was touched and grateful that they considered me close enough to share this experience with them.

We went to the hospital and were taken to the morgue by two police officers. As Sylvia's body was wheeled out on a trolley the police tactfully looked away, trying to give us some privacy at this difficult moment. Sarah cried and Richard embraced her, while I looked at Sylvia and tried to take it all in. She was a big, healthy woman who looked so peaceful she could almost have been asleep, although the back of her head was a dark purple from the congealed and settled blood of the haemorrhage. My shocked mind was reluctant to accept what my eyes were seeing. Somehow I expected her to breathe.

This was my first experience with a dead body. As I looked down at her I said out loud, 'Oh Sylvia, I just can't believe this,' and shook my head. Gently I started stroking her hair, from her forehead down over her crown. I let my hand gradually rest on her crown, as I would with a sick child, lost in my thoughts and emotions and a deep sense of disbelief.

What happened then was one of the most extraordinary experiences of my life. I saw a column of energy leaving from the crown of Sylvia's head. It passed through my palm and out through the back of my hand. It was palpable. It appeared as physical matter like a vapour jet and had a force of its own, which continued up my arm and down to my heart.

Time stood still for me. I glanced at the police, who were looking away. Then I looked at Richard and Sarah to check whether they could see what was happening, but they were immersed in their comforting embrace. I remember wanting to fully appreciate what was happening, knowing that it was something wild and very special.

When it eventually stopped, I took my hand away and stared transfixed at Sylvia's body. I was overwhelmed with the intensity of the experience. However, I needed to support Sarah and Richard, caught up in their grief and in all that lay ahead.

Back at the house, I offered to help them organise the funeral. It felt important for us to do it ourselves. I knew that wherever Sylvia's spirit was, she would be thinking, if Zenith's involved, it will all be alright!

On the way home, as I drove through a small town, I saw the tiny new office of a funeral director, which I hadn't noticed before. I went in and met Ron, and told him that my best friend had just died, that I worked in a legal firm and wanted to undertake her funeral myself. I asked him if he would guide me through the process. In half an hour, he had explained the whole legal procedure, the forms and possible pitfalls. Ron was a generous and caring man. He gave his advice and time freely. He even offered to be there in the background in case anything went wrong. I gratefully accepted his offer.

I went into action and began to organise everything. Richard was busy supporting Sarah and contacting Louise, who was trying to arrange a flight back home from overseas as soon as possible. Sarah was still in total shock. A friend built a simple coffin, and I did the paperwork with the Coroner, then went to collect Sylvia's body from the hospital morgue, where I met some resistance as this was new to them. But I was determined and not to be stopped. Sudden death requires the body to undergo an autopsy, so I had rung the hospital several times to explain that we were having an open coffin for family and friends to view her, and asked them to do a tidy job.

We took Sylvia's body to a friend's house where six women friends washed and dressed her. The friend who had built the coffin became very emotional and was unable to finish it, so we frantically stapled in a favourite fabric of Sylvia's to line it with before her body could be gently placed inside. The coffin was decorated with Sylvia's own artwork.

When all was finally ready, we lifted Sylvia in her beautiful coffin into the van, only to find we couldn't close the back door. The coffin was a little bit too long for the space. We took out the van's back seat and now the coffin fitted. Then I checked the petrol gauge, nearly empty. One of the women sat with the coffin for the journey to the service station, and on to Richard and Sylvia's house. This time was particularly important for Louise, who needed time to experience her loss on her own with her mother.

Richard's deeply spiritual outlook supported him through this challenging time, while also giving him the strength to support his grieving daughters. They were grateful to be able to spend a couple of hours at home with Sylvia before we headed to the crematorium for the ceremony. The funeral was held outside in the crematorium gardens where more than two hundred people gathered. I was also to be the celebrant. I had never done anything like this before. I stood there in front of everyone ready to begin reading what the family and I had written. I took in the scene and felt so sad. Taking a deep breath I calmed myself and from my deepest, most steady place I began the ceremony. Many people had asked to speak and sing, and I had a sense of order about how it would unfold. We talked, sang, cried, shared and laughed. We honoured her individually and collectively. Then at the end we let her body go.

I felt a great sense of achievement. It was my thirty-sixth birthday and it had been an amazing day. I looked across and saw Ron, the funeral director, and bowed my head to him in gratitude and completion. He had stood in the background at the hospital, at the house of preparation, at the house of viewing and at the ceremony. He had not been needed but his presence had been supportive. Ron had been my guiding angel and with his generosity he had set me on my path. I felt exhausted but very satisfied.

I have now been involved with hundreds of people with death and dying, in many different situations. Ron's example to me has been a guiding force. It taught me that when someone asks you for information, to always give it with generosity, as you never know what they will do with it. I always carry Sylvia in my heart and because of my love for her, many people have experienced meaningful and appropriate rites of passage, ones that fully support the bereaved. It has been and continues to be an extraordinary learning and a very privileged journey. I hope I will inspire others, just as Sylvia inspired me.[2]

I know that through Zenith's work she has lessened the sense of grief and confusion for thousands of people faced with losing loved ones, and equally increased the sense of joy and peace—what a great thing to do with your life!

Jean Linderman, the founder of Women Writing Women, has never forgotten how it felt to lose two of her best friends—she describes them as 'treasure' in the story below.

Even if you have a sister (and I cherish mine), I sometimes think that having a woman friend is like finding a treasure you did not know you deserved. Losing them hurts long, long after they are gone. I have lost two, and I guess I will miss them forever.

I met Inge when we were both young mothers married to naval officers who were often at sea. She was Danish, with a charming accent and an exuberant approach to life. Her daughter and mine were born within a few months of each other. We exchanged mothering hints and laughter in equal amounts. When she divorced her husband and moved back to Denmark, we wrote letters. When she married another American and moved to the United States, we visited, even though we lived several hundred miles apart. When our son died, she sent our children the biggest Lego set they had ever seen. Decades later Inge was diagnosed with Lou Gehrig's disease. On my visits to her during her illness, she never lost her no-holds-barred sense of humour. I was asked to speak at her memorial service. I wasn't asked to cry, but I did.

I met Carlene when our husbands were working for the same steel company in Pittsburgh. We became the kind of friends who could share anything and know that the other would hold your words safely in her heart. Half the recipes in my file have Carlene's name on them.

When her son battled mental problems she called me, often from the hospital. When I wanted to talk about marriage, life and her hilarious theory about short men, I called her. (Luckily, both our husbands are tall.) When she was diagnosed with lung cancer, I cried. How could someone who never smoked, who exercised and ate all the veggies receive such a diagnosis? When she had weeks left to live, I drove ten hours in one day to visit her. When she had bad days, I repeated the drive. Oh, I know life isn't fair, but I keep having to learn it all over again.

Life isn't fair. Perhaps the best we can do with that is simply admit and forget or forgive it! There is no point bashing ourselves or others up about the unfairness of life, as composer Yantra de Vilder found with the suddenly diagnosed illness of one of her oldest friends. It was a journey that, in the end, gave Yantra a rare and privileged experience, one which was not without humour as well, as she describes.

> Parampara and I first met when we shared a communal house. They were wild and heady days—lots of dancing, feasting and ecstatic moments. We were a part of a fantastic community and our life was rich and full, revolving around group meditations and music events.
>
> I was always really focused on my music career and she was yet to find her passion—this was the subject of many of our conversations. Parampara had always been interested in astrology but somehow hadn't realised that this was to be her path in life.
>
> One day I said to her, 'What about astrology? You're always talking about it in relation to yourself and your friends—maybe you already have your calling right here.'
>
> Little did I know the impact that this conversation would have on her. She went on to devote her life to this study, diving deeper and deeper into the stars until twenty years later she had become one

of Australia's leading astrologers and teachers. She set up her own school and had a huge clientele.

I often wonder if she had foreseen the signs of her death in the stars.

Our paths were constantly interwoven. We both bought properties in northern New South Wales in the coastal town of Nambucca Heads, where we were part of a small and intimate group of friends.

I did not live there all the time, and so at times we saw each other and at times we didn't. Our lives weaved in and out, as friends do—what is it that Kahil Gibran says about space? Allow the winds of change to blow ... and then, out of the blue, I got a phone call telling me that Parampara had developed lung cancer—and that the prognosis was not good.

I was shocked. I went to bed early and all that night I dreamt about her—and they were not good dreams. The signs were ominous.

I called her. She was scared. It was the nights that she was finding most difficult. She had always told me how important my music was to her and how healing she found it. Indeed, it was her support that had led me to studying music at university. I knew that there was a way I could support her in the dark hours of the night—when fear was at its worse and pain was acute.

I bought her an iPod and assembled a collection of my original music that I felt to be calming and relaxing. I interwove this with other pieces that I knew she loved.

It was a pink iPod—she loved pink, as she loved all the colours of the sun. The music provided a sanctuary for her during the dark nights.

The weeks drifted past and I didn't hear from her. I had told her to contact me when she needed me. And then came the phone call, 'I need you and want you here with me.'

As circumstances would have it, my partner and I were both at Nambucca. I had gone there to spend some weeks working on a music commission.

I went over to her place. I was shocked at the demise of my darling friend who had been so full of the sun. Her body had withered away. She was on morphine; she had gone through radiation and chemotherapy and nothing had worked. The end was near—all the signs were there.

'What do you want to do?' I asked her.

'Take me to the beach.' She had always loved the ocean, the sun, dolphins—anything to do with the beach.

There was a storm brewing, the sky was grey, but she didn't care. She wanted to go into the weather, whatever it was. I packed her into the car and we went down to the place where the river met the ocean. Her house had a track to the beach but she was too weak to walk the distance so we went to a place where I could drive right up to the sand.

As we walked gently along the water's edge, the sky becoming darker with ominous clouds, she started talking to me about her funeral. 'I want you to be in charge of it, Yantra,' She said. 'I want you to create a celebration of my life, with music and sacred elements.'

A soft rain had started falling and I opened the umbrella above our heads, holding onto her with one arm, the umbrella with the other. She walked with a beautiful African shaman's walking stick—dignified, regal, fragile and frail. Thunder was rumbling and a storm was imminent.

Suddenly out of the skies a huge bolt of lightning cracked through the black clouds. The umbrella I was holding had a steel frame and at that second a high-tensile electricity sound crackled through it as a deafening thunderclap enveloped us, accompanied by a blinding white light.

We both fell to the ground with the impact of the shock. We lay there for a while, stunned and shaking—and then we looked up at each other in shock … and started laughing and laughing, and crying and laughing.

'I thought I was going to die of cancer, not a lightning bolt,' she said, and we laughed again.

A surfer had been in the water and had seen what had happened to us. He came running toward us to see if we were OK and there we were, laughing hysterically because we felt we had been 'saved' and yet at the same time we had gone through an initiation of sorts together. It was profound.

I gathered her up and took her back to the car and we made our way home. That evening we were sitting together by candlelight and an owl flew to the window and looked in at her. She was riveted and they held each other's gaze for at least ten minutes. The owl wasn't interested in me … it had come for her and their communion was tangible.

We had many precious moments of stillness, sadness, joy and meditation together in the last days. I felt privileged to have been invited into her orbit in these challenging times. It was an honour to be there, to wash her, cook for her and be a friend to someone who was passing through the veils in such a brave and beautiful way.

My life has been enriched by the gift of sharing these last weeks with my dear friend.

She taught me to practice an exquisite attention to detail and gratitude of the small things. All this became intricately defined and took on a rarefied fragrance—the one that exists between the worlds where one door is closing and another is opening.

The moment between the breaths in and out … the magical time of surrender and letting go.

I had been given the glimpse of the beyond through the intimacy of shared moments with my dying friend.

Death is a private thing, and no one knows how it will be. It is the honouring of each person's individual process that I believe is the greatest gift—as it is in life. And this has been the greatest lesson for me—to honour all of our frailties and differences.

No two people can die the same or live the same. We are precious and unique jewels each with a different song to sing and path to be walked. To share the harmony and the road at certain times of quickening makes the joy of life even more exquisite.[3]

Yantra's journey with Parampara was full of love and compassion, but of course death is not always kind or pretty, sad as that truth is, and some people seem to receive more than their fair share of adversity, either personal or within their family.

A Bundjalung woman originally from Lismore, Rhoda Roberts is well known as an Australian arts presenter and now has her own art gallery near her home town. I first met Rhoda not long ago when I asked her if she would do the official 'Welcome to Country' at our local writers' festival, and also if she would participate in some panels. I took to her immediately—she has the most lovely smile, and a quiet dignity she has acquired during the tumultuous years of her life.

Rhoda's story is a searing tale of the difficulties of growing up 'mixed race'—with a white mother and an Aboriginal father—in the Australia of the 1960s, and the tragedies that befell her identical twin sister, Lois.

> The smell of antiseptic means something just for me, and it always conjures a place of safety—it's clean and bright. I have known this aroma since I was a babe with a beautiful mother who was fixated on cleanliness.
>
> 'You could eat off our bathroom floor,' she would announce proudly to me and my three siblings.
>
> 'But why would we want to do that, Mum?' we would snigger, thinking she had gone a little crazy in the heat of the summer as she tucked her fingers behind her ear attempting to push the gold strands of hair that would defy the Grace Kelly role and escape in the humid air.

So when I walked the linoleum hospital wards in my brown lace-up Halls, the starch in my uniform making a crisp swish, each step reminding me of my duties as a student nurse, I reflected on how far I had come. Who would have thought the little brown girl from the bush could adjust so quickly to routine? But for those who might have wondered, little did they know my mother.

I honestly felt more at home in the pan room with the smell of bleach and Betadine than dealing with Mrs Johnson, for instance, who had been admitted for a routine operation. She was so dignified and graceful. Her hands were soft, nails just the right colour and always with the coral polish she favoured. Every morning she would do her hair and tie it into the nape of her neck. It was luscious and thick and defied her senior years. But it was her eyes that made me warm to her; I was just eighteen with a shyness that belied the crisp image I presented. I also had a hidden secret—the fact that I had a crushing terror of authority.

Mrs Johnson made me feel like I was Florence Nightingale herself. She introduced me to her family and was one of the most vigorous ladies I have ever met, with a severe intelligence that must have made her formidable in her younger years.

A week later things had gone terribly wrong with the routine operation, and severe complications had set in. The luscious brown hair had been savagely hacked when Mrs Johnson had suffered from a bout of projectile vomiting that had stained her scalp with bile. I wondered why they had simply not washed her hair. Her crowning glory was now turning grey, and her nail polish had been removed for the theatre procedure. It was only the hushed whispers of her daughters that could stir those piercing blues to open. How could it be that in such a short time this life could almost be extinguished?

I spoke with the ward sister, who told me in no uncertain terms to 'toughen up' and prepare myself for her death. I had three days off at that point, and I went into a frenzy of cleaning the bathroom and surrounding myself with the smells of disinfectant that made me feel protected.

Three days later when I was on the afternoon shift and the sound of the cicadas had risen to a constant penetrating drone, I was assigned the 'special room' in the long post-war Nightingale-style ward. The ward had twenty beds either side, opening onto the verandahs. The handover nurse droned on: 'Bed 26 routine varicose veins now with bowel obstruction and renal failure,' she said. 'The patient occasionally stops breathing so will require constant checking, she is not for medical intervention.' I noted all this on my clipboard and prepared to schedule my evening. I was going to be busy with six other patients to look after as well.

Bed 26 was my Mrs Johnson, and as her daughters surrounded her bed, I took a deep breath and spoke to her, explaining the course of action I was about to undertake. I had noted the aroma of faecal matter in the room and wanted to give her a sponging to make her a little more comfortable. On hearing my words her eyes flew open, a hand grabbed mine and she attempted to smile. I looked deep into those eyes and saw the warmth and generosity of an incredible woman, and I only wished I had known more of her story.

Her eldest daughter's cry was audible. 'Oh my goodness, Rhoda,' she said. 'I think she has been waiting for you to say a cheerio to her.'

And so perhaps it was, because she died right at that moment.

As I prepared her body, I told her how she had impacted on my life and changed my fear of the unknown. I told her that she had accepted me, she had not judged my background. I knew as far as she was concerned I was little Ms Nightingale with the brown eyes who had made her feel special. Not the *Abo' from the bush, and let's see how long she lasts* ... I worked on in silence, thinking of the grandmothers who grace our lives.

I made a pact that day that even if I was busy and even if someone was short with me, I would think of my mother or grandmother and treat them with the love required no matter what. I would show them that behind all our facades our world has too many similarities to focus on the differences. As I sprayed the Lysol antiseptic across Mrs Johnson's now empty bed, I was once again cocooned with the odour of security.

Three years later it was a different matter for me when I walked into a ward not as a nurse but as a visitor. My darling twin sister lay unconscious in the Princess Alexandra ICU unit. She had severe head injuries as the result of a car accident, only three months before our twenty-first birthday.

I knew—we were twins, so I always knew—and I had felt something, and had howled to the wind. As Dad drove the Pacific Highway to Queensland I had tried to prepare myself for the worst but I was never going to be prepared for the sight of the girl I saw lying lifeless in a bed surrounded by the smell of the unconscious. A smell, if you have been lucky enough never to smell it, that somehow seems to be of sweet hay mixed with antiseptic. But this smell could no longer cocoon me—I felt lost, afraid, and the guilt set in. Was this payback? Had I done something wrong and now was the punishment that my sister should be so hurt? Warped views I know, but when you grow up of mixed blood, not one or the other—or so I thought at the time—often your feelings can be distorted.

I lit up a cigarette and once again I justified this new habit I had taken up. Smoking filled the void for me; it was about the ritual of silence.

'Think about words,' my dad would say. 'Words are to be treasured, they're too important to be wasted.'

I felt washed out, exhausted as if I had jetlag, but all I had done was cry, silently, sobbing like a lost spirit, and now my cries were silent daggers exploding inside my head. My tears had given me a bloody headache, a huge does of misplaced remorse and guilt and red-rimmed eyes.

It nearly broke my heart when I saw Dad emerge from the third floor lift that day. He looked somehow smaller, as if the weight of the last few days was heavy, far too substantial for his shoulders to carry. His face had lost its velvetiness but his gentle smile was as huge as it had always been and he held my eyes, mouthing: 'Love you so.'

Dad clutched the family Bible as he walked towards the ventilator, announcing like a preacher, 'Where there is breath there is life.' I knew, just like he had done when one of us was sick as children, that he would stay beside her bed and pray all night if necessary. I am sure he believed Mum's disinfectant and his prayers were going to save my sister.

'No Dad,' I said ever so softly, 'where there's breath there's a ventilator.' Respiratory equipment—a man-made machine—was keeping one of his dearest daughters alive.

He held me in a bear hug and I wanted to shake him and yell that his bloody God was of no use. But then he whispered in my ear, 'Have faith, she's got strong spirit, like Ngadhang, our Lois has.' With his eyes red-rimmed from crying, I wasn't sure whom Dad was trying to convince and give some hope to.

Against the odds the prayer worked, even if I secretly knew it was the comforting smells and the voices and the music we played daily that led to my sister's recovery. But although she 'recovered', my sister was the same soul in a different body; her gait different, her speech slower, but somehow she maintained her amazing strength and resilience and two years later she was living in her own house.

A new journey began and with each following decade I readjusted. No longer was the gregarious beautiful sister I had known at my side. We had always joked that she got the looks and I got the brains, but let me tell you as far as I'm concerned she also got the brains, and I often reflected on her intelligence and perception. Like the ancient culture that runs through our veins we constantly adapted to the new challenges. Lois was someone special—not just a sister, she was a light who showed me a new road to travel, accepting the differences and the limitations of people.

For the next two decades I would again have a twin sister to converse with, with whom I could share the most outrageous stories, hopes and dreams. However, in our forties, unbeknown to us at the time of course, a new crushing decade loomed. This was going to be our big celebration, but once again the spirit of the past crossed my path and with Lois's brutal murder began a new passage.

This is another story but it's one I now proudly share with my sister's daughter, Emily, who has now become my daughter. I am her other mother and we will walk the path together and learn from all those women, sisters and daughters who travel this unknown journey of life with us and before us.

My two girls, Emily and Sarah, show me that the voyage of life can be rocked with the wind, but the aromas and the memories embrace and nurture us and we must always appreciate the past—it is the teacher for our future.

You never lose by loving. You always lose by holding back.

BARBARA DE ANGELIS

30

The healing touch

I know for most women that once we have discovered the power of massage, or reiki, or the strength that can come to us from a woman's healing touch, we know when we need it; it becomes essential to find our way from time to time to someone who has the knowledge of the female self, to be able to take away our aches and pains, physical and emotional, if only for a brief space of time. I've often wondered whether the healers enjoy their work, and now, reading Carmen Paff's piece, I know they do!

I love my job. I really do. As a reiki healer and massage therapist, I get to connect on a deep level with women from all walks of life,

The healing touch

all ages, all backgrounds, at all stages of spiritual development. I feel privileged that they trust me with their fears, their worries, their daily battles, their many joys, triumphs, hopes and dreams, and above all, their wellbeing. I find it so rewarding to be able to share simple techniques for coping with everything from a nasty boss to a terminal illness. I love seeing women accept a healing with their entire being to feel sacred, whole, loved and healed once more. To see that look of contented calm when the lines of stress have dissolved from their faces, leaving room for their inner glow to radiate wellbeing again. What an honour! I am truly blessed.

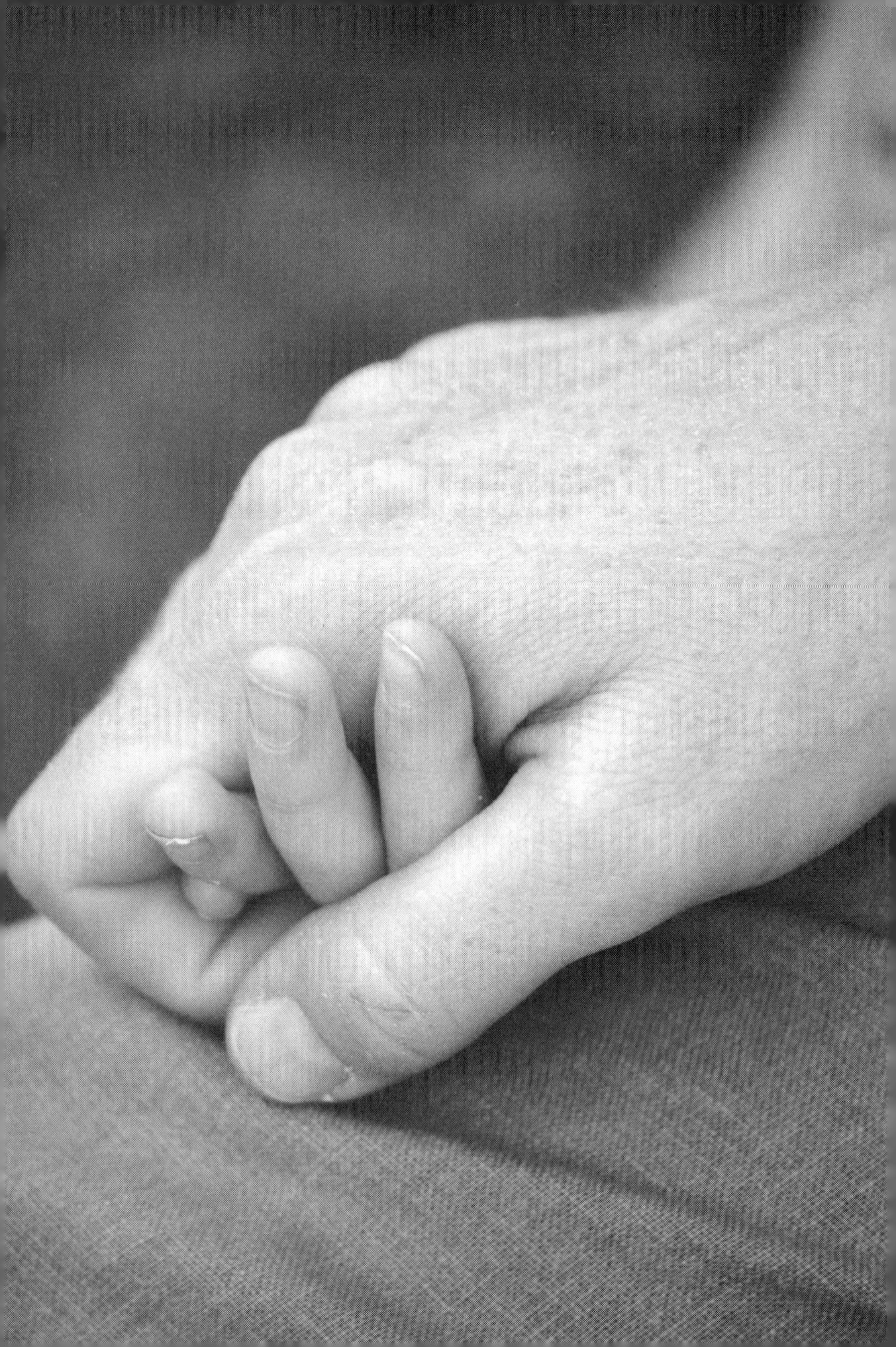

31

Hormones rule

I cannot begin to tell you how much I've envied women in my life who have said things to me like, 'Oh I've never had any bother with PMT' or 'Menopause was a breeze for me.' You what? I feel like screaming at them. That is so unfair. As a teenager I battled rampaging hormones, as a young woman I battled raging PMT, as a middle-aged woman I got run over by a truck full of menopause, and I'm still picking up the pieces. And I have to tell you for those of you who are not there yet, after twelve years (twelve!) I am still getting hot flushes. Not as bad as the early years, thank goodness, and at least I no longer suffer the feeling of Not Being Me, which is the worst of the worst, along with the awful chilled-to-the-marrow cold that likes to come along just prior to the hot flushes, but still I cannot wait to be 'ova' it, as the indomitable artist and coach Sally Swain puts it in her story.

Menopause is new, but old. It's a complete inner refurbishment, yet it reminds me of puberty—the last time my hormones ran riot.

I'm ova it! It's not just the flushes, which are intense but pass quickly. It's not just the alarming night sweats and grizzly insomnia. It's not just the sandpaper dry mouth that wakes me begging for a drink. It's not just the shock and humiliation of peeing when I sneeze. It's the emotions. I'm hypersensitive and anxious about little things. I bristle with calamitous thoughts. My sense of perspective is haywire. Yes. That's it. My Proportion Meter is out of whack. It's like an endless bout of PMT.

And then there's the anger. Oh my goddess! The fire that many of us were told to suppress, squish and subvert. Don't rock the boat. Don't lose your temper. Turn yourself inside out to please and placate. These well-worn habits are becoming an endangered species.

I'm early in the journey. I've just burst into it, or has it burst into me? It's happened in a fairly spectacular I'm-outta-control-what-the-hell-is-going-on way. One minute my body's doing what it's been doing for thirty-seven years. Next minute, there are serious internal communication errors. I've always had trouble understanding which hormones do what, when and why. The menstrual cycle is mysterious enough without the ovaries putting their hands over their ears and refusing to listen to directions.

Pituitary Gland: *Release your eggs.*
Ovaries: *Nope.*
PG: *Go on. Release your eggs. I'm sending down FSH, LH and other Hs to prompt you. That means hormones, in case you're in any doubt.*
O: *La la la. We're not listening. We're old and tired. We're ova it.*
PG: *Very funny. I'm telling you—eggs out now! Scrambled or boiled, I don't care. Do what you do.*
O: *Can't. We're ovacooked.*
PG: *Listen, pals, we've always worked well together. I'm going to have to do something different. I'll bring in the hyphothalamus and Sally's blood vessels will open up. Her face will burn and her chest will prickle. She won't know what hit her.*
O: *Sorry, it's our time to rest down here. Do what you like up top. We've done our job. Ova and out.*

The trouble is, no amount of *doing* things seems to help. There's a moment of clarity, then I'm feverish and prickly, then gluggy and fuggy. Then, oh I dunno, I don't want to do anything in particular and I'm tired tired tired. I'm lost. I feel I've lost a whole lot of the inner gains I've made over thirty-seven years. I don't like it.

I listen for a Wise Self to say, Darling, your gains are not lost; merely mislaid. You are growing up all over again, with the benefit of hindsight, foresight and insight. It's fundamental, this change.

Of course it's affecting your perceptions of everything, including your identity. Of course you feel loss. It will pass, I assure you. You will learn from this experience and emerge stronger.

She's cool, this Wise Self. Me? I'm hot. And exhausted. The fever, the inner conflict, the oestrogen and adrenaline up, down, up, down. Some call it Hormone Hell and some barely notice a thing. It's so variable. I've been in it three months. Some women are in it for ten years or more. Spare me!

In three months I've tried acupuncture and dong quai and other herbs, which cost a fortune and don't seem to have an effect. I've tried cutting back tea, sugar, chilli and alcohol. I've tried stepping up walking and yoga. I've discovered heaps of great books. I've been talking to anyone who will listen, and listening to anyone who will talk.

What about the herstory of menopausal women? The artists and writers? Was Enid Blyton menopausal? Beatrix Potter? Grace Cossington-Smith? Jane Austen wasn't. She didn't live that long, poor woman. Nor did Sylvia Plath. How about Virginia Woolf? Gertrude Stein?

Come on, Sally, are you nuts? How can you include Enid Blyton and Gertrude Stein in the same category?

Anyway, which writers and artists went through the Change? Germaine Greer, obviously. Rosalie Gascoigne started painting in her eighties or something. Where are the role models? Where are the women who can teach us how to not only survive this thing, but to do it with panache? To ride its transformative powers

Hormones rule

like a witch on a broomstick. Note to self: google witches and menopause.

I try to order my thoughts. *Heel! Or should I say Heal!*

My thoughts say: *This is not a disease or disorder. We have nothing to heal from.*

I say: *But you sure the hell feel like a disease or disorder.*

Thoughts: *You need to reframe.*

Here's my purpose: I want to share my experiences. I might help someone. I don't want to be a victim. I want to do this with strength and grace; and without HRT or axe-murder. Can I seize the spiritual learnings available in this fiery change? I can paint it out, write it out, do menopause with power. I hope to find ways of dancing with what's uncontrollable—to inspire others to burn through without burning out.

Why is it still taboo? I hang out mainly with women who are mid- or post-menopause. Strangely, I've not heard many actual conversations about it. My friends are broad-minded, feminist, alternative types, aren't they? Where is the acknowledgement of menopause? The talk, support and exploration? I'd like to find creative ways to be on the journey and to turn it into something of value. I don't want to be dragged into a medical model. I don't want to see it as a nasty disease with symptoms to be treated, even though this is how it feels.

It's easy to medicalise. That's the recent attitude to the Change. And let's face it—middle-aged and older women are not exactly regarded as the glamour queens of our culture. We have pretty low status in general. Bugger that! I refuse to buy into it. It's taken all these years to build a bit of confidence and believe I have something to offer ... some wisdom, even.

Let's not swallow our words or stifle boldness. Let's harness the energy of this powerful time and use it to create life, art and community.

PS. A month later, most of my menopausal 'symptoms' have disappeared. Whether it's due to black cohosh, soy milk, artmaking or salsa dancing, who knows? I suspect the shift is my body doing its own thing, regardless of my efforts. I won't be surprised if the whole shebang returns with a she-bang.

Though I am grateful for the blessings of wealth, it hasn't changed who I am. My feet are still on the ground. I'm just wearing better shoes.

OPRAH WINFREY

32

Aunts and great aunts

I had a great aunt—Great Aunt Ethel, my paternal grandfather's sister, as my sister just reminded me! It took me years, decades even, to work out exactly who or what a great aunt or uncle is, and so for those of you who might still find it confusing, a great aunt is the sister of one of your grandparents.

What I remember about my great aunt is how gentle and kind she was. She had very soft skin, I recall, and a soft voice. I do also remember that I was surprised at how much my mother cried when she died—more than she did when her own mother died, I recall now, so I think that Auntie Ethel, as we called her, must have meant much more to my mother than, as a self-obsessed child, I ever realised.

Aunts and great aunts

The lovely thing, of course, about aunts and great aunts is that they are part of this wonderful circle of female connection that allows us to feel and understand our inclusion in the family tribe.

Writer Helen Brown remembers her Aunt Lila with great affection.

Aunt Lila was a post–global crash eco-warrior—though she didn't know it.

We smiled at her habit of hoarding pieces of string and old paper bags in a kitchen drawer. Even then it was surprising how often a paper bag came in handy. She always had spare lemons on her tree. Four or five would fit perfectly in a used paper bag to be left on a neighbour's back step. String was useful, too, for tying a tomato to a stake or wrapping a birthday present to be posted to a niece.

Under the kitchen drawer a cupboard brimmed with treasures, some of them familiar. If I looked closely enough, I'd be able to identify the ribbon I'd tied her last birthday present in, and Santa wrap (wrinkles smoothed, though not completely) from two Christmases ago. Sometimes I could make out boxes of writing paper waiting to be 're-gifted' to unsuspecting relatives. Deeper investigation was discouraged.

Aunt Lila indulged in unusual activities like screeching to a halt in her car whenever she spotted a superior mound of horse poo on the road. Out of the driver's seat she'd spring to swing the shovel she kept in the car boot for just such occasions. The boot was lined with sacks, enabling her to gather not only horse poo but armfuls of kelp from Ohawe beach, ten minutes drive from her Hawera home on the west coast of New Zealand's North Island.

Everyone understood the horse poo was for her garden, but some thought seaweed was going a bit far. They rolled their eyes when Aunt Lila said kelp was good for her vegetable patch. She understood how much information adults could handle. We kids were the only ones who knew she'd also fill her bath with kelp and hot water, and lie in it. Skin treatment, apparently.

We loved Aunt Lila because, like us, she didn't tell the grown-ups everything. At the same time she let us completely into her world. To her nieces and nephews who were bright enough she taught poker. The rest of us were introduced to the thrill of horseracing.

A day with her was never dull. It started with porridge and brown sugar steaming under the disapproving eyes of our ancestors on her dining-room wall. A phone call later we'd be off to visit some startled members of a distant branch of the family tree, usually farmers.

On the way we'd be instructed to keep an eye out for mushrooms or blackberries. If some were spotted and Aunt Lila was confident the farmer wouldn't shoot, she'd stop the car and we'd scramble over the fence. Fortunately, Aunt Lila kept a supply of cardboard cartons (along with the sacks) for impromptu foraging.

Once the relatives had stuffed us with roast hogget and cream from their own cows, conversation dried up. Aunt Lila judged when our welcome had worn thin and we'd say goodbye. If we were lucky, she might take a detour straight up Mount Egmont. The best part would be the ride home when, in the interests of saving petrol, she'd turn the motor off and let the car glide down the mountain. We'd invariably sail past the National Park gates, crawling to a halt in lush dairy land. Desperate to keep the car moving, we'd climb out of the back seat and push till we ran out of puff.

Aunt Lila was visionary. If modern cars were designed so steering wheels didn't lock up, children could be encouraged to push themselves to school and ballet lessons. Child obesity would shrink along with carbon footprints.

Back at her place, we'd try to eat the mushrooms, then tumble into beds warmed with eiderdowns and hot water bottles (electric blankets? Pah!).

Aunt Lila wasted nothing, recycled everything, and lived almost self-sufficiently till just past her ninetieth birthday. People thought she was crazy, but the woman was just ahead of her time.

Then there were the aunts who were perhaps not quite what they seemed. Emma Ashmore tells the tale of her Great Aunt Joyce, whose long-term relationship with another woman was disguised in familial terms, as was not unusual back in those days.

> It is 1948. My mother is sixteen. She has caught the train all the way from the city and has walked seven miles from the tiny station in the rain. I imagine she's crying as she wades past the sodden paddocks and steps over the gushing cattle grids, relieved to see a line of smoke feathering up from the homestead's chimney.

When she reaches the verandah, she wipes her nose and removes her dripping coat and mud-caked shoes. She sees the orange light of the sitting room. Aunt Joyce is leaning against the roaring fire in her trademark moleskin trousers, a cigarette moving on her lip as she holds up a glass to propose a toast.

When my mother is spotted at the window she is hurried inside and directed to a steaming bath. She is given clean dry clothes, a bowl of barley soup and an eggnog charged with a good shake of rum. Nobody asks her why she's run away (again) as she huddles on a sofa staring at the fire, her aunt's friends chatting and laughing around her.

There's Miss Harriet Olsen, a headmistress of an exclusive girls boarding school, always ready with the silver flask secreted in her coat. Beside Miss Olsen sits Miss Bryce Lamont, a garden designer who, according to the December 1950 edition of the *Australian Home Gardener*, is making a name for herself by championing the subtle beauty and remarkable hardiness of Australian plants. Mrs Katherine Forsyth, art collector and frequently controversial reviewer in the *Southern Art Digest*, is yet to become notorious for the 'unusual marital arrangements' with her Russian cellist husband, the details of which are later splashed across the front pages of the evening press. And there's Violet—or Cousin Violet, as my mother always called her. Violet is bringing in another tray of pigs-in-blankets and plump cheese scones.

'Did everyone stay at the homestead?' I ask my mother.

She can't remember.

'And what did they all talk about?'

Another blank.

'Cousin Violet. She wasn't really a cousin, was she Mum? You think she was Scottish. Was she regarded as "just the housekeeper"? Is that how it worked in those days?'

My mother looks past me. She is tired.

I can only just remember my Great Aunt Joyce, leaning against the white truck eyeing us kids as she rolled a needle-thin cigarette. Her face was lined like an old map. Her arms were as brown and lean as sticks. A single photograph survives of her—she is frowning behind Cousin Violet, who is playing a piano on the back of a truck.

'That's them, isn't it?'

My mother raises a finger to trace the soft pale face of Violet, circa 1958.

'Hmm,' she says. 'Cousin Violet had no head for music.'

'You used to say she was a marvellous cook.'

My mother smiles as if inhaling the smell of freshly baked bread. We concentrate on that, the safe territory of remembering Violet elbow-deep kneading dough, humming flatly as she popped legs of lamb and apple pies into the roaring Aga, or sighing as she wielded an oar to stir the vats of homemade wine she kept in the washhouse, next to the terrifying mangle machine Joyce had cobbled together from old car parts.

My mother's memory stalls at the mangle machine. She lies back and closes her eyes. I leave the photograph by her bed.

I've driven two and a half hours from the city for a regional history conference to present a paper on 'Setting the record straight on women settlers'. Nobody in the audience asks any questions at the end. Fortunately a friend has come along and raises her hand.

'Could you perhaps touch on any challenges you encountered when you were researching women settlers?' she asks.

A few people turn around and look at her, then back at me as I race through an abbreviated version of the usual complaints of women's history researchers: the paucity of records detailing women's daily lives; the difficulty in finding their original voice; the disappointment of entering the archive only to find the shelves bare.

Our reward is the drive home through wine-growing country.

'Stop,' I say, as we speed past the turnoff for a town.

We turn back, nosing our way into the broad main street, the newsagency with its *New Idea* headlines, the miniature supermarket with its blackboard announcing 'Quince Paste' and 'Local Camembert', the obligatory abandoned corner bank. There's barely a soul on the street but for a few men standing outside the sandstone pub, staring at us as we pass.

I tell my friend to drive on until we come to the little church on the hill.

The wind sighs as it tramps through the dark branches of the pine trees. I try to remember where they are, my mother's parents.

I never met them. We only came here once to lay a bunch of lilacs on their graves.

There they are. *In loving memory of... beloved wife of... much loved husband of...*

'Look,' says my friend, who has wandered off, camera in hand.

Violet Nelly McGregor, 19th June 1896–20th January 1970. Loved deeply.

Joyce Therese Guilford, 1st August 1892–7th April 1974. Deeply loved.

'You never mentioned Great Aunt Joyce and Cousin Violet were buried together,' I say to my mother the next time I visit.

She looks past me, smiles and closes her eyes.

Australia-New Zealand
Direct Line
TRANSMISSION DEVICES
CASINO RACING CLUB
LIMITED
CARLTON
DRAUGHT
Australia-New Zealand
Direct Line
BEEF WEEK CUP DAY

33

Forever young

I have had many close friendships with women throughout my life. My friend Lizzie deserves a special mention, partly because she was the first friend I made when I arrived in Australia, partly because we have stayed friends through thick and thin for thirty-six years, and partly because of the delightful way in which we met.

Lizzie told me the other day that she is now on the pension.

No, my mind screamed. *How can this possibly be? How on earth can Lizzie be 65?!*

We met in 1976 when I was on my first trip to Australia.

I was twenty and had managed to land a job as an understudy and wardrobe assistant on a theatre tour with the Royal Shakespeare Company. We were travelling overland from England to Australia and spending three months playing in country towns right across New South Wales and Queensland. Four actors, one musician, me, our technical director, a general manager and the bus driver—and that's a whole other story!

I had a friend back then—a friendship that has sadly gone wrong since—who was married to an Australian. When we were playing in Calcutta my friend was in America visiting her mother, but her husband and I had dinner together. He told me about his brother and his sister-in-law who had a property near a place called Bathurst.

'If you go near there you should visit them,' he said. 'You'd like them—they've got three small kids, dogs and horses, and they live on 4000 acres of beautiful land.'

I filed the information away but I didn't think much more about it—we were so busy travelling from place to place and I really couldn't imagine what our time in Australia would be like.

A few months later we were touring around the country, going from town to town, and we were booked into a hotel in a town called Orange. When we checked in, the manager told me there was a message for me—someone called Lizzie Barlow had called for me.

John had contacted Lizzie; Lizzie had found out our tour schedule from the Arts Council and had discovered we had a day and a night off in Orange. 'I'm coming to get you,' she said, 'and you're coming out to Cheshire Creek to get a dose of home life.'

She turned up shortly afterwards. A tall, dark-haired beauty, she looked as exotic as a gypsy or a Spanish dancer in the daggy hotel reception in country Australia circa 1976.

I think it would be fair to say that my soul recognised her immediately—it was as if I was meeting my older sister. We started talking, and basically we've never stopped. These days our conversations are further apart. The young woman who went riding with me, brought up her three wonderful children, managed more than her fair share of tribulations, is now a grandmother, and spends a lot of time with her children and grandchildren. Somewhere along the line she left her husband and managed to acquire her own 100-acre block on which she put a collection of old railway carriages, doing them up with her usual artistic and eclectic flair.

Over the years we've shared so much. Lizzie is godmother to my son, and I have known her children, who are now all married with children of their own, since the youngest was in nappies. Parents have died, children have been born, jobs gained and lost, marriages made and left; beloved horses and dogs have also lived out their earthly journeys during our friendship. Add up the years of living we have both done since we met and it's over seventy! How on earth did that happen?

In the early years we rode together—one memorable day we were out from early morning until late afternoon, riding the full 4000 acres. We saw places no-one ever went; startled a herd of Black Angus cattle who decided to try and round us up; saw wallabies, eagles, kangaroos and wild goats.

I lost her once. In the midst of an emotional crisis she suddenly moved country for a relationship and was in such turmoil that she did not tell me where she had gone. When I rang her house for one of our normal chats and found that she had left, I was devastated; I felt as if my heart had been ripped from my body. Fortunately I found her, and fortunately for her the turn her life had taken was temporary. All of those who loved her breathed a sigh of relief when she was back on her beautiful block of land, safe and sound. We breathed even more of a sigh of relief when she found a wonderful partner to share her life with.

One of my few regrets about moving 800 kilometres from where I lived is that now Lizzie is a long way from me, but all I have to do is imagine her and her beautiful railway carriages sitting on the hills, with their view down among the gum trees to the she-oaks that line the winding river, and I am there, with the woman who has been my support and friend for over thirty-six years.

But still I ask myself—where did the time go?

Carmen Paff, too, sums up the support system that our women friends give us, even in the midst of continuing difficulties.

> I cannot imagine my life without my amazing group of close female friends. They are there for me at every joy and every sorrow. Their happiness is contagious when I am feeling down; they rush to my side armed with hugs and hot cups of tea when I am in crisis; they send flowers and champagne when I can't face the world. And I have tested them in past years, having a partner with multiple brain tumours and constant health issues, a difficult birth and emergency caesarean, almost losing our house when both incomes dried to a trickle. These are not fairweather friends! They are in it through the storms and tsunamis of life, boots and all. And I love them. They

have taught me that I am not alone, that it is essential to ask for help, and how to accept it graciously. They have taught me that it is OK to not be OK. It is OK to cry, to yell, to break, to fall apart, to rest, to take time out, to be selfish, vulnerable, and above all to be myself and be loved.

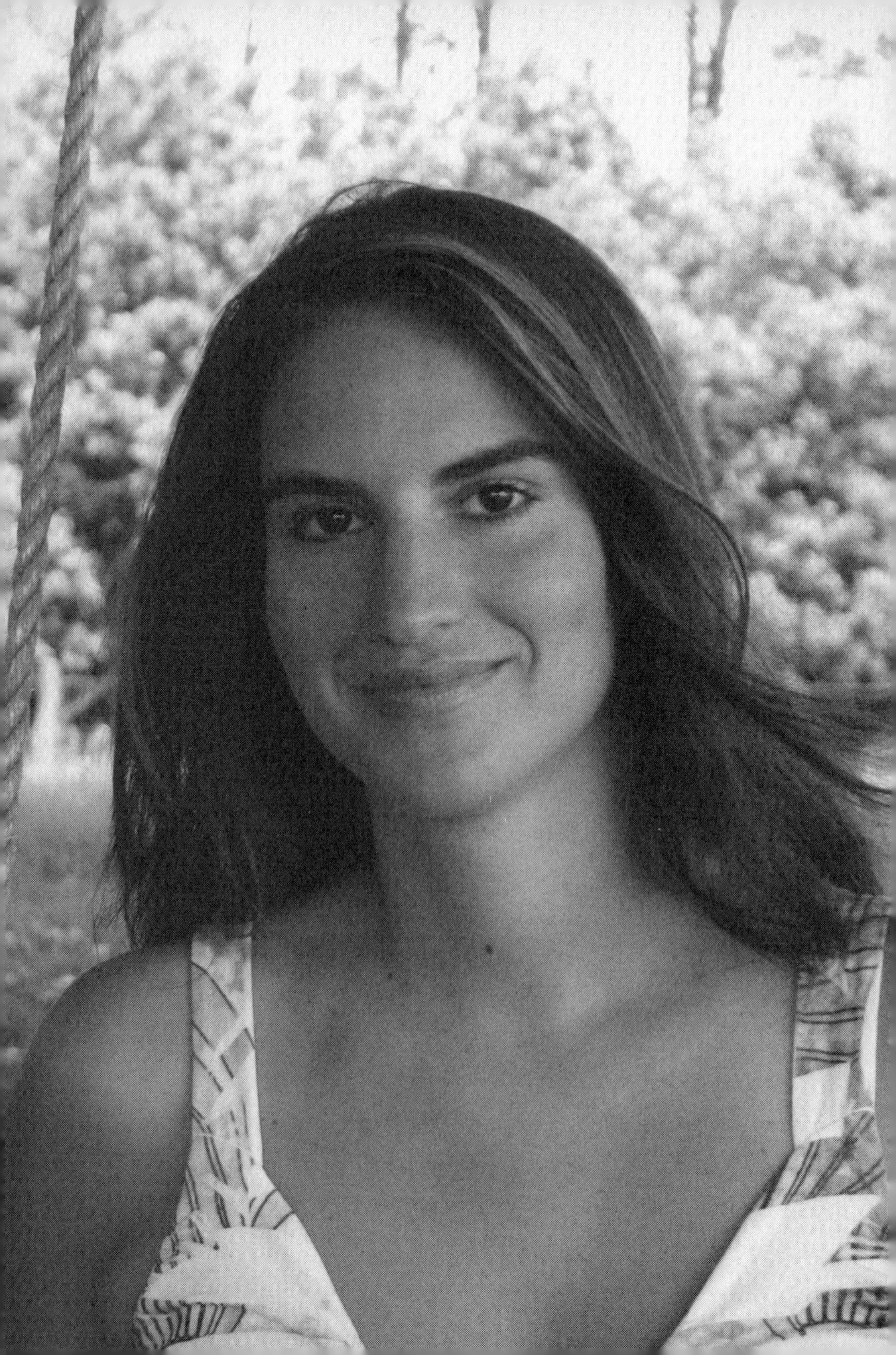

34

Growing older gracefully—almost

The other day I decided to eat my lunch in front of a bit of daytime television, and there was a doctor on who specialised in women's health. He told the audience that every decade after forty, we lose five per cent of our metabolic rate, so even if we have always been careful eaters we will still end up putting on weight. Even increasing our exercise by five per cent won't help us much as you might think because our bodies also use less energy when we exercise.

Hmmm, I thought, looking down at my plate of cold pizza and salad, and the little folds of tummy sitting comfortably over the top of my jeans—that explains it!

I was born in 1955, which makes me fifty-six while I sit here and write this. I am not into Botox or cosmetic surgery, or even make-up or facials, but I can't say I'm entirely happy with what gravity is deciding to do with my physical appearance, just as I can't say that I'm entirely happy with the fact that my hearing is a little less acute than it was, and that I now have to wear multifocal glasses. I'm also not ecstatic about the fact that my memory is not what it used to be, and neither, most importantly to me, is my energy.

On the plus side, there are some things I like more about myself as I've got older. I'm more compassionate—I hope! I am less reactive, less angry, more sure of who I am, and more fluid—I have a lot of different personalities in my garden of souls, as Jung described it, and I think I've come to terms with most of them, although there are a few that could still do with a good weeding. And I'm working on them, I truly am.

The only problem with this ageing business is that apparently I can't stop it.

I may have only thirty-odd years left with this particular lifetime—now that's a scary thought. But I look back at myself thirty years ago at twenty-six and see what an amazing life I've led, and if the next thirty are anything like the same I will be a lucky woman—although possibly somewhat exhausted!

I was visiting a friend the other day, and her 23-year-old daughter came into the room. She was gorgeous—blonde and slim and very pretty. But looking at her I could see something—what? An anger perhaps, an inner tension, a lack of grace, and I actually thought to myself that I really wouldn't want to be like that again.

What I do want to do is hold on to a belief that the best is yet to come. I think that the inevitable disappointments of our lives, the failures and, for women, the hurricane force of the menopause, can often crush our spirit. We perhaps believe that we are not worthy, that once we get past a certain age our dreams can't happen.

I am buying this less and less. We are worthy, we are deserving of the life that will see us fulfil our potential. We are all beloved of the universal spirit and we are all here in the earth school to learn lessons, some painful, some happy, some just plain old boring.

It's never too early to aim for your dreams, and it's never too late. But in the meantime, if the weariness of motherhood overcomes you, or indeed the weariness of life, there is no harm in collapsing and giving into tiredness from time to time.

Clare Wishart, a full-time mum, knows all about family life. With children come babysitters, often reminders of times gone by and our younger selves, as Clare describes in her story.

> My babysitter came today and said, 'I have something to show you.' She pulled a white envelope from her metallic handbag and shyly extracted two photos. They were of her all dressed up for her school formal. She looked beautiful. Her make-up was professionally done but still natural; her black dress with blue ribbon complemented her skin colour. I couldn't get over the transformation from schoolgirl to accomplished young woman.
>
> My babysitter is exactly twenty years younger than me. A few weeks ago, as I was driving her home, we were talking about the

future. 'I don't know what I want to do,' she said. I remember the burden of the future very well from my teenage years. I didn't know whom I was going to marry, where I was going to work or even in which country I would reside. It all weighed heavily on me. This is one of the benefits of growing older. Some questions are answered. The balance of your life swings so that you have equal amounts of past and future.

I want to tell my babysitter so much. I want to tell her that when you grow older, you will look back with nostalgia on events such as your school formal. Enjoy it for what it is: a great night out with friends at a certain time in your life. I want to tell her that she should look into work culture and think about where she will fit in and thrive, and not so much about 'what she will do'. I want to tell her that the great issues of her life will probably not be what she does, but who she is. How she relates to her body and the healthy respect she has for it. How she finds escape from a clamouring society and its endless appeal for more, how she nurtures her creative spirit when all around is calling for destruction and decay. I want to say that she will always be herself, at seventeen, at twenty-seven and at thirty-seven. This is my gift to her. I have become older and more settled in who I am. It has been a long and bumpy road, but now I want to share it with those who come after.

Someone who is definitely growing young rather than old is photographer, writer and adventurer Claire Leimbach, who only last year, in her mid-sixties, went galloping on a horse across the Mongolian Steppe!

In our mid-sixties most of us are slowing down and have half the energy we used to, but not so our spirits. We still like to get out there and protest against war or violations to the land and its original inhabitants. Fortunately I live in an area where people feel passionate about their environment and we protest regularly, the most recent being against exploration for coal seam gas. However, the most memorable was when over six hundred women sat naked on a hillside and spelt out NO WAR. Photographed from the air it sent a clear message of opposition to the war in Iraq. The women ranged in age from teenagers to seventy-year-olds and the sense of solidarity and desire for peace touched us all.

For more than twenty years now I have been part of a sisterhood who were drawn together in the Pacific Islands for the South Pacific Arts Festival, which was hosted every four years by a different island nation. We fell in love with the islands and have been going back regularly ever since.

We call ourselves 'the Ministers of Fun'. Our credo is, 'If it's not fun don't do it, and if you must do it, make it fun.'

We all love dancing and singing, especially the hula. I have always believed dancing and singing were the best tonic and in Pacific Island cultures they are an essential part of life.

Having been an adventurer all my life, I have no intention of stopping now. Fortunately I have a number of dear women friends who feel as I do and are always ready to join me in some remote wilderness, often in the Himalayas. Here we enjoy the challenge of the magnificent mountain scenery and can support each other when the going gets tough.

Last year my girlfriend Lisa and I went to Mongolia together and had the thrill of galloping across the Steppe; our knees weren't happy but our souls were singing. These are magic moments we will always remember and enjoy telling our grandchildren about.

I have been looking forward to having grandchildren but since this has not happened yet I have acquired several surrogate or 'heart' grandchildren. I am lucky in being able to act for some absent grannies and I get huge pleasure from spending time with new young mums as we share our experiences of the joys and pains of motherhood together.

It is wonderful, now the responsibilities of child-rearing are over, to be free to explore one's creativity. I have had the most rewarding time taking up sculpture, something I had never done before. I have joined a group of women who meet each week with a model to sculpt in clay. I feel no pressure to produce a saleable piece, only to enjoy the total focus it takes while doing it. I am not always happy with what I produce but that doesn't matter, it is the commitment to trying and the shared pleasure developed within the group.

My women friends bring countless blessings to my life. They are always there in times of need, with either a sympathetic ear or chicken soup if I am sick. I simply cannot imagine life without them and can only hope we will grow old disgracefully together.

Of course many of us will not be quite so physically adventurous as Claire as we get older, and I am sure even the brave souls among us get wobbly moments from time to time. Perhaps ageing in its best sense is about acknowledging the fears it produces for us, but at the same time not being defined by them and realising that choices about how we live our lives still present themselves every day, as life coach Kim Townsend tells us.

> I suppose you could say that I have recently become obsessed with growing old or ageing. I constantly hear friends sigh and say, 'Oh my god, I'm turning 50!' They say it with an air of shock that it has apparently happened overnight, and with a sense of disappointment, foreboding and fear.
>
> I don't get it! I'm turning the big '5–0' in five months and I'm excited! I'm 'coming of age', not growing old. It is actually a time for a reality check. First, we have been dying and ageing since we were born so one would think we could get a grip on this phenomenon by now. Second, it is just another transition in life—why is it labelled a 'crisis'? To me, it is transformation time.
>
> I'm finally at a stage in my life where I know what I want and I'm consciously working towards getting it. I'll admit, it is not always easy, but, understanding the necessity of persistence and perseverance, I keep on going. Every step in the 'right' direction is an achievement to be celebrated. I'm at peace with myself and my health is great. My finances are a bit of a worry, as chasing the dollar has not been important to me until now. And even now, I'm not really chasing the dollar—I'm living my passion and getting financially rewarded for it. That's why I'm excited—I still have a lifetime ahead of me to really enjoy. When I'm doing what I love and it won't feel work.
>
> People say, 'I wish I knew what I know now when I was twenty, I would have done things differently.' What I say is, 'You now

know what you know because you were once twenty—so utilise that wisdom and get on with the life you still have ahead of you.' I know I have a lifetime left to live and more knowledge, wisdom and experiences to draw from than ever before, so why is the future anything other than bright? I am set on focusing on what I can do. I refuse to live in fear of ageing and death.

Bella Vendramini, a writer's daughter and herself a writer, is one of those finding that learning to become her true self is part of the ageing process—time spent away from her path resulted in depression, but now she says the older she gets, the more she knows how to grow.

> There aren't many things I'm sure of in this strange old world, but there is one thing that I am sure of: as I get older, I feel 'it' growing stronger. I'm not even entirely sure what 'it' is, but what it feels like is a strength, an ease, a balance.
>
> People say 'it' grows from an accumulation of trials and adventures, an understanding of your own processes as well as others. I don't really know. But it continues to grow the older I get; a clearer heart, a softer anger, an even balance to my chin. Not high and proving, not low and afraid, but an even chin, level to the ground, my eyes clear and looking straight ahead. My smile real, not forced. I taste 'it' like a berry on my tongue; bone-honest and fresh—and I want more. Every year goes by and my desire for it increases.
>
> Like most of us, I've tasted extremes in life—I've fallen ass over tit and even shared in a couple of successes. As a child, I was like a

small, freckled, knobbly-kneed, tomboy fairy, and kind of odd. But eventually I started to grow out of my freckles and wipe my face clean. Then I pushed my hair a brighter shade of 'I want to fit in' and wore red gloss on my lips. In my twenties I became an adventurer and travelled madly with a hell-bent curiosity to climb mountains, love hard, push my limits and get into trouble. At one stage I even learnt to hush my passions, wear grown-up women's clothes and work in administration. With depression I learned that life was too short and depression too dangerous a friend to give up on your dreams for.

Looking back on it all now, it feels like a kaleidoscope. There were so many highs and lows, so many mistakes and red-blooded excitement, so much uncertainty and searching. I was unsure of how to be, what I wanted or where I belonged.

I'm in my thirties now and even though I haven't found total peace, I sure can smell it from here. Now, all those different parts of my past have become a part of me, and they have lost their sharp edges. I am more at ease with myself. Age has helped me lose the panic yet keep the joy. I am so deeply thankful for that. It's the 'it' growing stronger with age. As lovely age continues to blossom, my curves soften and grow round, my hair is brushed, I am an adult, tall and even. The fury of youth, the insistence, danger and curiosity like a smack of crazy in my blood has gone. I am no longer at the mercy of it. Of any of it: the oddity, the mud splatters, the pushed hair, the proving, the travels, the nine to five, the uncertainty. I am standing above it (and not *just* because I get to wear stilettos now), and I am adaptable. I feel my past is this big bag of experience that I can use now, plucking out lessons at will, helping me in everyday life.

The older I get, the more I know how to grow, turn the other cheek, communicate better, live fearlessly or fix a tap. I even know the wise small ways to keep depression at bay. I feel this ripening in me—and I love it. My berry ripening. I love growing older more than I can say. I see myself in years to come with crinkly old skin, smiling that deep satisfied smile of a woman who has fought her battles and won. Who knows that lovely dazy feeling of her past integrating and her happiness being balanced. I can only imagine the roundness, the final completion and joining of all my parts, the curvy berry roundness of old age to come.

It is not easy to find happiness in ourselves, and it is not possible to find it elsewhere.

AGNES REPPLIER

35

Time flies

*I*t's impossible to imagine when we hold our newborns in our arms that twenty years can pass in a flash.

Like Ros Brenner in her story below, I imagined almost from the moment of my children's birth that it would be a great thing when they left home, and indeed, in some ways right from the moment they were born, the preparation for that time began.

But when the reality arrives, it can be very painful.

I remember vividly the day I left to emigrate to Australia permanently. My mother was putting on a brave face but I could feel how devastated she was to be losing me. My younger sisters later told me they found her crying in my clothes cupboard—not an easy image to carry with you over the ensuing decades.

I suppose in many ways life is about reconciling dualities, and the tiny baby and the independent adult are at the opposite ends of the spectrum of those dualities.

I looked forward to the day that my children could look after themselves. In fact I spent years grooming them and teaching them how to be independent. I didn't at any point consider that having an adult child living at home was an option.

At one stage I joked about a new mattress that I bought with a five-year guarantee. I said it would last my eldest daughter until she was eighteen, and then she, like the mattress, would have to leave. I had no idea how much it would hurt me to have her leave, especially since childbirth seemed like the worst possible pain that I could ever have imagined.

By the time I had reached forty-eight, my three children were living their own independent lives, and I had thought I was doing alright with finding my own path in a new country with new and exciting adventures.

Recently I broke my arm and it was much more painful than I had imagined it might be. I became depressed and finally understood the connection between pain and depression; I realised that I had been living in a state of depression for some time and making choices based on my pessimistic outlook. My depression, I realised, was caused by the loss of the role as a mother; I was in denial of the distress that it was causing me. But it still didn't make any sense—I was happy, my job done. It was supposed to be my time.

When I was a child, my dream for when I grew up was to get married and have two children. My most favourite game was pretending I was a mother, and making believe I had a husband and babies. Mothering was all I ever thought of; I even left high school and didn't even consider getting a university degree as I was so sure that becoming a mother would be all I needed to fulfil my life. At eighteen I married and by the time I was twenty I had my two children.

However, I was totally unprepared for how different my life would become with children. All of a sudden there was this new little person to consider. My first reaction once at home and alone with my daughter was fear, I remember wondering how I would cope, asking myself if I had the ability to cater to her needs. My fear made me wish that the years would roll by very quickly and that she would grow up and look after herself in as short an amount of time as possible. She grew into an independent person—even by the age of two she knew how to manage herself, and the whole household!

I suspect that I lived for years after her birth without realising I had depression. I sought no help, just tried to cope on my own, mainly in denial. After my youngest was born nine years later, I had more knowledge about what mothering her would entail. But I remember after being at home with her for a week feeling the dread of getting up out of bed, and my lack of confidence in feeding her, as well as taking care of the rest of the family.

Time flies

For a mother, the time of childbirth is a link with the earth. But in modern times there are no rites or rituals, and the quick disconnection with the umbilical cord is another reminder of the pain that we are separated from nature. At least while the child is in the home, this pain is kept at bay, the reminder of separation and longing to be connected resurfacing again at the time when the child leaves and the great mother role is left empty.

It is far too easy to dismiss the significance the empty nest has on mothers. To make the journey through the pain, many mothers will find, as I have, that there is a new life waiting to be lived, and that in learning how to nurture yourself you obtain a wealth of wisdom and a level of satisfaction far more important than any amount of material wealth.

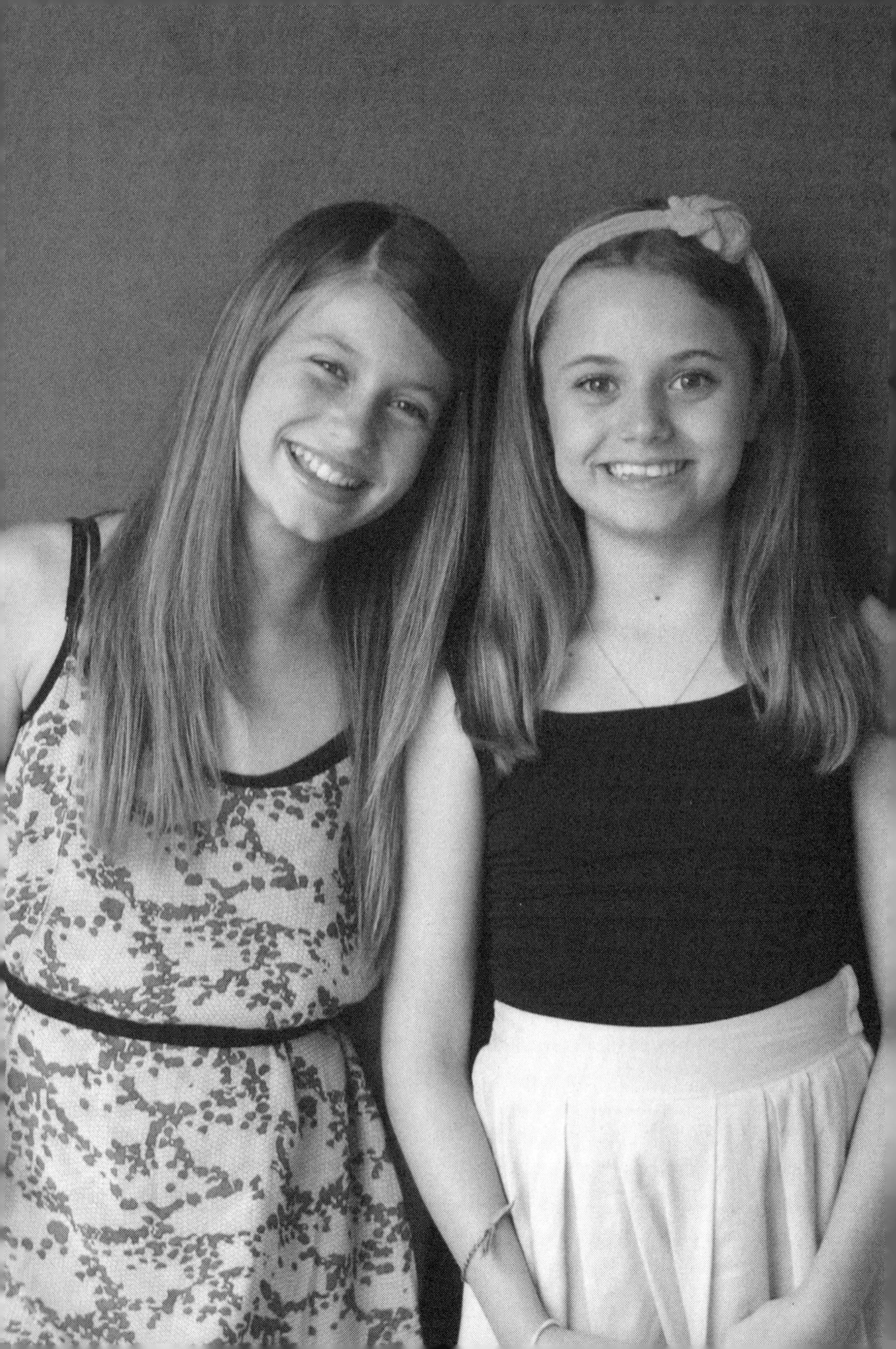

36

Taking time out

I think it is very hard for women to take time away from their busy lives without feeling guilty, and perhaps even harder to take solitary time—time to contemplate their own place in the world and their connection to the sacred.

As I get older words like 'still', 'profound' and 'quiet' are becoming more and more important to me. It is in these still, profound and quiet times that we reconnect with the earth, with our belief in the creators of the universe (in whatever form that may be) and also, most importantly, with ourselves.

It's in these times that we gain the sense of how small and large our lives are and how, by stepping away from all the mundane, everyday things we have to do, we can connect with the higher energies of nature—the unconditional love, support and harmony that exists out there for us, beyond judgement, criticism of or blame, either of ourselves or from others.

I think it is a fundamental need for us to reconnect with landscape from time to time, as Grace McKenna so beautifully describes in her story about travelling with her family to Uluru.

> We're driving in the outback, having been on the road for three months now with no particular destination in mind, and that, suddenly, after all this time, has become a focal point of mine. I'm no longer happy to just take in the sights. I need to sense a purpose to this journey.
>
> And so the little things have begun to irritate me—the chafing of my adolescent son's hairy legs against mine as the car wends its way over rough roads; the back-breaking nappy changes on the rear seat; the dinner menu choice of baked beans on toast or lentil stew enhanced with a tin of vegetarian sausage. You see, we're a family of six getting about in a rather gypsy fashion, with our bench-seat station wagon and a caravan designed before wind resistance was even a concept.
>
> It's hot, and the air conditioning goes by the name of Open Window, replete with dust. In the far distance I can just see the outline of Mt Connor, and the excitement level buzzes up a few notches as we contemplate this most extraordinary event unfolding—we, from coastal Australia, are getting closer and closer to our mysterious and famous monolith, Uluru.

We unhitch the van in this caravan park in the centre of the continent. The kids wander off in various directions, the youngest happy to cling to my legs as I attend to essentials like placing bricks behind the wheels, connecting water and electricity, and sticking a bucket under the sink outlet pipe. While husband levels the van, I eye off the van next door—it is shiny, positively glowing (dust-repellent paint, maybe?), and comes with aircon and a TV antenna perched conspicuously on the top. It is also huge.

Tomorrow we will check out The Rock.

Father and three sons make the climb, an activity the traditional Anangu owners tolerate rather than encourage. Somewhere in every Australian boy's heart is the longing to climb this massive rock. It's a steep climb, treacherous in parts, and about thirty-five people have died trying. Husband comes down (complete with full complement of original party), clearly shaken by the terrible responsibility he has encountered. Now that he's back I give him the one-year-old to mind as I climb as far as the start of the chain to a little jutting-out bit that is quite high enough for me, thank you. I also know that I don't want to climb it; I can feel that the Anangu people don't want me to climb it.

But something has opened up in me during the time I have spent at the base with the baby. There is a mystery about this huge lump of rock that seems to have propelled itself out of the very ground it was formed on. I, who have given birth four times, feel this is a place of birth. I, who have been driving around for three months still in post-natal stupor, am feeling. A mass of unidentifiable emotions have been awakened and I need time out.

THE WISDOM OF WOMEN

I tell my husband that I want to walk around the rock. He is quite incredulous: Why walk around it when you can go up? he asks. But that is what I want to do, and I want to do it alone. He drops me off early the next morning and we arrange to meet in the car park in four hours time. This is a measure of his babysitting tolerance rather than how long it takes to do the walk. Fortunately, that is about how long it takes to walk the 10.6 kilometre marked track.

I am grateful for this path. It's early morning and I can feel the cool night air warming up as it brushes my bare knees and arms in my walking rhythm. Incredibly, there are drops of dew on the small yellow flowers that grace the clumps of jagged stones scattered along the ground. How long does a stone have to sit still before one of these plants will grow in its lee?

I'm walking along the west side, heading south with a sense of urgency to get as far away from the car park area as soon as I can.

I want to be alone.

The path begins to curve gently in a south-easterly direction and suddenly I sense I am in the middle of nowhere, this massive dark rock on my left flank, and now I am really heading off. Hell, I could go anywhere from here! The sense of the vastness of the continent is almost tangible, and certainly realised in ways other than pure mathematical calculation. My pace slips into a rhythmic cadence as the path nudges the rock. It's simply enormous, its mass speaking of permanence, of endurance, of something that always was and always will be.

The silence is astounding. It fills my ears and the occasional twittering sound of a small bird is part of a greater symphony out

Taking time out

here. I remember hearing an Anangu man saying this place wasn't about the climb, but about listening to everything. Well, I'm listening. As the track curves again I'm facing east, sun in my face, a slight breeze susurrating through the mulga scrub. It passes and I hear my footfall, a soft, sure tread on the red claypan. A striped skink crosses my path and I bend down to examine its delicate footprints, its silent passing a reminder that there are sounds and voices that I can't hear. With a conscious action of my brain I take a mental snapshot, one that covers the colours, the light, this absence of sound, the fine impression of the little beast's claws in the red sand—the beauty I long to possess, captured in a fleeting moment.

The track hugs the rock, which is now flaring red with the eastern sun full on it. I am bedazzled by it, this geological mix of sandstone and feldspar; I want to touch it. A little further on I turn to make sure no-one is looking and lie down on the ground. Arms spread-eagled, I want to feel the vibration of the ground beneath me. Who will talk to me out here? What words can I hear that I would hear nowhere else on this ball in space?

There are caves and gorges, deep grooves carved in the rock from millennia of water falling down its steep sides. There are springs and a permanent waterhole and paintings created over a vast stretch of time. There are areas forbidden to visit and to photograph. There is a history, and I am a small person on this planet, but I am invigorated by a sense of purpose, of belonging, of not-aloneness. The rock acts as though it is hugging me, rather than the other way around. When I take my final steps back into the car park to await the pick-up, I know I am ready for the world again.

To me Grace's story is a perfect summation of why we need time out. To slow down, to get in touch with our senses, to enjoy being part of this infinite universe and to just step away from our busy schedules for a moment. It's curious, isn't it, that when we are on overload we can be with family and friends and feel completely alone, yet when we are truly alone in the right space we can feel completely connected to the universe in all its glory.

Ros Moriarty writes about the power of rediscovering her connection with her homeland and the ancient culture she was born into.

Ngalki: my inner spirit is my substance in the world.

My inner spirit holds the unique beauty and meaning of my being. It is the essence of who I am in the world.

It feels like 4 a.m. when we stir at the desert camp. It is dark, and cold. Annie sits up on her mattress next to me and calls across the camp in language. Everyone starts to stir. It's actually after six. The sky is the clear, translucent indigo of pre-dawn. It gradually turns to the familiar night-and-morning sponge cake of palest pink and powder blue layers, until the sun rises to bleach the colour and the morning star away. We get up and stoke the fire. The billy is filled with water and put on the coals to boil. We fossick around for Weet-Bix and powdered milk.

Before we can eat we are called to the ceremony ground for the first of the rituals. Before coming here, Annie told me just once, but

Taking time out

with authority, that I am not permitted to write about any content of the ceremonies or the sacred objects. No detail. I can only say that Annie takes me with her in the line, and tells me: 'This will make you strong.' It is solemn, simple, deep. I can feel it. I have sensed moments of similar spiritual calm in foreign places, burning a single candle in a quiet moment in another country's cathedral. But this is just a big circle of red sand inside a ring of desert grass and scattered, spindly trees. In my own country.

The dancing, the singing and the beat of clap sticks start soon after. The other mob first.

'We respect them,' Annie tells me. 'It's their country.'

They are the same sacred songs handed down for thousands of generations to those who have the authority to receive them. They have deep meaning. They encapsulate the Law. The rules of the culture to keep everything right. Season follows season with abundance. The species procreate and people are in balance with the earth, the sea and the universe. There is renewal for the human spirit. We are quiet. Respectful. Looking from a way away.

The wind is whipping the sand around the dancers. It is *a-Mardu*—the south cold weather wind, Yuwani Annie tells me. I like its lemony sharpness on my face. It counters the intensity of the sun that I know will rise by midday. It is early winter in the desert, but the days are still hot. Annie tells me it is good for me to come to these ceremonies. Really strong. All women. Really good.

Annie and the others tell me who everyone is. 'Your mum, *kujaka*, your sister, *baba*, your auntie, *narna*, your mother's brother's daughter, *kathakatha*, your father's brother's daughter, *kulhakulha*, your mother-in-law, *yuwani*.' I start to remember the words more often. 'You call her Kujaka, she's straight sister for your mother.' Only family here. No dislocation or ambiguity. Clear and straight. No exclusion. The Law has joined these women of many bloodlines. There is no fear to include, to embrace with unconditional permanency.

I feel a tranquillity, a strength, from the non-negotiable rules of connection around me. Inclusion is a powerful thing. I am a sister, auntie, niece, daughter-in-law. I wait, and Yuwani Annie tells me what to do. Every step of the way. She looks after John for his mother, and that includes looking after me. I feel emotionally nurtured, supported. In Sydney, I look after my mother and I look after my children. Here, I have simply stopped in the middle: they all look after me. It is deeply calming.

We are called to the ceremony ground. The women from Central Australia call the Borroloola women over. Protocols. We are seated on the ground on one side of the dance area. The ritual starts. It is feminine, sensual, lyrical. There is parody, symbolism, charade. Rhythm and form. Irony and humour. It is expressive, sophisticated. Pared down to a richly devised essence. 'Very important one,' Annie whispers. 'Strong Dreamin'.' It is a long time out there on the ceremony ground. Yet the minutes and hours merge, as if time is not passing at all.

Taking time out

It occurs to me that the invisibility of the occasion is remarkable. The modern sophisticated nation I live in has no idea that the singing of the continent it sits on continues in the heart of its landscapes. We newcomers have barely scratched the surface of the power of the land we occupy to inspire and nourish. To stir the senses and lift the heart. We see the stillness of dawn at the ocean, the cacophony of summer cicadas, the ripples of red dunes in the desert, and marvel at Australia's natural endowments. But we are far from at one with it. We sip at its physicality when we could gulp from the well of its spirit.

Back in our own area, the camp is collegiate. Women enjoying time when time stalls. I look at my watch, expecting it to be late afternoon. It's 2 p.m. We sit, talk, laugh, sing. We sew strips of cotton for ceremonial headbands for tomorrow. The crisp-edged wind that was blowing across the ceremony ground this morning is blocked out of our camp by a pile of leafy windbreaks. It is still and hot. I move to the shade to sit with one group, then another. They all have stories to tell me. Guidance to give me. If I interrupt their contemplation, or ask brazen questions, they don't tell me so. They excuse my ignorance. They speak gently to me. Sharing food, laughs and truths about their world. They take me carefully with them on this journey of the heart and mind. I am profoundly moved. And grateful.[4]

The interesting thing about taking time out or setting ourselves journeys is that what is important about them is the spiritual pilgrimage or process of self-discovery, rather than the actual length of the journey. Eunice Mosher discovered this when, recovering from a stroke, she set herself the goal of getting to the fourth light pole on her street.

On sunny days I walk to the fourth light pole. Coming home always seems longer than going there, and I ask myself why I walked that far. Not that the fourth light pole is far; it is less than one-sixth of a mile from our driveway. An able walker might think six miles far, but for me the fourth light pole is far.

Metal light poles situated along the sidewalk tower above tiled roofs, saguaros and our mesquite tree. A metal arm atop each pole arches toward the street like a lone tree branch. At the branch's end, an inverted nest holds a single iridescent egg, which glows above the street from sundown to sun-up. Birds find the horizontal arms convenient lookout perches. One must step with care when walking under light poles.

From our driveway I turn left and walk along the sidewalk to the first light pole; that is, to the far edge of our lot. I recall a day last year when walking there to supervise pruning of our desert willow seemed unduly far. Two years ago, walking from bed to chair seemed far, despite being half-carried by strong arms. Fortunately those days are behind me.

The second light pole stands at the end of our block where the sidewalk bells like a cul-de-sac, then straightens right to face the sun. Not that it is always toward the sun, but that is true for my usual walking time, mid-afternoon. Viewed from above one might think the cul-de-sac corner appeared to be a huge question mark. The predominating question is whether or not I will fall. Manoeuvring past the bird droppings at the cul-de-sac corner was exhilarating. With that behind me, I could advance 'Full speed ahead!' toward the third light pole.

To walk toward the sun on a spring afternoon is its own reward. Nonetheless, by the time I reach the third pole my left arm usually begins to feel tired from leaning heavily on my cane, which I must do to maintain equilibrium. My right arm hangs from my shoulder like the arm of an ape. My right hand, however, cannot grasp a pencil, let alone a tree limb. Not that I long to swing about in trees. What I long for is simply to walk.

By the time I reach the fourth light pole, fatigue and light-headedness are catching up with me. I become obsessed with thoughts of sitting. Even a flat boulder like those in my neighbour's yard would suffice, although I cannot envision trespassing to perch on one of his rocks.

This measured pace allows ample time to close-read the coloured rocks homeowners have chosen for their ground cover. Rocks grow in around roots of shrubs and cactuses, from lot edge to lot edge and from houses to the sidewalk. Walking past the gravelled lots is like inspecting root vegetables in a supermarket, enormous bins of beets, parsnips, potatoes or yams. Man-made pebble creeks wind through gardens. I see only two grass lawns along the way. The variegated rocks are as far away from Kentucky blue grass as I can imagine.

I have read that in England it takes several hundred years to develop a truly splendid lawn. Two workers with strong arms and backs, shovels and a wheelbarrow, can spread a rock lawn in one afternoon. How many eons went by while the earth layered sandstone, quartz and granite to form mountains? It seems a regrettable turn that mountains have been degraded and used to upgrade this level street.

Paving dominates the landscape. Nineteenth-century poet Gerard Manley Hopkins observed that feet, 'being shod', could no longer feel. I cannot feel the soil through these thick soles and the concrete sidewalk, nor is any soil visible. The street is sealed tarmac. A wavy concrete curb connects street to sidewalk.

Wide concrete driveways cover a sizeable portion of lots. Yet, though my feet cannot feel the soil, its presence is profoundly seen in thriving desert trees and shrubs.

I reach my doorstep convinced that going to the fourth light pole and back was going too far. Before resting, however, I must crawl across the burning sand to the kitchen oasis for a glass of water.

My doctor tells me when we walk the brain plays a set of instructions. Normally this 'walk tape' is automatic. My walk tape having been erased, every step I take is an effort to imprint a new tape. If someone approaches from rear or sides, turning my head to look in their direction could well cause the tape to unravel and spin away down the street. Oftentimes I sense, rather than see, the passing car or the bird in flight. 'Look both ways before crossing!' carries an additional caveat: 'Plant your feet before looking!'

Taking time out

Early on it seemed the slightest breeze might whisk me up and away beyond the treetops. Even now I resist gazing at trees or sky until I stop to brace myself. Preoccupation with the mechanics of walking causes me to withdraw from surrounding distractions. Concentration is not only necessary—it has become a safe haven, compared with which the sky seems almost irrelevant. Faces of people I meet drift by like clouds.

My hobbling gait is another detraction. Among picture book houses and orderly rock gardens, I am erratic as the trucked-in boulders, a maverick on a stony field, a wanderer in this desert suburb. There are few pedestrians, fewer canes. Occasionally I hear the sound of a garage door closing. I imagine people whisking their children inside, closing their doors and watching from a window until I have passed by. Not that there are any children in these houses—their occupants are baby boomers or beyond.

Since the event of my stroke, I live exiled inside a tunnel. My words dissolve in air, losing their way before they reach an ear. I am a ghost.

Two years ago bees swarmed into my attic and buzzed my brain, killing movement, but generating an avalanche of images: crystalline sea wands, moons and stars, Vincent van Gogh irises, pink flamingos, intricate geometric art, *ein, zwei, drei* polkas and ideas never before imagined spilling out.

My stroke: It has taken me two years to own those words. In the hospital they wheeled us into a communal dining room to take our meals. I'm not sure if they did that to give us a sense of belonging, or of despair. Each patient able to communicate had a different story, all with the same ending. 'Conversation' came around to: 'Why me? Why us?' I said I thought we were like the 'chosen ones', chosen not for the suffering (those around us suffer more), rather, to glimpse the future—a sneak preview of what the future inevitably holds for all of us.

On a Thursday, black garbage sacks set out on the sidewalk for collection hinder my progress and I wonder if walking is worth the steps. I play the walk tape over and over, every step a monotonous uphill climb from heel to ball of foot: Lift right foot, move it forward. Shift weight to right hip. Touch down with right heel. Roll weight forward to ball of foot. Lift left foot … moving in an endless processional toward a distant graduation. Strains of 'Pomp and Circumstance' echo inside my head, yet I never reach the stage nor collect a diploma. Am I destined to walk on until the composer has forgotten the melody?

As I turn toward home my feet refuse to leave the sidewalk. The voice of my sea-going brother echoes in my ears, 'Aboard ship, Sis, sailors paint everything that is not moving, so either move on or be painted!' With his advice, I step off the wavy curb and set out across the blacktop sea, lured by the siren song of a rose garden on the far shore.

There is another side to this street. Pink, lavender and yellow roses appear even more gorgeous close-up. An elderly gentleman by the curb fumbles with the twist-tie on his garbage sack and adds a forgotten bit of trash. He tells me he used to walk two miles, but because of cancer he now walks one. I tell him I walk about one-sixth. He advises me to walk a bit further each day, and before I know it I'll be walking a mile.

'The thing is,' he says, 'be consistent.'

One meets the nicest people along the maverick trail!

My friend, who knows him, told me later this man had spent time in a concentration camp, and that is the reason for his kindness.

The sun lays warm hands on my shoulders. My shadow leaps ahead, cutting across the coloured stones, urging me toward my door. It's getting late and I have poems to write.

It is a wholesome and necessary thing for us to turn again to the earth and in the contemplation of her beauties to know of wonder and humility...

RACHEL CARSON

37

Leaving children

I've always found it hard to be away from my kids. In fact from being someone who was always a brave and fairly constant traveller, I've become much more stay-at-home since I've had children. For me, nurturing the children we have seems vital, although of course I know many good mothers who travel for work. Last year, however, I had to go back to England because my father was not expected to last much longer. It seemed, the doctors said, to be a matter of weeks, not months—even, at the time, possibly days. My stepmother had also died only a few weeks before and so it seemed as if this was the time to go and say the goodbyes that needed to be said.

What turned the trip from something hard and difficult into something lovely was being able to spend time with all my northern hemisphere sisters—and I got to see all three of them.

My sister Ellie had moved to Devon since I had last been to England, and that was a delight to discover, but of course, because it was so beautiful, I immediately wanted my daughter there to share it with me.

When I'm away from her, I miss her with an almost physical aching. I feel as if a bit of my soul has been temporarily misplaced.

Thank goodness for Skype is all I can say!

Where I live, in the country, I have many backpackers who come and stay for a while to help out in return for food and accommodation. It's not difficult to spot whom they are all connected to—their mums! No matter how young or old they are, it's their mums they want to see and talk to on Skype. Not that significant others, dads, siblings and friends don't get a look in, but it's their mums that seem to be their touchstones while they're travelling—and how lovely is that?

When I was away from Anna I wrote her the little letter below.

> Dearest darling Anna Julia Drewe,
> Today Ellie and I had a lovely day, even though it was pouring with rain. We snuggled down, and lit Ellie's fires, and I did a lot of writing on my cat book, and then in the afternoon when it stopped raining we went for a lovely long walk through the woods, with all the little primroses and thousands and thousands and even thousands of golden daffodils nodding their trumpet heads to us as we passed, and delicate white

snowdrops, and a beautiful river, and it was all VERY English, right down to the mud and the gumboots and the people coming past saying, 'Good Afternoon ... good afternoon ... good afternoon ...'

When we got back from the walk we went to a garden centre with a deli that sold lovely things and I bought a ten-year-old girl I know another little present, and then we came home to the fires and cups of tea, and I painted a beautiful little painting. Well, at least I think it's a beautiful little painting! Then I did some MORE writing, and then Ellie and I walked in the chilly evening mist down to her favourite pub which is right by the river, with all the pretty boats and moorings, and we sat inside in the warm and I had crab soup, and fish and mashed potatoes, and toffee pudding!!! Crikey, how English is that????

And now I have come home to go to bed, so I am sending you this because in the morning we will be up and about and off back to see George, and to celebrate his 80th birthday, even if he doesn't realise what we are celebrating, I am sure he will enjoy it—especially the cake, because he has got very fond of sweet things! Yummy, yummy, he says.

One day I shall bring you to Devon to Ellie's house because Devon is absolutely beautiful—probably the most beautiful bit of England I've ever been to I think, and it is lovely with its beaches which actually have golden sand, and its rivers and estuaries, and hills behind—a bit like an English version of near us.

Anyway my gorgeous girl, I love you to infinity and beyond 57 000 times and I always will, and you are the light and love of my life too, and I will see you quite soon now, and I can't wait to give you the world's biggest hug.

I will talk to you on your Friday night, my Friday morning.

Have a great day at school.

xxx

Love you

Mum

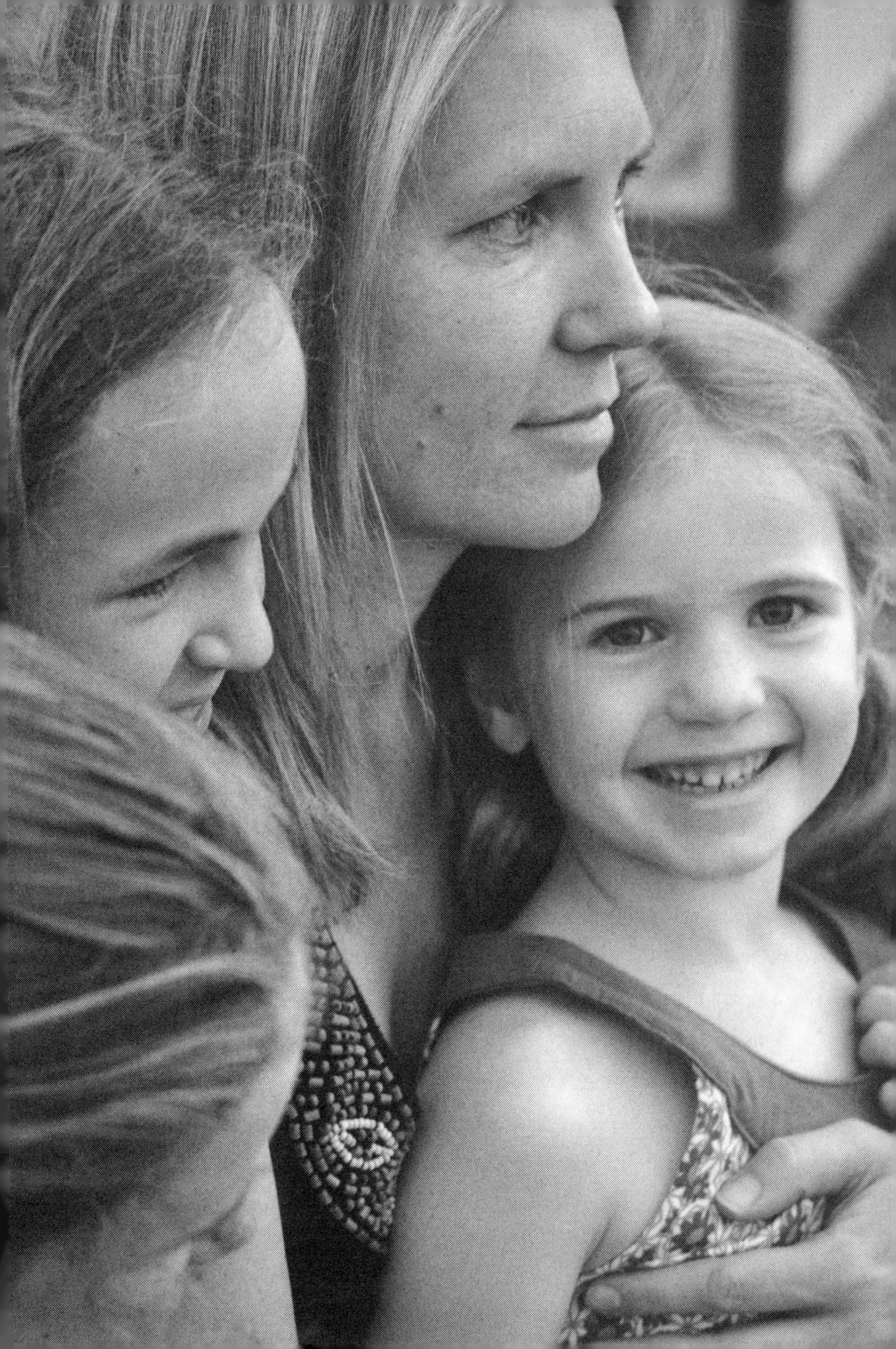

38

As mothers move on

*I*t's inevitable that at some point we will lose our mothers, or the women who have mothered us. I can still remember, twenty-six years later, the unforgettable grief and anguish when my mother died, even though it was a blessed relief and release for her from her alcoholism and what her life had become, and even though it was many years since I had received any mothering from her. The loss of our mothers, or those women who become our mothers and are the first ones to love us, cuts deep and stays with us forever. Despite the loss, what I found was that when I had adjusted to Mum's passing, we continued our relationship in a much easier way once she had shed her recalcitrant and tired body. This is

As mothers move on

something many people find comforting after they've experienced the loss of a mother, including writer Stella Vance in her moving story about her mother's presence after her death.

My mother discovered she had kidney cancer at the age of seventy-three. I'd known all along, due to her eating habits, that she wouldn't live to be a hundred, but it was shocking that this happened in her early seventies. Mum took the doctors' advice and tried interferon. When she came to San Diego for a month, she was a shadow of her former self. Dropping down to her ideal weight pleased her, but she had no energy for the walks on the beach that we'd formerly enjoyed.

Seeing that even the interferon was not working, she went off the drugs. In about a week, her vitality came back. She was again able to walk, hike and trim the hedges. The sparkle and enthusiasm returned.

One night I had the distinct urge to call her to share with her an inspiring passage I'd read about someone overcoming cancer. 'I think you can beat this cancer, Mum!' I told her.

'Oh, yes! I know I will!' came her reply. Then she said to me: 'Stella, have you forgiven everyone? After seeing a healer, I realise now how important it is to forgive.'

'Yes, I think I've forgiven everyone,' I replied.

'Are you sure? Dig deeper! It's so important!'

Little did I know these would be the final words of wisdom to me from my mother. The next day, 21 September 2000, I received a hospital call informing me that my mother had suffered a stroke. The cancer had metastasised to her brain. The doctors said that no-one ever recovered from this type of stroke.

My sister Stephanie and I rushed to be with her. We spent the next five days at her side, talking to her even though she was in a coma. I went days without much sleep, holding her hand and telling her it was okay to pass on.

At one point, I said to myself—not out loud—'Mum, you know you have to cross over. If you agree, please cough.' To my astonishment, *she coughed immediately*. And that was the only time I heard her cough during those five days.

Finally, on 25 September, the nurse could tell from her breathing that the end was near. I witnessed Mum's final moments in her body. Watching her breathe ever more slowly, stop a little, then gasp some more was very intense. Stephanie and I held her hands, stroked her forehead, and reassured her that it was okay to go into the light, and that we would be okay without her. Though Mum was unconscious, tears streamed from her eyes as she silently said goodbye. Watching Mum's *final* breath and rebirth into a higher dimension was probably as intense as *her* watching our *first* breaths and births into this dimensional plane had been. Stephanie and I felt very privileged to have witnessed this passage. We hung around a while, as the room felt lit up with Mum's energy. I gave her body one final hug.

Stephanie, meanwhile, also reacted strongly to Mum's death, feeling very sad. Then after a few weeks, something right out of the movie *Ghost* occurred. Periodically, according to my sister, my mother channelled through her or even briefly entered her body (with her permission). I felt this was true, because at times Stephanie told me things that sounded like they were coming from Mum. All of this caused my sister to be open to the ideas Mum had taught, rather than traditional Christianity.

My family had been divided between the traditional belief of 'eternal hellfire and brimstone' and reincarnation, with the men siding with hell and Mum and I with reincarnation. My sister wavered between the two. Since she'd recently opened up to the idea of reincarnation, she was very disturbed to learn that Dad had told our brother he feared she would go to hell.

Puzzled, I asked her, 'Really? I didn't think he was that dogmatic. He never conveyed any concern over *my* eternal damnation!'

'Well, Stella,' Stephanie replied, 'Dad gave up on you a long time ago. He just figures you're going to hell and there's *nothing* he can do about it!'

Mum left behind her many journals, and reading them comforted me after her transition. I was astounded to read that during the divorce with Dad she was awakened with what she called 'a vision of Jesus' who assured her that she was making the right decision to proceed with the divorce.

'Everything will be OK!' came the response from the light being.

I think many people who get a vision of these sorts claim it is Jesus because they can't imagine who else it could be. Could it have been a guardian angel? Some people believe that such visitations are actually from one's future enlightened self who has learned to go back into the past.

A couple of months after Mum passed, on 1 December 2000, I woke up at about two in the morning, as I frequently do. Only this time it was due to the startling noise of footsteps coming closer to my bed. I opened my eyes to see if it was my husband, but no-one was there. It was spooky, but I wasn't afraid.

Suddenly, my whole body was enveloped in a warm, vibrating energy of love. I smiled. Mum wanted to say hello. And she undoubtedly knew that my intention was to begin writing on post-death communication precisely on December first!

Now, by nature I'm a real sceptic, especially when it comes to *my own* psychic experiences. I somehow feel that everyone else is more sensitive and psychic than I am. So when something like this happens to me, it has to hit pretty hard and be pretty intense to convince me it's not a dream or my imagination.

Mum, knowing my mental nature and left-brain tendencies, must have known I still had some doubt. So *again*, after another REM sleep cycle, I was awakened by the distinct noise of approaching footsteps. When they got closer, I was *again* surrounded by and enveloped in the same warm, loving energy! This time I was fully convinced I'd just experienced an 'after-death communication'.

Why did Mum wait a few months to demonstrate her ability and reach out so profoundly? She knew I didn't need comfort; she knew I had no doubt as to where and how she was and how happy she was. But she had always encouraged me to use my writing ability, and this personal testimony of her visitation was her gift to me as a writer.

My mother is not dead, I am totally convinced. She is right here by me, in another dimension—and only a thought away![5]

How we do miss our mums! Even though I truly believe my mother's death was a blessed relief for her—and for us—from what had become the pain of her life, I still missed her most dreadfully. Kerry Littrich discovered that sitting with her sick mum gave her a sense of peace and quiet that she still remembers. In her original letter to me Kerry wrote: 'I recently lost my mum to brain cancer, after a heart-wrenching five year battle. Over the last few years of her life, Mum and I shared a special closeness and appreciation of one another, and we were blessed to be able to say our final goodbye without any angst or misunderstanding sitting between us. Our past had been quite dysfunctional, so achieving this sense of peace and unity was indeed a gift.'

What a wonderful thing that a journey none of us exactly look forward to can contain such hidden treasure.

I really miss visiting Mum's nursing home. Most Mondays, and sometimes days in between, I would take a few hours break away from the frenzy of the rat race and go and sit quietly with her. Over time these quiet hours became an invaluable part of my week. Mum would greet me with a radiant smile, so happy to see me, and for an hour or two we would be encased in the purity of love without agenda or selfishness. Those hours spent with Mum were precious interludes where I could sort through the clutter in my mind, smooth out the wrinkles in my emotions and allow myself to breathe. Mum's presence was a tonic, allowing me to see with renewed clarity how foolish my worries were. As I held her shaky hand and stared into her warm eyes, I'd throw my anxiety into the rubbish bin, realising the triviality of my fears.

The nurses loved to care for Mum as she smiled at each of them as special and valued friends. It wasn't only her daughters and the nurses who received her beautiful smiles—she lavished her kindness and affection on all around her, whether doctor, cleaner or stranger. Everyone who entered her room came out smiling—her love was infectious. I will never forget the impact one little lady, severely impaired by a brain tumour, made on the world around her.

I remember how repugnant it was when Mum lost a tooth and the dentist told me the procedure to re-insert a crown would be too much for her fragile health. The kindest thing would be for her to live without a front tooth. Mum had always been so well-groomed and conscious of her looks, I felt I had let her down. Yet she went on smiling just the same, her face lighting up with joy, and nobody seemed to notice her missing tooth.

Now Mum is gone and there is a void. The trivial and mundane loom large and my moments of reflection are shrinking. It is rare to find a smiling face that is happy to see me for who I am, rather than for what I can do for them. Some days it is rare to find a smile at all as people rush from one appointment to the next, tense and preoccupied. I long for quiet moments of closeness to another person who has time to sit and simply be. It was such a privilege to have those hours where I was able to sit in the presence of pure love.

This week I walked into our old family home, empty now the tenants have moved on. Once the home was warm, buzzing with noise and activity, messy in places, tidy in others, expanding and contracting with the rise and fall of emotions within its walls. I recall dark times—the chaotic sounds of arguments, doors slamming, and weeks of icy silence. I learnt to walk on eggshells and hold my breath for long periods. Mum seemed impossible to please, and I never felt good enough.

I look beyond the shadows and remember Mum's beautiful smile—happier days when fragrant casseroles bubbled on the stove, shrill laughter lit the air, and the telephone always rang. Cancer robbed Mum of her life, but also taught us how to hold each other's hands and walk through the valley together. The hurts of the past no longer mattered.

It is only the people we love who turn houses into homes, transform bland nursing home rooms into sanctuaries of grace, and bring meaning to our lives.

The more I live, the more I see the value of real love. I will close my eyes and hold onto the memory of Mum's beautiful smile. The memory inspires me to inhabit my own home with warmth and kindness, and to smile not only at those I love, but at the lonely stranger I see on the streets. Her smile taught me how fruitless it is to try too hard and do too much, and the wisdom in slowing down and cherishing the quiet moments with the special people in my life. Mum showed me the profound difference one genuine loving soul can make to the world around them—one beautiful smile at a time.

To be kind to all, to like many and love a few, to be needed and wanted by those we love, is certainly the nearest we can come to happiness.

MARY STUART

39

The importance of rituals, writing and nurturing

At the age of eleven, my daughter already understands the importance of female ritual. I am somewhat stunned by this because, loving as my mother was, the idea of rituals, or celebrations of friendship or womanhood, were not something she would have countenanced.

A year ago, a new family came to live close by. One of their three daughters, Ainslie, was the same age as Anna and was put into the same class at school. Anna's 'bestie', Amber, was also in the class, so suddenly the two As became, as the headmaster nicknamed them, The Triple As.

Over the past year they've played together, worked together and done homework together. Ainslie brought to our school her prodigious skipping talent, resulting in the creation of the school's first skipping team. The three girls even produced their own news show—*The Triple A News*.

There are, of course, other friends in the group, and a lot of the time the three were four, because Chloe was one (although not an A of course!).

Sadly, after a year in our area, Ainslie's family made the decision to move back to their home town, and there was much sadness among the friends. Anna, Amber and Chloe got together and made a plan. During Ainslie's last week they would have a surprise gathering of the four of them for her.

They arranged it down to the most minute detail. Four identical necklaces were bought in the company of one mother. I was nominated hostess for the event, which meant spending several hours tidying Anna's room when I should have been finishing this book—and putting on the disco, butterfly and fairy lights so that everything sparkled and shone. Ainslie's mother, in on the act, delivered beautiful cakes from our local patisserie, and teenagers were coerced into blowing up balloons.

Amber's mother delivered Amber and Chloe early and directly from school, and as soon as they heard Anna and Ainslie arriving (they'd been dawdled home by Anna's brother), they hid in Anna's cupboard.

Ainslie wandered into Anna's room thinking she had come for a play, and when the two girls leaped out of the cupboard, I think you could literally have knocked her down with a feather.

There was much hilarity, exchanging of presents, eating of food, dancing and laughing. We even had toasts and speeches, with my (Leo) daughter leading the way. Dinner—pasta, ice-cream and melted chocolate—came all too quickly, even for me, and soon the girls were off home, leaving one slightly emotional and overtired eleven-year-old behind.

She had done a great job, I told her. They all had.

I was amazed at the thought they had put into the whole event, and their care and love for their friend; Ainslie was obviously touched and thrilled.

I absolutely know they will stay friends, and I know they will all remember that evening. So will I, because the one moment of motherly reluctance I experienced when the idea was first mooted was well and truly buried under the avalanche of pride and love I felt for them all.

And anyway, I love melted chocolate too ...

Anna and I love to spend what we call 'mummy and daughter' evenings together. They don't happen often, these little times, and I hope that Anna treasures them as much as I do. I often feel guilty that due to my split with her dad, and the various animals, projects and jobs competing for my attention, she seems to get less individual time with me than she should, so when we do get some substantial time together it's particularly precious.

Last night was one of our mummy and daughter nights, and what we did was make dinner together. We chopped potatoes, and she made meatballs, and I made a salad, which we served in separate salad bowls; then while the potatoes were cooking she had a long bath with lots of bubble bath and oil. After her bath we cooked the meatballs together. We decided to watch a movie, and settled on *Marley and Me*, putting our three badly behaved dogs outside so we could claim our sofa and sit inside and watch a movie about a badly behaved dog.

The importance of rituals, writing and nurturing

After dinner, Anna decided she would like a massage, so I got the table out, lit the oil burner, and gave her a massage for half an hour, and being my little Leo, she bossed me about and told me exactly where to rub and how to do it! The massage was followed by a leisurely dessert of jelly, frozen yoghurt and a chocolate biscuit—what use would a treat night be without chocolate? Then, because she was now covered in oil, the Princess required a warm shower before bed, and bed in this instance was with me, because how nice is it to snuggle up to a warm, clean, sweet-smelling child, and how many years do I have left of that?

I've learnt some things about these times with children—if it is going to be 'special', leave judgement aside for the duration of the special time, give into the moment, and go with their flow. It's a way to help them make decisions about what they would like to do.

These nights are always different. Sometimes Anna has me lie on the massage table, and gives me her 'healing', which she seems to do quite naturally. Sometimes we make a beautiful floor space with doonas and cushions and lie on our backs together and chat, or get my crystals out and discuss each one. Sometimes we listen to music, sometimes we read, sometimes we dance or draw or sing, and sometimes we simply cuddle and watch television.

By the time my mother was my age she was lost to alcoholism, and it had been many years since I had received any nurturing from her. But when I was little, I do remember how much she loved me, and how I used to cook with her and cuddle with her, and I think that for me it is a way to reconnect with all that was loving and good about my mother, as well as trying to convey silently to Anna how much I love her—to infinity and beyond, as we say every night at bedtime.

Biographical details

Emma Ashmere

Emma Ashmere is a writer. Her work has appeared in *Sleepers Almanac, Etchings* and *Griffith Review*. She lives in northern New South Wales.

'My mother gave me love—and books.'

Ros Brenner

I am a mother of three adult children and a grandmother of one special granddaughter. I have spent many years supporting women through their addiction toward sobriety while working in a women's rehabilitation facility. I am in the midst of writing a novel based on my history as the daughter of a Holocaust survivor.

'I have spent a long time grappling with what gift my mother, who suffered with manic depression, left me, but I see she gave me a great sense of spiritual strength that has helped me to navigate my own journey and grow.'

Charlotte Brooks

Charlie was born in England. She moved to Australia when she was sixteen and is currently living happily in Sydney with her husband.

As Emerson said 'the earth laughs in flowers', and Charlie finds her soul is fed when she listens to the flowers.

'We all have turning points in our lives. I had one when I had the great fortune to meet a woman named Kamala when I was in my twenties who freed me from some very deep and tightly wound energetic threads that bound me. I am quite sure that without her my personal healing journey would have taken a lot longer.'

Helen Brown

Helen is an author based in Melbourne. Her book *Cleo*, about a little black cat's impact on her family, is an international bestseller and about to become a major movie.

'Aunt Lila taught me to believe in magic, and that grown-ups aren't always right.'

Jane Camens

Jane is a writer and literary events manager who spent twenty years in Asia. She writes and consults from her home in Byron Bay which she shares with her husband, Ian, who, sadly, did not meet Jane's wonderful mother before she died.

'My mother's greatest gifts were my memories of the songs she held in her heart, her respect for higher education, and her advice to "Get out of Brisbane, Jane. There's a lot more to the world."'

Marian Clarke

Marian Clarke was born in London in 1932. When World War II broke out, she was sent to the country to escape the bombing, where she suffered repeated abuse. After four years she was awarded a scholarship to a school in London, and became a shorthand typist. She married in 1955, and, to overcome shyness, began to drink. She and her husband moved to Australia for a job in 1970, and Marian was hospitalised four years later with health problems. She spent five months in the hospital and has never drunk or taken prescription drugs again. Her husband died some years ago, and Marian now lives in Balmain with her cat. 'Life,' she says, 'is beautiful.'

Jessie Cole

Jessie grew up in an isolated valley in northern New South Wales, and lived a bush childhood of creek swimming and general barefoot free-range adventuring. Her first novel, *Darkness on the Edge of Town*, is scheduled for release in June 2012.

'It is the women in my life who call on me to be myself, and no matter how joyous or lonely, to give expression to this self—to create.'

Bernadette Curtin

Bernadette was born at Crystal Brook in South Australia and now lives with her husband near Byron Bay in New South Wales. In her painting practice she explores water in all its forms, and she also conducts painting workshops.

'My mother has shown me courage and acceptance while enduring illness and incapacity in old age.'

Louisa Deasey

Louisa has been a freelance journalist for over a decade and writes about health, psychology, travel and medicine. She is also the author of *Love and Other U-Turns*.

'My mum was an artist, and she gave me the gift of understanding the meaning of true creativity—the ability to transform trash into treasure, an onion into a soup, a tired plant into a blossoming tree, a rainy day inside into a hive of activity. That there's no real rubbish in this world, just things we haven't yet found a use for.'

Yantra de Vilder

Yantra de Vilder is an accomplished composer and sound artist. She has spent the last twenty-five years working on many different forms of music, both nationally and internationally, including a range of projects with the BBC in London, Bangladesh, Afghanistan and Burma, to name a few. Writing words is also a passion for her, and she always accompanies her exciting musical projects in the form of blogging or published works for books and magazines.

'My mother gave me the gift of Faith in myself.'

Kim Falconer

A speculative fiction author and professional daydreamer, Kim writes imaginative stories of intimacy and adventure, magic and astrology, environments and social satire. She lives with a host of critters on the north-east coast of Australia.

'My mother's gift to me wasn't wrapped in a box and tied with ribbon. I didn't even know, growing up, I was receiving it, but in her everyday voice, in her wit and style, she taught me how to love words. That gift has made all the difference in the world to me.'

Mel Fleming

Mel (Melanie) Fleming travels the country teaching 'Connecting with Horses' and 'Riding with Synchronicity'—a holistic approach that encompasses all aspects of the mind, emotions, body and spirit of horse and rider.

'The gifts that both Aunty Pauline and my mother gave to me and my two sisters, Rose and Catherine, were the gifts of love and compassion.'

Susanna Freymark

After being selected to work on her first novel at Varuna, the Writers' House, Susanna Freymark has had four short stories published. She divides her time between journalism, working on her novel and studying her Masters in Creative Writing at UTS in Sydney.

'I learnt from my mother that judging others based on looks or status or what they own meant nothing, and that serving a shop-bought cake for afternoon tea wasn't the end of the world.'

Lynn Gecso

A mother, carer, homeschool teacher, volunteer worker and writer of spiritual poetry, Lynn has been blessed with three beautiful children, two of whom are hearing-impaired. She is also a dreamer! Both her daughters are featured in *The Wisdom of Women*.

'My mum gave me the gift of imagination. She used to call me a dreamer, which I didn't like, but now I embrace it and proudly own it!'

Zali Gecso

Zali is a fifteen-year-old high school student who loves to be creative. She sketches, designs, writes poetry and is currently being homeschooled.

Maya Gecso

Maya Gecso is twelve years old and almost finished primary school. She loves drawing, painting, doing craft activities and playing with her two puppies. Maya's second language is Australian Sign Language.

Maggie Hamilton

Maggie writes books and magazine articles, and is publisher of Allen & Unwin's Inspired Living imprint. She is also a passionate campaigner against the sexualisation and commercialisation of our children. Sustained by the kindness and nurture of a wonderful husband and good women friends, Maggie loves to lose herself in dance, theatre and film, in nature and all things sacred, and to travel to faraway places.

'My mother, Joan, taught me the joy of laughter, knitting and cooking, sewing and spinning; the importance of curiosity and thinking outside the square; and finding the courage and tenacity to follow one's heart.'

Elaine Harris

Elaine was born and educated in England where she began her work in radio. She emigrated to Australia to marry in 1982 and has since worked in radio and television, and as a theatre performer and writer. Her writing has featured in numerous publications and is included in numerous anthologies; *The Wonderful World of Dogs*, *The Amazing Life of Cats* and the US book *Two Plus Four Equals One* are among them. Elaine lives in Tasmania with her husband, Chris, two crazy dogs and a wonderfully wild garden.

'The greatest gift Mum ever gave me was the example of selfless acceptance: during her treatment for leukaemia I enquired, 'Do you never ask yourself "Why me?"' The reply was unequivocal. 'Of course not! If I asked "Why me?" I'm really saying "Why not somebody else?", and I could never do that.'

Zoe Humphreys

Zoe considers herself fortunate to be a mother, grandmother, adult education practitioner and curious creature. She feels that her students, friends and family have blessed her with their time and attention and taught her so much that she strives to put into practice.

'My mother gave me the gift of life and the opportunity to learn from our shared experience of growing up alongside one another; she was my first love and that love has shaped me.'

Noelene Kelly

Noelene has held multiple roles in leadership and education. After profound immersion in the Western mystical tradition and studies of Eastern and Indigenous traditions, she is now engaged in transformational work with those who wish to evolve their consciousness or create new cultural models (www.noelenekelly.com.au).

'The precious gift I have received from my mother and from all the women in my life is a love mirror. This mirror is offered by soul contract and allows me to see Who-I-Truly-Am.'

Fay Knight

Fay is a journalist and author of two non-fiction books, and has contributed to various anthologies. She now lives in Sydney and works in communications for a national charity.

'My mother gave me the gift of an adventurous spirit—she and a girlfriend were the first women to ride motorbikes to Cape York in the very early 1950s, and at eighty-three she still goes backpacking around Australia.'

Trish Landsberger

Trish works and lives in Brisbane with her husband and two grown boys. Family is dear to her. As she is far away from her place of birth, extended family are very precious. In her work she notices the effect that positive and supportive families have on a life, and the struggle people have when this love and support is absent.

'My mum gave me the ability to give and accept cuddles that envelop and warm your soul.'

Claire Leimbach

Claire Leimbach, a photographer and writer, was commissioning editor on various magazines, including *Geo*. She has also worked on anthropological documentaries and remains passionate about the plight of indigenous peoples and the environments in which they live.

'The greatest gifts my mother gave me were a deep love and respect for the natural world and the security of knowing I was loved unconditionally.'

Deb Lennon

Deb is a New South Wales state gold medallist in netball and marathon running. She is also a radio DJ, sings in a band, and is currently writing her memoir.

'Mum is my best friend, my shining light, my inspiration and the nurturer of my hopes and dreams. I love her so much.'

Jean Linderman

Jean started Women Writing Women in 2003 in response to her concerns about the need for heartfelt communication between women of different cultures and beliefs. She is married to her high school sweetheart, has four children and six grandchildren, and is the author of the book *Sacred Stories: What Hospice Workers Know that Can Change Your Life*. For information and letter-writing guidelines, visit the website http://womenwritingwomen.org.

'The gift my mother gave me was just this: pay attention to each moment of life and listen: *really* listen.'

Kerry Littrich

Kerry is mum to two soccer-crazed boys. She writes for magazines and is working on a novel. She also paints, draws, blogs and teaches Buddhism and meditation.

'My darling Nana gave me the great gift of love for all by showing everyone she met, without exception, great kindness and respect. "You catch more bees with honey," she once told me with a twinkle in her eye.'

Grace McKenna

Grace lives between the forest and the beach in northern New South Wales. She is a member of the Dangerously Poetic Society and also a sometime potter who sometimes also goes for very long walks.

'My mother taught me to step up to what is in front of me, and have faith in the landing of my feet.'

Tryphena McShane

Trypheyna McShane is an award-winning artist with artwork in international venues. She has a background in environmental education, a Masters in Applied Science (Social Ecology), and was wildlife artist/educator for the Zoological Parks Board of New South Wales. A published author and community artist, she has worked with a diverse number of Australian communities and is co-creator of We Wise Women (www.wewisewomen.com).

'My mother's special gift was having the courage to ask people she met about their family history and where they came from. Invariably she discovered close links with them. She befriended people all over the world, who loved her dearly and kept contact with her until she died, because she was so interested in them.'

Ros Moriarty

Ros Moriarty was formerly a journalist with Radio Australia in indigenous affairs, women's issues and the environment. She has also held senior positions in the Federal Department of Aboriginal Affairs in Canberra and Sydney. She is currently Designer and Managing Director of Balarinji Studio, Australia's leading indigenous art and design group. Balarinji is possibly best known for covering Qantas jumbos in Aboriginal design. Ros's book *Listening to Country* was published by Allen & Unwin in 2010.

'My mother gave me the gift of moving to live close by us in her later years, when I found inspiration and joy in her unfailing humility, resilience and generous spirit.'

Eunice Mosher

Eunice Mosher was born on a small farm in the mid-west of America. After her father's death, she moved to California with her mother, who pined for her childhood home. There, Eunice met her first husband and was a stay-at-home mum while her son and daughter were young. She continued studies in three community colleges, received her degree nine years later, and taught medical office courses in two community colleges. She moved to Monterey and met her second husband. Later they moved to Arizona to be near his family. She has been writing poems and short stories most of her life, and is still writing.

'Evenings were often spent listening to our mum retelling her history from faraway places. She also played and taught piano, not to mention gathering us in mandatory prayer. I did not fully realise my mother's strength and endurance until after she had passed away and I had borne and raised three children of my own. She truly taught me to bloom where you are planted.'

Cecilia Novy

Cecilia Novy was born in Switzerland in 1925. She graduated from business school, married a Czechoslovakian student and moved to Geneva. When the communists took over Czechoslovakia, the couple became stateless. They applied and were accepted into Australia, and arrived in 1950 on a refugee ship to Melbourne, where Cecilia became a kindergarten teacher in South Melbourne. In 1962 the family, with their three children, moved to Sydney. Cecilia later divorced after eighteen years of marriage, working for many years for the Theosophical Society. She retired in 2008 to live on her daughter's land near Byron Bay.

'My mother's gift was familiarity with death. I was one year old when my mother died of TB, despite her prolonged stay in the Swiss mountains. As a little girl, I always wore a small gold pendant with her photo, cheerfully showing it to everyone who asked me about her. Her presence was accompanying me in my dream-life, consoling me when I felt lonely. Even as a grown-up I was well aware of her presence, especially when I too had babies. She would always wake me when the children needed help during the night. Gradually her visits faded away as I matured.'

Carmen Paff

For the past ten years Carmen has run Corps De Lumiere Reiki and Massage Healing in Melbourne, and has also taught reiki and crystal healing. She has a loving French partner, a beautiful baby boy, Byron, and an amazing group of beautiful women as friends.

'The gift my mother gave me was the knowledge that I Can Do Anything, and to this very day I live by that and hope to pass it on to my son.'

Jenny Palmer

Jenny has been a lecturer and ABC broadcaster, and her passions now are her family (including dogs), friends, art, books, food, wine and Italy. She is not growing old gracefully, has no intention of doing so, and remains a champagne-loving leftie.

'My mother fed me books for the entirety of my childhood and took me to the theatre, the art gallery and the movies, so I always knew there was a wider world beyond the boundaries of our suburban existence. She established my appetite for learning and being open to both the wisdom and love of other women wanting to share their world with me as teachers and friends. I am eternally grateful to her.'

Liz Porter

Liz is the Melbourne-based author of one novel and two books on forensic science, *Written on the Skin* and *Cold Case Files*.

'The gift my mother gave me (I hope): the ability to be a tolerant, helpful but non-smothering mother.'

Ally Redding

Ally is a wife and the mother of three children based in the Byron Bay hinterland, New South Wales. She feels that her life has begun anew after losing over thirty kilograms. She is passionate about supporting children with special needs, particularly autism, and their parents, at which she has a front-row seat.

'The greatest gift my mother gave me (and continues to give) is honesty, loyalty, a wicked sense of fun, generosity, perseverance and a strong work ethic. Unfortunately, I also inherited her love of food.'

Rhoda Roberts

Rhoda Roberts is an Australian journalist, broadcaster, actor, producer, director, writer, arts advisor and artistic director. Rhoda is a member of the Bundjalung Nation, Wiyebal Clan, of northern New South Wales and south-east Queensland. She is the daughter of the late Pastor Frank Roberts, an Aboriginal activist and a minister with the Church of Christ, and Muriel Roberts, a white woman. Having been told by her mother she would never get work as writer, Rhoda initially trained as a nurse, before moving into acting and writing. She is married to landscape designer Stephen Field. They have two children and are also raising the daughter of Rhoda's murdered twin sister, Lois. Rhoda is the presenter of a radio show, *Deadly Sounds*, for Vibe Australia. She is also working on her first novel, *Tullymorgan*.

'My mother, Muriel, had two favourite sayings that impacted on our lives—and still do. One was to have faith in everything we do . . . the other was to always outclass people—then they can't box you in. But her love for my father and her humanity was the greatest gift of all and still is. I only wish I had inherited her skill as a dressmaker . . . but you can't have everything.'

Melissa Sanghera

Melissa Sanghera is an intellectual property lawyer and writes poetry, short stories, feature articles and scripts. Melissa loves classical Indian films and dancing.

'Mum always worked hard to give us everything she could, including all her love, and taught me the value of education and honesty.'

Virginia Satir

Virginia Satir (1916–1988) was an American author and psychotherapist, known especially for her approach to family therapy. She is widely regarded as the 'mother of family therapy'. Her best-known books are *Conjoint Family Therapy*, 1964; *Peoplemaking*, 1972; and *The New Peoplemaking*, 1988. She is also known for creating the Virginia Satir Change Process Model, a psychological model that was developed through clinical studies. Change management and organisational gurus of the 1990s and 2000s continue to embrace this model to define how change impacts organisations.

Simone Smith

Simone travels Australia working as television producer. She holds a BA in Communications in Writing, and loves travelling, reading, practising yoga and scooting around on her sky-blue Vespa, 'Bluey Smith II'. She dreams of one day writing a novel, when she can sit still long enough to start.

'The greatest gift my mother has given me is her time. I will be eternally grateful for the many amateur theatre productions, softball games and TV shows she has lovingly sat through. Her encouragement has meant the world to me and is why I am the person I am today.'

Sally Swain

Sally is an artist, writer, creativity coach and spiritual 'worrier'. She says you can find bits of her at www.artandsoul.cc, other bits at Sally Swain Art on Facebook, and the remaining bits collapsed on the floor. She loves helping people blossom.

'My mother gave me the gift of reading. When I was three, Mum wrote the alphabet on a blackboard, with a picture for each letter. I loved the chalk elephant.'

Sarah Taylor

Sarah is an aspiring writer, better known, she says, for the ranting and raving that won her the Australian Poetry Slam in 2009 (www.sarahslampoetry.com). She performed in 2010 at the Sydney Writers' Festival and the Ubud Writers and Readers Festival. She is currently working on a memoir about growing up with a father suffering from mental illness.

Kim Townsend

Kim has journeyed through many experiences, challenges and lessons to find peace of mind and her life purpose. Now, she is passionate about sharing her wisdom and strength to help others to embrace change so they too can 'anti-age' from the inside, create their dream lifestyle and ultimately rest in peace with no regrets.

'To my grandmother—Nan, Nanna, Grandma, Aunty Ed, Mrs T, the Pink Lady, the "Hat Lady"—known to so many for her generosity of heart—thank you for sharing your gift.'

Stella Vance

Stella Vance's piece is an edited extract from the book *Dancing with Duality: Confessions of a Free Spirit*. The life of Stella Vance embodies all the adventure, drama, romance, humour, and philosophy of a free spirit let loose in the seventies and finding its way into the new millennium.

'All her life, my mum was giving me bits and pieces of wisdom that continue to inspire and guide me today!'

Bella Vendramini

Bella is the author of bestselling memoir *Biting the Big Apple* and the sequel *Naked in Public*. She was nominated in 2008 and 2011 for the Cosmopolitan 'Fun Fearless Woman of the Year' Awards. She lives in Sydney and New York.

'My mother taught me that strength, flexibility and love are the ingredients for a happy life, and even though I sometimes lose faith, if I hold that notion close enough it'll keep my darkness at bay and my optimism bravely to the fore.'

Zenith Virago

Zenith has lived in Byron Bay for nearly twenty years. She is a celebrant and a deathwalker—someone who walks the journey with the dying and their family. She lives her life as honourably and as fully as she can.

'When I was young, my mother once told me that I had a superiority complex as a girl. She was right, and I have lived my life never feeling less because of my gender.'

Linda Walker

Linda lives in regional New South Wales with the love of her life, Andy, two dogs and a fearsome cat, Jeff, who thinks she's a lion. According to Linda, she shops too much, eats too much, occasionally drinks too much and is all together too much. She has a very patient family of whom she thinks the world.

'My nan Myrtle was such a fun woman, well before her time in so many ways. She taught me life was short. Her favourite saying was "You're a long time dead, you know!" She was a real live-in-the-moment woman. It was her greatest gift she left behind—her legacy of enjoying every second. She never wasted an opportunity to put on lipstick and fling on her brightest beads. Don't save them for a special occasion. Just living is a special occasion.'

Clare Wishart

Clare is a full-time mother raising a family in the suburbs. Her dream to write is slowly taking shape with each new article or story accepted for publication. She has written for parenting magazines and motivational Christian literature.

'My mother's gift to me has been her reassuring presence and support at all times and in all circumstances.'

Susan Wyndham

Susan is literary editor of *The Sydney Morning Herald* and has been a journalist for thirty years. She is the author of *Life In His Hands: The true story of a neurosurgeon and a pianist* and has edited and contributed to several other books.

'The day before my mother died in August 2011, I told her, "I couldn't have a more loving mother" and she replied, "No, I don't think you could." It was no exaggeration, and I understand now more than ever how her love gave me security, confidence and happiness. I miss her but I still feel that love.'

Acknowledgements

The Wisdom of Women owes an enormous debt to one person—my wonderful publisher Maggie Hamilton. Conceived as an idea some years ago, it went through various incarnations while my other anthologies, *The Infinite Magic of Horses*, *The Wonderful World of Dogs* and *The Amazing Life of Cats*, were compiled and published. With Maggie's constant support, *The Wisdom of Women* was able to find its true voice and I thank her from the bottom of my heart.

One of the most rewarding aspects of compiling an anthology is working with the contributors on their stories. For me, learning about other women's lives and reading and working on their heartfelt stories has been an amazing journey, and I thank every single woman who has contributed to the book for her amazing honesty, humour, and in some cases courage in bringing forth their experiences for the world to share. In particular I would like to thank my sister Charlotte for her kind words about me, and the close friends of mine who allowed themselves to be persuaded to contribute!

I would also like to thank Kathryn Knight for her careful carriage of the project and Sue Harvey for her judicious line editing; my original agent for the project Fitzroy Boulting for his patience and support of the book; Jacklyn Wagner for her contribution to the photographs; and those women who allowed me to photograph them for the book.

The Wisdom of Women was a project close to my heart, and I hope readers find it as inspirational to read as I found it to create!

Notes

1. Extract from, Kim Falconer, *Strange Attractors*, HarperVoyager, Pymble, 2010, pp. 346–8.
2. Story first published in Claire Leimbach, Trypheyna McShane and Zenith Virago, *The Intimacy of Death and Dying*, Allen & Unwin, Crows Nest, 2009, pp. 129–33.
3. Story first published in Claire Leimbach, Trypheyna McShane and Zenith Virago, *The Intimacy of Death and Dying*, Allen & Unwin, Crows Nest, 2009, pp. 78–80.
4. Extract from Ros Moriarty, *Listening to Country*, Allen & Unwin, Crows Nest, 2010, pp. 72–6.
5. Edited extract from Stella Vance, *Dancing with Duality: Confessions of a Free Spirit*, CreateSpace, Charleston, 2011, pp. 237–41.